*The Indian History of an American Institution*

# The INDIAN HISTORY *of an*

# AMERICAN INSTITUTION

*Native Americans
and Dartmouth*

COLIN G. CALLOWAY

DARTMOUTH COLLEGE PRESS
*Hanover, New Hampshire*

*Published by*
*University Press of New England*
*Hanover and London*

Dartmouth College Press
Published by University Press of New England
One Court Street, Lebanon NH 03766
www.upne.com
© 2010 Trustees of Dartmouth College
Manufactured in the United States of America
Designed by Katherine B. Kimball
Typeset in Minion by Passumpsic Publishing

University Press of New England is a member of the
Green Press Initiative. The paper used in this book meets
their minimum requirement for recycled paper.

For permission to reproduce any of the material in this book,
contact Permissions, University Press of New England,
One Court Street, Lebanon NH 03766; or visit www.upne.com

Library of Congress Cataloging-in-Publication Data
Calloway, Colin G. (Colin Gordon), 1953–
The Indian history of an American institution:
Native Americans and Dartmouth / Colin G. Calloway.
p. cm.
Includes bibliographical references and index.
ISBN 978-1-58465-844-3 (pbk. : alk. paper)
1. Indians of North America — Education (Higher) — New Hampshire —
Hanover — History. 2. Dartmouth College — History. I. Title.
E97.65.N4C35     2010
378.1′9829970742—dc22     2009047233

5  4  3  2  1

A portion of the royalties from this book helps fund the Native American
Writing Prize at Dartmouth. The award was established with the royalties
from *After King Philip's War: Presence and Persistence in Indian New England*,
ed. Colin G. Calloway, also published by UPNE.

FRONTISPIECE: Weathervane representing Eleazar Wheelock and an Indian
under a pine tree. Designed by Stanley Orcutt, crafted by A. N. Merryman,
c. 1928. Made of copper, the weathervane measures 8 feet 9 inches in
length, 6 feet 8 inches in height, and weighs 600 pounds. Mounted
atop Baker Library, it stands 200 feet above the Dartmouth campus.
Photograph courtesy of Dartmouth College, Rauner Library.

*To Dartmouth's Native American students,*
*past, present, and future*

*And to Marcia, Graeme, and Meg,*
*always*

*"Wo unto that poor Indian or white man that Should
Ever Com to this School, with out he is rich."*
—DANIEL SIMON, Narragansett, Class of 1777

*"It was here that I had most of my savage gentleness
and native refinement knocked out of me."*
—CHARLES EASTMAN, Sioux, Class of 1887

*"We owe a debt to Dartmouth College which we can never repay."*
—HENRY MASTA, Abenaki teacher at "the Dartmouth school"
at Odanak (St. Francis), Quebec, 1924

# CONTENTS

# ACKNOWLEDGMENTS

I have many people to thank throughout Dartmouth College and within the Native American community for their help and support in making this book possible:

Former College president James Wright for suggesting to me that Dartmouth needed a book like this and for his forty-year support of Dartmouth's Native American programs.

Presidential scholars and research assistants Courtney Collins, Ibrahim Elshamy, Brook Jacklin, Marcus Luciano, Sarah Part, and Melinda Wilson; I am particularly indebted to Brook and Courtney for their diligence and enthusiasm in helping to track down individual Native students in the financial records of the College and Moor's Charity School.

In the Dartmouth Libraries, Peter Carini, Sarah Hartwell, Barbara Krieger, Jay Sutterfield, Josh Shaw, and their colleagues for assistance, answers, suggestions, and an environment that makes Dartmouth a very good place to do research. Rebecca Fawcett provided prompt assistance with pictures and permissions from the Hood Museum of Art.

For reading the entire manuscript in an earlier and unpolished version, and offering valuable suggestions, thanks to Peter Carini, Jere Daniell, Bruce Duthu, and John Moody; thanks to Ivy Schweitzer for reading the first three chapters.

For answering queries, for correspondence and conversation, for offering suggestions and sources: Rick Behrens, for his information and enthusiasm about Dartmouth alumni in the West; Dave Bonga; Brent Burgin, archivist at the University of South Carolina, Lancaster, for information about Frell Owl's early life in the Thomas John Blumer Collection on the Catawba Nation; Patrick Frazier; Neil Goodwin; Michael D. Green; Michael Hanitchak; Colleen Larimore; John D. Manning and John W. (Jack) Manning; Anne Margaret Meyers; Theda Perdue; Amanda Prentiss; Jeffrey Siemers; David Raynolds; Jean-Pierre Sawaya; Donald Smith; John Stearns; Linda M. Welch.

For assistance with Abenaki place names: John Moody and Donna Roberts Moody.

At the University Press of New England, I am grateful to Richard Pult for his early and sustained interest in the project, to Lys Weiss for steering the manuscript through production, and to freelance copyeditor Martha Ramsey for her careful copyediting.

This is not an institutional history. Nor is it a Native American history of the institution. Over the years, I have talked with hundreds of Native American students and conversed daily with my Native colleagues, and their attitudes, experiences, and statements of course have shaped my understanding of Dartmouth's Indian history. Ultimately, however, this is just *my* history of Dartmouth's Native American history, and I bear responsibility for all errors, inaccuracies, and omissions. It is a story with many subplots, some twists and turns, and a multitude of individual human experiences that cannot all be included here. It is also a story that deserves to be remembered, told, and retold by many people.

# INTRODUCTION

## A School in the Heart of the Indian Country

Like many people, I vividly remember the day I first arrived at Dartmouth. A Friday, February 1982, snowing. My wife and I had driven up from Bellows Falls, Vermont, in an old Subaru we had bought for $800 a couple of weeks earlier. The car quit on the last hill on Interstate 91 before coming into White River Junction, but a couple of good Samaritans helped get us on our way, and we limped into Hanover and parked in the slush.

I didn't know much about Dartmouth but I wanted to see its library. It would not be too much to say I was desperate to see the library. Just a couple of months before, I had given up a tenured position at a college in York, England, a walled city with a Roman history, a medieval cathedral, and, so it is said, a church for every Sunday and a pub for every day in the year. Now I was living with my new in-laws, had no job or prospects of employment in American academia, and wondered what on earth I was going to do with myself in a northern New England backwater. In those days, Baker Library's holdings were recorded in card catalogues contained in wooden cabinets in the entrance hall. I spent hours leafing through them, trying to get a sense of the riches within. The entries under *Indians* seemed to go on forever. I had found a lifeline.

For the next few years, while I received rejection letters from what seemed like every college and university in the country, I was fortunate to land a teaching position at Springfield High School in Vermont. ("You're English; teach 'em English," was the principal's rationale for hiring me). After school and at weekends, I would frequently drive up to Dartmouth, get a day pass into the stacks, or pay to borrow books. No one would hire me, so I wrote my way into American academia. After two years at the D'Arcy McNickle Center for the History of the American Indian at the Newberry Library in Chicago, I moved to the University of Wyoming. From there I came back to Dartmouth as a visiting professor on three occasions (for several years I commuted between Laramie, Wyoming, and Bellows Falls, Vermont). In 1995, Dartmouth hired me as Professor of History and Native American Studies.

I've been here ever since, and for a dozen years I was chair of the Native American Studies Program.

I relate the above not as some kind of academic rags-to-riches story but to show that, like many other people, I have many reasons to be deeply grateful to Dartmouth and feel a loyalty to the institution. I have also felt sympathy, respect, and fondness for Dartmouth's Native American students, and a kind of loyalty to them. The two loyalties have sometimes been in tension. Dartmouth is a place with a special history and a special pledge. From my office window in the Native American Studies Program I can see the weathervane atop Baker Tower: a colonial figure in three-cornered hat (representing the College's founder, Eleazar Wheelock) and an Indian sitting, presumably learning at his knee, both in the shadow of a pine tree. This "college in the woods" was ostensibly founded for the education of Indian students. It has not always lived up to that pledge and when it has tried to do so, its efforts have sometimes been hampered by incidents, attitudes, and traditions that make Dartmouth a hard place to be Native American.

When Eleazar Wheelock planned the school that became Dartmouth College, he wanted to locate it "in the Heart of the Indian Country."[1] He built it on Abenaki land. Old by American standards, Dartmouth is actually quite a recent development in Abenaki country, where history stretches back thousands of years to a time beyond memory. It is perhaps difficult to think of the upper Connecticut River Valley today as Indian country, even though Indian people still live here. But two and a half centuries ago things were very different. Twenty-five years before Dartmouth was founded, fourteen-year-old Susanna Johnson moved with her family to Charlestown, New Hampshire, now just a half-hour drive down the interstate from Hanover. Charlestown in 1744 was a collection of wooden huts inhabited by nine or ten families. "The Indians were numerous, and associated in a friendly manner with the whites. It was the most northerly settlement on Connecticut River, and the adjacent country was terribly wild," Susanna recalled in her old age. "In those days there was such a mixture on the frontiers of savages and settlers, without established laws to govern them, that the state of society cannot easily be described."[2] "Vox Clamantis in Deserto" proclaims the College motto, "A Voice Crying in the Wilderness," invoking the founding mission to educate the Indians of the region. But wilderness, like beauty and civilization, lies in the eye of the beholder. "Only to the white man was nature a 'wilderness' and only to him was the land 'infested' with 'wild' animals and 'savage' people," wrote Luther Standing Bear, a Lakota author and actor who was one of the first students to graduate from Carlisle Indian Industrial School, a boarding school opened at Carlisle, Pennsylvania in 1879.[3] Abenaki people could say much the same thing. The monumental architecture of Dartmouth conveys to its students, alumni, benefactors, and those of us who work here the solidity of an institution of higher learning. But like the monumental architecture of regimes and empires in other times and places, it can convey quite different messages to the people whose land it occupies and who feel themselves excluded from its power and privileges.

Yet while some Indian people have undoubtedly felt excluded from Dartmouth, others have studied here, made a home here, and managed to make an Indian community within the Dartmouth community. Despite early failings and recurrent mistakes, there is much that is laudable about Dartmouth's Indian history, if only in comparison with greater failings or less effort at educational institutions elsewhere. Dartmouth's historic role in educating Indians was far greater than the rather paltry numbers of Natives who actually graduated from the College in its early years would attest. Before the middle of the nineteenth century many more Indians attended Moor's Charity School than attended the College. Eleazar Wheelock moved Moor's School from Lebanon, Connecticut, to Hanover when he established Dartmouth College and, despite periodic interruptions in its operations, Moor's School remained attached to Dartmouth and came under the responsibility of the Dartmouth president. Some students stayed at Moor's only for a short while. Some made the transition from the Charity School to the College. Most did not, and many never intended to do so; they came to complete a course of study that they hoped would benefit themselves or their people, and they left. Some who transferred to the College only stayed a term or two. Many of the students at Moor's were teenagers and even children, and the president supervised their care, instruction, and progress, and reported their expenses. Moor's Charity School closed its doors in 1849 or '50, but President Nathan Lord insisted in 1853, in one of his many attempts to persuade the Society in Scotland for Propagating Christian Knowledge in the Highlands and Islands and the Foreign Parts of the World (SSPCK) to take a less tightfisted approach in administering the funds in its care for Indian education, that "The school & college virtually constitute a complex being, unique, peculiar, having a very indefinable relation of parts, as to form, but morally & essentially united."[4] Indian students also attended the Chandler School of Arts and Sciences

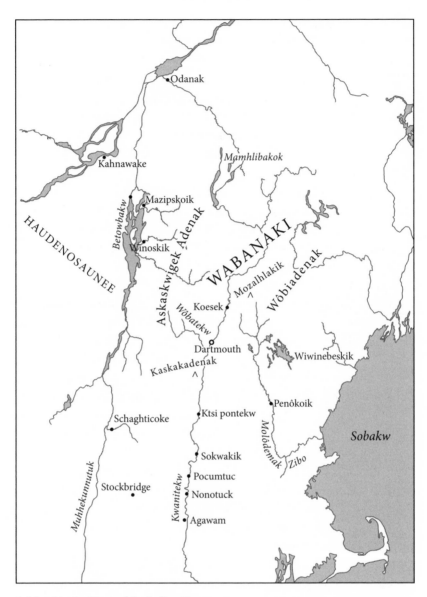

A School in the Heart of the Indian Country.

# MAP KEY*

| | |
|---|---|
| Agawam | Springfield, Massachusetts |
| Askaskwigek Adenak | Green Mountains of Vermont |
| Betowbakw | Lake Champlain |
| Kahnawake | Caughnawaga |
| Kaskakadenak ("wide mountain") | Mount Ascutney |
| Koesek ("at the pines") | Coos, Newbury, Haverhill |
| Ktsi pontekw ("great falls") | Bellows Falls |
| Kwanitekw ("long river") | Connecticut River |
| Mamhlibakok ("wide lake/expansive lake") | Lake Memphremagog |
| Mazipskoik | Missisquoi, Swanton |
| Molôdemak Zibo ("deep water river") | Merrimack River |
| Mozalhlakik | Mt. Moosilauke |
| Muhhekunnutuk | Hudson River |
| Nonotuck | Northampton, Mass |
| Penôkoik ("at falling hill") | Concord, New Hampshire |
| Pocumtuc | Deerfield, Massacusetts |
| Odanak | St. Francis, Quebec |
| Schaghticoke | Mahican village |
| Sobakw | Atlantic Ocean |
| Sokwakik | Squakheag, Northfield |
| Stockbridge | Mission village |
| Winoskik | Winooski |
| Wiwinebeskik | Lake Winnipesaukee |
| Wôbatekw | White River |
| Wôbiadenak | White Mountains |
| Haudenosaunee | The Six Nations of the Iroquois (east to west: Mohawk, Oneida, Tuscarora, Onondaga, Cayuga, Seneca) |
| Wabanaki | Abenaki peoples of Vermont, New Hampshire, and Quebec, plus Penobscot and Passamaquoddy of Maine |

*Lisa Brooks, Donna Roberts Moody, and John Moody, "Native Space," in Rebecca A. Brown, ed., *Where the Great River Rises: An Atlas of the Connecticut River Watershed in Vermont and New Hampshire* (Hanover, N.H.: University Press of New England, 2009), 133–37.

or Scientific School established in 1857, and the Agricultural College, then located in Hanover and affiliated with Dartmouth until 1892, when it moved to Durham and then evolved into the University of New Hampshire. The so-called Scotch Fund administered by the sspck also supported Indian students at Kimball Union Academy in Meriden, New Hampshire, and at Thetford Academy, a dozen miles north across the river in Vermont, usually with a view to helping them advance to college in Hanover. In its first 200 years, Dartmouth admitted only a trickle of Indian students and graduated only a handful. Since 1970, the number of Native American students attending Dartmouth has soared, and few institutions of higher education — perhaps only the tribal colleges — can match Dartmouth's recent record in recruiting, retaining, and graduating Native students.

Joseph Johnson, a Mohegan Indian, was educated at Moor's Charity School when it was located in Connecticut. He received his license to preach at Dartmouth in August 1774, and preached at College Hall on more than one occasion. He wrote (admittedly to Eleazar Wheelock): "I do ever retain in my mind with pleasure, and respects, DARTMOUTH AND HER SONS."[5] Like other alumni, Native students have often had fond memories of Dartmouth. But they also have had mixed and sometimes bitter memories of their experiences at this privileged, East Coast, Ivy League institution. One Native alumnus, who attended for just one year in the 1920s, reflected half a century later on what he described as Dartmouth's "agony, sort of, in trying to find ways for responding to the indian [*sic*] conundrum Wheelock saddled the school with in the first place."[6] The experiences of American Indians at Dartmouth mirror the experiences of Indian peoples in America. What happened here happened elsewhere; what happened elsewhere affected what happened here. Since its founding, in the view of another Native alumnus, Dartmouth "has alternately used, courted, tossed aside, enticed, mocked, ignored, and, occasionally, educated Native Americans. In some ways, it is almost a mini-America."[7]

In some ways, Dartmouth's Native American community represents a mini–Indian country as well. Different from other Indian communities in the huge tribal diversity, lack of on-campus generational diversity, and temporary residence of its members, it has nonetheless often experienced differing attitudes, generational changes, and shifting strategies that reflected what was going on Indian country as a whole. In addition, Native American graduates of Dartmouth have gone home to help Indian people reshape policies and forge new strategies and have gone national in helping to shape federal

Indian policy. Native Americans have also traveled far and wide after leaving Dartmouth, joining other "Indians in unexpected places."[8]

Dartmouth's Indian history involves not only the Indian students who have come to campus but also non-Indians associated with the College who have gone into Indian country and into Indian affairs. Sometimes they went with honorable intentions, sometimes not. Indian and non-Indian students from Moor's and from Dartmouth went to work as missionaries and teachers in Indian country. As missionaries, Indian agents, and politicians, non-Native alumni often participated in assaults on Indian cultures, lands, resources, and independence. In the eighteenth and nineteenth centuries, going into the "Indian business" often meant getting involved in the land business. In the nineteenth and twentieth centuries, going into politics sometimes meant getting involved in Indian affairs.

Michael Dorris, the founding chair of Dartmouth's Native American Studies Program, once said that Dartmouth's Indian history really began in 1971, when the College finally committed itself to Native education in a meaningful way. In a sense he was right. But Dartmouth has a much longer history that is Native American. In fact, the bulk of its story pertains to the period *before* 1971 and before most of its Native American students attended Dartmouth. Members of the Dartmouth community often invoke that history as part of an honorable or not-so-honorable tradition, but few people really know much about it beyond some words in the College charter, some knowledge of Samson Occom's fund-raising efforts in England, and some awareness that the College failed for a long time to live up to its pledge and then struggled to get things right. This book is an attempt to tell the whole story, though not an attempt to cover every detail or mention every individual involved.

One of the obstacles faced by historians of Native America is dispelling the myth that Indians were "people without history" because they produced no written records or histories of their own. Of course, Indian people have as much history as anyone else, and oral cultures typically preserve memories of the past in traditions, songs, and stories passed from generation to generation, but a dearth of documents written by Native people does constitute one of the challenges in doing Indian history. It is less of an issue, however, when reconstructing the Indian history of an institution whose historical foundations rested on teaching young Indians to read and write English. Indian students of Eleazar Wheelock wrote, sometimes wrote well, and sometimes wrote often. As with all historical documents, one must consider the circumstances, motivations, and restrictions of the writer. Wheelock's Indian students clearly were expected to adopt a subordinate, even self-abnegating, tone in their writing, to confess their frequent failings and their many sins, and to express appropriate gratitude for their education. The fact that the students knew Wheelock might use their letters for fund-raising also no doubt affected their content. It is as if Wheelock is looking over their shoulders as they write; sometimes it is clear that Wheelock is the real author of letters attributed to his students. Some letters conceal more than they reveal: Indian students often shielded their individual humanity and their quiet resistance behind the veil of their writing. Nevertheless, Indians who attended Moor's Charity School and Dartmouth College produced a body of writing and an important documentary source for understanding the institution's Native American history. Many years ago, as a graduate student poring over manuscript records in London dealing with colonial Indian affairs, I learned to recognize the handwriting of Joseph Brant, a prominent Mohawk war chief; Brant had studied as a young man under Wheelock, and I appreciated the clarity that distinguished his letters from those of many of the non-Indian correspondents in the files. Samson Occom is generally recognized as the first Native American to write an autobiography. In addition, he wrote diaries, letters, ethnographies, sermons, hymns, and petitions to colonial assemblies and state legislatures, complaining about encroachments on Indian lands and infringements of Indian rights. "Mastering the dominant voice," notes Bernd Peyer, "enabled him to defend himself against colonial repression." About 1,000 manuscript pages of his writings survive. Occom scholar Joanna Brooks describes it as "the largest extant body of writing produced by an American Indian author before Santee Sioux intellectual Charles Eastman (1858–1939) began his writing career in the early twentieth century."[9] Eastman, Dartmouth class of 1887, went on to become an author as well as a physician, and wrote several books on Native American issues. Some Indian students wrote about their experiences at Dartmouth; some who traveled far afield kept in touch with the College after they graduated. More recently, Dartmouth's Native American students and faculty have written dissertations, books, novels, poems, news editorials, and court decisions.

Brant, Occom, and Eastman all, on occasion, used their pens to defend their Indian world and to critique the non-Indian society that presumed to call them savage. "I am afraid the Poor Indians will never Stand a good Chance with the English, in their Land Controversies," Occom wrote in 1773, "because they are very Poor they have no Money, Money is almighty now a Days, and the Indians have no Learning, no Wit nor Couning the English have all." Ten years later, at the end of the American Revolution, he reflected: "when I Come to Consider and See the Conduct of the Most Learned, Polite, and Rich Nations of the World, I find them to be the Most Tyranacal, Cruel, and inhuman oppressors of their Fellow Creatures in the World."[10] Not all Indian students attained the degree of literacy shown by Occom, Brant, and Eastman, but many acquired an appreciation of the "power of print" and understood that literacy could serve Indian people as a weapon in the war for cultural and political survival as well as it served the English and Americans in the campaign for conversion and as an instrument for dispossession.[11]

Eighteenth-century writing lacked modern consistencies in spelling, punctuation, and capitalization. In quoting from the sources, I have retained the original spellings and forms, inserting letters, punctuation, or capitals only when it seemed necessary to clarify meaning, and indicating the insertion within square brackets. In some cases records are incomplete and sketchy. In an age when literate Anglo-Americans did not always standardize spelling even of their own names, it is not surprising that they spelled Native Americans' names without much consistency. Outsiders — in the students' home communities, for instance — did not always make the distinction between Moor's Charity School and the College and simply described the students as going "to Dartmouth." Sometimes even the College records are not always clear or consistent. Some students attended the Agricultural College, some the Chandler Scientific School. Others attended neighboring preparatory schools — Kimball Union Academy and Newport Academy in New Hampshire, Thetford Academy in Vermont, and Northfield Mount Hermon in Massachusetts — with a view to enrolling at Dartmouth, but did not always succeed in doing so. Many students enrolled in the College and its associated schools but did not graduate, and some stayed less than a year. Sometimes the records briefly mention an individual identified as an Indian or bearing a recognizable Indian name who was at the school for an indeterminate period of time and for an indeterminate purpose. In a few cases, there are doubts about a student's Indian identity.

Despite their gaps and silences, Dartmouth records afford scattered glimpses into the lives of the Indian students who attended the Charity School and the College. Obliged to provide the sspck with a detailed accounting of how money was being spent — and that it was indeed being spent on

Indians—Dartmouth itemized every expense. Ledger books and receipts record costs for tuition, board, and lodging, books and Bibles, paper, quills, and ink, shirts, waistcoats, pants, woolen stockings, coats, hats, and gloves, shoes and buckles, buttons and thread, handkerchiefs, washing and mending of clothes, candles and lamp oil, cords of firewood, doctor's bills, and travel expenses (which often entailed renting a horse at 3 or 4 cents per mile and sometimes required hiring a sleigh as well). Such entries reveal much about who was at the school, about what they were studying, about what their lives were like, and about ordinary incidents in individuals' day-to-day experience.

Dartmouth's involvement in Indian history has taken many forms: an institution at the forefront of the English assault on Native American cultures; a colonial project physically located in Abenaki country; a college that lost sight of its founding mission though it never relinquished its founding story; an "Indian school" without Indians; a place where young white men "played Indian" and established traditions associated with their notions of what constituted "Indianness"; a college that recommitted itself to Native American education and achieved levels of success unmatched by other institutions, but largely by default; a place Native Americans have regarded with anger, bitterness, nostalgia, and affection.

Two hundred years ago, convinced that Indians could survive only if they ceased to be Indians, Dartmouth attempted to change its Native students. Convinced of the rightness of their mission, the College and its affiliated charity school directly affected the lives of dozens of Indian people, and indirectly affected the lives of hundreds more. But Indian people had something to say about how much they changed, about what they did with what they learned, and about Indian education at Dartmouth. The Native students at Dartmouth today are more likely to apply the skills and knowledge they gain to make sure that Indians survive as Indians in a rapidly changing world. Few people today think of Dartmouth as a school in the heart of Indian country— quite the contrary: for many Indian students and their families in the West, Dartmouth is "out there" in a remote northeastern corner of the country, far from the Indian communities they know—yet it is a school with a role in Indian country.

Dartmouth's Indian history is a troubled one, as is the history of Native Americans in this country. In its failings, contradictions, and attempts (sometimes misguided) to do the right thing, it mirrors the larger story of English and American dealings with Native peoples over time and across the continent. Yet it also has its own stories that are, for better or worse, unique. It is a history about which Dartmouth itself would not agree, which is as it should be in a liberal arts college that encourages multiple perspectives and understandings, but it is a history that Native and non-Native members of the Dartmouth community — at different levels and with different experiences — have shared, and it is a past that continues to shape Dartmouth present.

Eleazar Wheelock. Joseph Steward painted this portrait of Dartmouth's first president from memory or from a miniature some fifteen years after Wheelock's death.
*Courtesy Hood Museum of Art, Dartmouth College, P. 793.2. Commissioned by the Trustees of Dartmouth College, Hanover, New Hampshire.*

*Chapter One*

# ELEAZAR WHEELOCK AND THE INDIAN CHARITY SCHOOL, 1743–69

❦ IN THIS DAY AND AGE, Eleazar Wheelock is a difficult man to understand, let alone like. He stares out from his portrait wearing a snow-white wig and clerical gown, with one hand on the Dartmouth College charter and a look that could be calculating or self-satisfied. As historian Jere Daniell has clearly demonstrated, Wheelock was a shrewd politician with an eye to the main chance.[1] Pious and moralizing, he amassed hundreds of acres of land through his educational ventures, he owned slaves, and his prescription for the education and salvation of Native Americans was predicated on the unquestioned superiority of his own culture and the eradication of theirs. Domineering, scheming, and hypocritical, he did pretty well for himself in the business of converting and educating Indians — what historian Francis Jennings characterized as "the missionary racket."[2]

Yet there was more to Wheelock than that. David McClure and Elijah Parish, who knew him, described Wheelock as a "great and good man" who was selfless in his efforts to bring civilization and Christianity to the Indians he held in his paternal care.[3] Published in 1811, their book about Wheelock was largely a eulogy, but more recent and more objective authors also have been favorably impressed with his commitment to Indian education.[4] Although his goals for Indians have long since been discredited as a form of cultural imperialism from which many Native American communities are still struggling to recover, Wheelock believed himself to be doing good work — and God's work. He displayed concern for the fate and future of Indians, at a time when few did. In fact, to read Wheelock's own writings, he dedicated his life to their cause. "I have for many years past, had my tho'ts much on the piteous state of the Indian Natives of this Continent who have been perishing in vast numbers from Age to Age for lack of vision," he wrote to Rev. George

Whitefield in 1756.[5] "I have had you upon my heart ever since I was a boy," he told the Mohawks, Oneidas, and Tuscaroras the same year.

I have pitied you on account of your worldly poverty; but much more on account of the perishing case your precious souls are in, without the knowledge of the only true God and Savior of sinners. I have prayed for you daily for more than thirty years, that a way might be opened to send the gospel among you, and you be made willing to receive it. And I hope God is now answering the prayers that have long been made for you, and that the time of his mercy to your perishing nation is near at hand.

He was sending them ministers, he said, and he intended "by God's help to do all the good I can to the poor miserable Indians as long as I live."[6]

The Mohawks, Oneidas, and Tuscaroras would not have considered themselves poor and miserable or felt that their nations and souls were perishing. Together with the Onondagas, Cayugas, and Senecas, they constituted the Six Nations of the Iroquois League, which stretched across what is now upstate New York from the Mohawk Valley to the Allegheny Valley. Even after massive losses from war and disease, the Iroquois, or Haudenosaunee, still exercised considerable power in the intertribal and international contests that raged across northeastern North America. It is doubtful too whether the Iroquois agreed with Wheelock's solution to their problems: like Thomas Jefferson and many later U.S. Indian policy-makers, Wheelock believed that giving up hunting, settling down as farmers, and embracing Christianity was key to the Indians' survival in this world and to their happiness in the next. "It looks to me more & more as though God designs to make a Short work with the Natives, that they will be Soon christianised, or destroyed," he wrote in 1766; "If they will not embrace the Gospel it is likely in a few Generations more, there will be no more Opportunity to Shew our Charity towards their naked Starving Bodies or perishing Souls." [7]Iroquois women, who for centuries had cultivated and harvested crops of corn, beans, and squash — the sacred three sisters at the core of the Iroquois diet and economy — were likely bemused by the notion that they needed to learn how to farm, but reformers like Wheelock and Jefferson thought Indian women were engaged in the wrong pursuit: farming was men's work; women should restrict themselves to more domestic chores. An economy based on hunting and seasonal mobility was a barrier to Indians ever becoming Christianized and civilized, so missionaries and reformers felt they had to change the Indians' way of life and dismantle their gendered division of labor as well as preach the Gospel to them and teach them English. The Iroquois would prove recurrently resistant to Wheelock's prescription for change and his philosophy for education.

Wheelock blamed many of the Indians' woes on unscrupulous, liquor-peddling traders and lack of concern on the part of society. He intended "to clear myself, and Family, of partaking in the public Guilt of our Land and Nation in such a Neglect of them."[8] He developed what he called "the great Design" as the best strategy for saving Indians: take "their own Children (two or more of a Tribe, that they may not lose their own Language) and give them an Education among ourselves, under the Tuition, & Guidance of a godly, & Skillful Master; where they may, not only, have means to Make them Schollars, but the best Means to Make them Christians indeed, . . . to fit them for the Gospel Ministry among their respective Tribes." Indian missionaries, who spoke Native languages, understood Native customs, and had influence in their own communities, would be more effective than English missionaries and, noted Wheelock, "may be supported with less than half the Expence."[9]

Anticipating Henry Knox—George Washington's secretary of war who argued that money was better spent dealing fairly with Indians rather than fighting them—Wheelock argued that if half the expense that had gone into building and garrisoning forts had been invested in missionaries and school-teachers for the Indians, "the instructed and civilized Party would have been a far better Defence than all our expensive Fortresses, and prevented the laying waste so many Towns and Villages."[10] With Britain engaged in a life-and-death struggle against Catholic France for hegemony in North America, a struggle that involved Indians on both sides and sometimes caught them in the middle, Wheelock was not blind to the benefits that English teachers and a strategically-located school might offer. "The Nations will not make war with us while their Children, and especially the Children of their Chiefs, are with us," he explained to the Earl of Dartmouth. In competing for Indian allegiance as well as Indian souls, Wheelock's "great design" combined "mundane incentives with heaven-sent obligations."[11]

There was ample precedent for what Wheelock tried to do, and for the attitudes and assumptions he brought to the work.[12] The English had been teaching and preaching to the Indians of New England for more than a century. In the mid–seventeenth century, John Eliot established a ring of "praying towns" in Massachusetts. With the help of an Indian translator and an

Indian printer (James Printer), he translated the Bible into the Massachusett dialect of the Algonquian language. It was the first Bible printed in British North America.[13] Harvard's charter of 1650 declared that the institution's purpose was "the education of the English and Indian Youth of this Country," and Harvard built an Indian college in 1656. Caleb Chaesahteaumuk was the first to graduate in 1665, but he died of "consumption" — tuberculosis — soon after.[14] In 1674, Daniel Gookin estimated that 1,100 Indian converts lived in the fourteen praying towns,[15] but neither the praying towns nor Harvard's Indian college survived the devastation of King Philip's War, which broke out the next year. After years of neglect, the Indian college was torn down in 1698. More enduring was the work of Thomas Mayhew and his sons on Martha's Vineyard, where Wampanoags embraced Christianity, established their own church, and made their religion a source of community cohesion and resilience in perilous times.[16] In western Massachusetts, John Sergeant established an Indian mission town at Stockbridge in the 1730s, drawing in Mahican and other neighboring peoples.[17]

After Eleazar Wheelock graduated from Yale and was ordained as minister at the Second Congregational Church in Lebanon, Connecticut, in 1735, he opened a small school—he called it his "Lattin School"—for "a few English youth, preparing for admission into college."[18] Eight years later a twenty-year-old Mohegan Indian named Samson Occom entered the school. It was the beginning of a relationship between Wheelock and Occom that would stretch across three decades, produce Dartmouth College, and end in bitterness and recrimination.

The Mohegans had once been a force in southern Connecticut. Under their leader Uncas, they had allied with the English in both the Pequot War (1636–37) and King Philip's War (1675–76) and increased their own power as that of rival tribes collapsed.[19] But they could not escape the disease, dispossession, and disruption that accompanied English colonialism. By the time of Occom's birth a mere 350 Mohegans were eking out an existence on the remnants of their former homeland. Many peddled baskets and brooms or worked as servants and laborers for Englishmen. Some sought escape in alcohol. Others turned to Christianity. In the first draft of his autobiographical narrative in 1765—the first written by a Native American—Occom said he was "Born a Heathen" and educated in his parents' "Heathenish Notions" until he was sixteen. Then "there was a great Stir of Religion in these Parts of the World amongst the Indians as Well as the English, and about this Time I began to think about the Christian Religion, and was under great trouble of Mind for Some Time." The emotional intensity of the religious revival known as the Great Awakening appealed to the poor and powerless. At seventeen, Occom "received a Hope, and as I began to think about Religion So I began to learn to read." In the second and longer draft of his autobiography, written in 1768, Occom said he put his trust in Christ, and "From this Time the Distress and Burden of my mind was removed, and I found Serenity and Pleasure of Soul, in Serving God." He taught himself to read and write so he could better understand "the Word of God" and teach Mohegan children.[20]

Occom and the Mohegans also had good reason to appreciate the power of literacy in more temporal matters. The tribe's experiences with land cases in the 1730s demonstrated the need to understand and command the legal language of the English colonial world. At nineteen, Occom was elected to the tribe's twelve-person governing council, at a time when the Mohegans were renewing their efforts to reclaim lost lands. In 1743, they took their suit to court. In December of that year, Occom sought out Wheelock.[21] Hearing of Wheelock's preparatory school in Lebanon, where his mother may have worked as a house servant, he had his mother ask Wheelock if he would be willing to give him instruction in reading. Occom's initiative was the important first step in Wheelock's career in Indian education: "it was Occom who sought out Wheelock and not Wheelock who sought out Occom."[22] Wheelock agreed, and Occom went to Lebanon, expecting to stay a matter of days or weeks; instead he spent four years with Wheelock, much of the time living in Wheelock's household.

Occom entered Wheelock's school with financial assistance from the Boston commissioners of the London-based Society for the Propagation of the Gospel in Foreign Parts. Although considerably older than the other students, and despite poor health and failing eyesight, Occom became fluent in English and proficient in Latin, Greek, and Hebrew, a remarkable achievement by any standards and particularly at a time when few people were literate even in their own language. Occom became a schoolmaster, and in 1756 the Society finally recommended that he be ordained. He ministered to the Montauk community on Long Island and served his own people and the neighboring Niantic Indians as an itinerant preacher. He was paid only a fraction of what English ministers earned, and he supplemented his income with hunting and fishing, carpentry, bookbinding, and making and selling brooms and wooden spoons.

Following the path Occom chose could not have been easy. Exhorting Indian people to look to Christianity to overcome the problems that beset them was a hard message to sell when Christians were responsible for so many of the problems. He faced opposition from among his own people, even resistance within his own family. David McClure, who visited him in his two-story frame home at Mohegan, said Occom "wished to live in english style," but his Montauk wife, Mary, with whom he had ten children, "retained a fondness for her Indian customs. She declined, evening & morning setting at table. Her dress was mostly Indian, & when he spake to her in english, she answered in her native language, although she could speak good english. His children when they left him, adopted the wild & roving life of Savages."[23]

Nevertheless, Occom's success prompted Wheelock to do more. His Mohegan student had been more useful than "could have been Reasonably expected of an English Man" at "less than half ye Expence," he said.[24] In 1754, Wheelock asked John Brainerd, a missionary in New Jersey, to find "two likely Boys" from the Delaware tribe to join his school. Brainerd sent fourteen-year-old John Pumshire and Jacob Woolley, a "naturally modest" and rather bashful eleven year-old. The boys set out on foot to walk some 200 miles "thro' a Country, in which they knew not one Mortal, and Where they had never pass'd before, to throw themselves for an Education upon a stranger," and arrived in Lebanon a week before Christmas.[25] Wheelock taught them to read, speak, and write English. Tragedy often struck Indian students at colonial schools, and later at American boarding schools. According to Wheelock, John Pumshire became ill, was sent home, and died soon after. (A "Jersey Delaware Indian" named John Pumpshire [*sic*] or Cawkeeponen was serving his people as an interpreter a couple of years later, but this may have been the student's father or uncle.)[26] Two more young Delawares, Joseph Woolley and Hezekiah Calvin, arrived, riding the same horse John had ridden home. Joseph was Jacob's cousin. Hezekiah, said Brainerd, was "a smart little fellow" but "will want taking care of. He loves to play, and will have his hat in one place and his mittens in another."[27] By July 1758 the three boys had "almost shaken off the Indian." Jacob could "read Virgil and Tully and the Greek Testament very handsomely."[28]

Wheelock persuaded Joshua More, a wealthy farmer in Mansfield, Connecticut, to donate a house and a school building on two acres of land "more or less." The school sat alongside the green in Lebanon, near Wheelock's house and the meetinghouse. One suggestion at the time was to call it "The Indian Charity School in America";[29] it became known as Moor's [*sic*] Charity School or the Indian Charity School. Its declared purpose was "Educating Such of the Indian Natives, of any or all the Indian tribes in North America, or other poor Persons, in Reading, Writing, and all Liberal Arts, and Sciences . . . & More Especially for instructing them in the Knowledge & Practice of the Protestant Christian Religion." More than 100 Indian students enrolled in the school during Wheelock's lifetime; McClure and Parish said as many as 150. In addition to Samson Occom, between thirteen and fifteen Indians educated at Moor's Charity School served as missionaries, teachers, or assistants. As he would at Dartmouth, Wheelock also admitted English youths who showed promise of becoming missionaries. Eight of his non-Indian students went on to become missionaries, including Samuel Kirkland, David McClure, and David Avery.[30]

Two hundred and twenty years before Dartmouth College went coeducational, Wheelock admitted girls. In his view, educating girls was essential to promoting Christianity and proper ways of living. The first was Amy Johnson, sister of Mohegan Joseph Johnson, who arrived in June 1761; Miriam Storrs, a Delaware, arrived soon after, and in the next eight years as many as nineteen attended. But Wheelock was no more interested in promoting gender quality than he was in racial equality: woman and Indians occupied assigned and subordinate places in his educational mission and in his hierarchical world. What Wheelock called the "female school" was part of the Charity School, but it had its own curriculum to educate young Indian women "in all parts of good Housewifery," which included tending a dairy, sewing, and spinning as well as reading and writing. Whereas boys lived at the school and attended class five or six days each week, girls were placed "in pious families," who were expected to teach them English in return for housework, "or under the care of a skilful governess," where they were "instructed in domestic business and other accomplishments adapted to their sex." Once a week they went to Wheelock's house for instruction in writing. The girls were also expected to teach the younger children. As in U.S. boarding schools for Indians in the late nineteenth century, the young Indian women at Moor's were being prepared to take their place at the lower rungs of society's ladder, working as domestic servants in non-Indian homes. But Wheelock had other hopes for them: that, like his male students, they would become missionaries to the tribes, or at least the wives and helpmates of missionaries.[31]

Although he began by educating Indians from southern New England, he was more interested in recruiting students from the Iroquois, whom he considered "a much better breed," less corrupted by contact with colonial society.[32] He obtained the cooperation of Sir William Johnson, an Irish trader in the Mohawk Valley who rose to become Britain's superintendent of Indian affairs north of the Ohio River. Johnson, who had married an influential Mohawk, Molly Brant, exerted considerable influence among the Iroquois and used his position to build up substantial landholdings.[33] In 1761 Wheelock began sending graduates from his school into Iroquois country as missionaries and teachers and asked Johnson for help in recruiting "Six likely Male youth of the Six Nations to be conducted hither to the School Under My care for an Education in such Parts of Learning as may render them Most useful among their Tribes." Educating young Iroquois "in the liberal arts and sciences, as well as in the knowledge and practice of the protestant religion" and training some to be missionaries among their tribes would, he assured Johnson, "guard them against the influence of Jesuits; be an antidote to their idolatrous and savage practices [and] attach them to the English interest." Johnson was optimistic that as word of Wheelock's "Laudable design" spread, more gentlemen would lend financial support and the number of students would increase. Johnson himself pledged "to contribute my mite."[34]

Samson Occom made three trips to the Oneidas in two years. In the summer of 1761, Molly's brother, Joseph Brant, a protégé of Sir William, and two other young Mohawks sent by Johnson arrived in Lebanon. They were edgy and apprehensive. Each had brought a horse, ready to make a speedy getaway if necessary. Brant was well dressed and understood some English; his companions, Center and Negyes, were almost naked and could not speak a word of English. Center was ill, and was soon sent home, where he died. Negyes escorted Center home and never came back, apparently having fallen in love and married there. But two other Mohawks — Moses and Johannes — came in their place. Meanwhile, Wheelock reported, Brant proved a good pupil, learned to "read handsomely in the Bible," and "much Endeard himself to Me (and I think to everybody Else) by his good Behaviour." Brant's education and his influential connections in Mohawk and English society served him well as he rose to prominence as a chief and cultural intermediary. Wheelock hoped Johnson would help recruit more students from the Mohawks "and from Tribes as remote as may be."[35]

When fifteen-year-old David McClure went to Wheelock's school to prepare to become a missionary, half of the thirty students in the school were Indian and half English. Arriving in Lebanon, he saw "a number of Indian & English youth playing on the spacious green" in front of Wheelock's house and the school.[36] On the surface there was perhaps nothing remarkable about that, but this was 1764. The long and brutal "French and Indian war" had just ended, and Pontiac's multi-tribal war of Indian independence had set the frontiers ablaze. As evidenced by the notorious slaughter of twenty peaceable Conestoga Indians by the "Paxton Boys" in Pennsylvania the previous December, it was an era of intense and escalating Indian-hating. Colonists generally were more interested in killing and scalping Indians than in educating them: at Windsor, Connecticut, a collection plate for the school came back empty except for a bullet and a flint. Wheelock's English and Indian students did not always get along—there were fistfights on more than one occasion[37]—and he clearly did not treat all students equally; nevertheless, a bicultural school and community of the kind Wheelock was building was remarkable.

But there was never enough money. Wheelock struggled perennially to finance his school. In June 1763, for instance, during a journey to Boston and Portsmouth, Wheelock solicited donations from private individuals, many of them contributing only shillings and pence, raising a total of £114. 6s. 11d.[38] In addition, Wheelock was constantly petitioning the colonial legislatures of Connecticut, Massachusetts, and New Hampshire, churches, and individuals for funds. He was not always very subtle: Writing to the governor of New Hampshire, Benning Wentworth, in 1764, Wheelock reminded him that he was not getting any younger, and had plenty of money but no children: so why not "impart Some part of the Abundance with Which God has blessed You, for the education of the Children of the Natives of this Land?"[39]

Support came from the Society for the Propagation of the Gospel in London and the sspck in Edinburgh, which was engaged in similar work in the Highlands of Scotland, endeavoring to evangelize peoples who were culturally distinct from the rest of English-speaking Britain. In 1701 "a few private gentlemen in Edinburgh" who were "deeply affected by the unhappy situation of their countrymen in the Highlands and Islands, sunk in ignorance, and destitute of all means of improvement," had begun raising money to establish schools in the Highlands, and in 1709 Queen Anne had approved the founding of the sspck. The sspck established charity schools in the Highlands and Islands of Scotland and sent schoolmasters to spread Presbyterian

Christianity, teach the English language, and promote "civilized" values. The sspck's evangelicals worked zealously to eradicate "immoral" music, dancing, drunkenness, and fighting and to curb sexual laxity. The first teachers were Lowlanders, but some Highlanders subsequently took up the work of educating their own people, just as some of Wheelock's Indian students did in America. In the second half of the century, sspck schools added spinning, weaving, and other crafts to their curriculum. The society initially worked to replace Gaelic with English, and students caught speaking Gaelic were chastised. But, realizing that tolerating the native language could help facilitate religious instruction, the sspck published the New Testament in Gaelic, and the Old Testament in 1801.[40]

After two decades of educational missionary work in the Highlands, the sspck extended its efforts to other "heathen and infidel lands" and began to support missionary work among American Indians. Seeing the wild lands of both the Scottish Highlands and North America as spiritually destitute "foreign mission fields," both part of a "North Atlantic circuit," the sspck supported missionary activities and educational colonialism in both places; its work among Highlanders and Indians followed some parallel courses. Twenty years after it was founded, the sspck set up boards of correspondents in Boston and New York through which it subsidized projects, and it sent missionaries to Indians in Connecticut and Long Island.[41] According to a committee report, the sspck's primary goal was "to *seize* upon young untutored minds, as yet undepraved by vicious habits and examples, but utterly destitute of all means of cultivation; to rescue them from savage ignorance, superstition, and vice; to furnish them with the means of knowledge and grace, and to train them up into fitness for being useful members of the church, as well as of human society." The goal was not just to teach children to read English and do numbers; it was "the SALVATION OF SOULS."[42] The sspck was to have a long and influential role in the history of both Moor's Charity School and Dartmouth College.

Wheelock educated with a heavy hand. He "monitored his students, controlled their actions, and demanded that they reconceptualize their thoughts and deeds in terms of sin and damnation."[43] Some Native students resisted and refused, of course—so did some non-Natives—but the letters his Indian students wrote to him were not only deferential, as befitted the conventions of the time, and humble, as befitted good Christians, but so much so as to suggest that Wheelock demanded unquestioning obedience, subordination, and even expressions of self-loathing. Some letters were in the form of confessions, dictated by Wheelock or at least with the minister literally or figuratively looking on. Hannah Nonesuch, a Niantic or Narragansett , wrote a confession on March 11, 1768, the very day she entered the school. Three nights before — she blamed Sarah Wyog, a Mohegan, for leading her astray — she was "guilty of being at the tavern and tarrying there with a company of Indian boys & girls, for (what is commonly called) a frolick where was much spirituous liquor drank, & much dancing & rude conduct" late into the night. Wheelock made her write (or at least affix her mark to what he wrote): "I am heartily sorrey, & desire to lie low in the dust & do now beg forgiveness of God, the Revd. & worthy Doctor Wheelock, his family, & school, and all whom I have hereby offended." Mary Secutor, a Narragansett, was at the same "frolick." Mary had been in trouble before. A couple of evenings after Christmas, she confessed, "I went into the School while I was intoxicated with Liquor and there behaved myself in a Lude and very immodest Manner among the School Boys, I also in a vile Manner profaned the Sacred Name of God." After her latest offense, Wheelock made her sign the same abject confession as Hannah and admit to having committed "many gross sins" while under the influence of alcohol. The first confession was "not her own composition"; the second was in Wheelock's handwriting. In July, Mary dropped out of school, an event recorded by a short letter to Wheelock thanking him for his paternal care and assuming all blame for her failure: "dont think I desarve ye honour of being in your School."[44] Female students did not always earn Wheelock's censure, however. The same July, he wrote a letter of recommendation for "Susanna, a Mohawk Girl," who had "obtained a universal character among us for a young woman of virtue."[45]

Other students confessed to backsliding, drinking, swearing, impure thoughts, and, in the case of Joseph Woolley, "the Carnal effections, rising in my Heart." When Joseph began to court newly arrived Hannah Garret, a Pequot teenager who had been living with the Narragansetts, Wheelock sent him to New York to teach Mohawk children. Joseph proposed marriage to Hannah, but he never saw her again; he died of consumption a year later. Hannah subsequently married fellow student David Fowler, a Montauk fourteen years her senior (who had previously hoped to marry Amy Johnson and gave her "a Gold Ring, which cost two Dollars"). Hannah accompanied Fowler on missions and had nine children with him, but none of the other female students showed much inclination for missionary work. Nathan Clap, an Indian from Cape Cod, confessed to "sinful Lusts" and asked Wheelock to let him marry his maid, Mary (presumably the object of his desires), "or vanish me away from the School." Wheelock promptly sent him to work with Samuel Kirkland in Oneida country, where he evidently found other female companionship.[46]

The regimen at Moor's was hard. In common with other schools at the time, but in total disregard of Native American child-rearing practices, corporal punishment was standard. At home, Wheelock knew, the Indians' "great Fondness for their Children" would not permit such treatment, but at his school, he wrote, "I can correct & punish them as I please, and as I find necessary, to humble them, and reform their manners."[47] The students' day began with prayers before sunrise; school began with prayer at nine o'clock, ended at twelve, began again at two, and ended at five o'clock with prayer. "Evening prayers were attended before daylight was gone. Afterward they applied to their studies."[48] In addition to the scriptures, students studied Greek and Latin and practiced penmanship. They also learned "husbandry," both to help support the school and to begin their adoption of the agricultural way of life that Wheelock regarded as crucial to their future. As they would at Dartmouth, the students sometimes felt they were being exploited as cheap labor and complained that they spent more time laboring than they did studying. When Molly Brant learned that Joseph, her brother, was required to do farm labor, she sent him a letter in Mohawk insisting that he withdraw from school, which caused Wheelock "no small Exercises to my Mind, and many Turnings of Thoughts what should be the Occasion of or meaning of it."[49] The father of Charles Daniel, a Narragansett, pulled him out of school after two years: he could just as well have taught him to farm himself and enjoy the profits of his labor, he told Wheelock, "being myself bro't up with ye best of Farmers," a reminder of the agricultural competence of Algonquian women and that the English enjoyed no monopoly on the agriculture that they held as an essential tenet of civilization.[50]

Several Narragansetts attended Moor's Charity School. Formerly one of the major powers in southern New England, the Narragansetts were devastated during King Philip's War, when an English army attacked and burned their village stronghold in December 1675, an event commonly referred to as the Great Swamp Fight, but frequently and perhaps more accurately described as a massacre. Narragansett numbers continued to decline as more and more English settled in Rhode Island. Many Narragansetts converted to Christianity during the Great Awakening, and they established their own church with their own minister.[51] Other Narragansetts sought an education for their children.

Sarah Simon, described as "a pious Narragansett widow," sent four sons and a daughter to Wheelock. In a letter Sarah wrote , or dictated, to Wheelock in the fall of 1767, she thanked him for "Your pious care of those Children which are under Your tuition," especially her daughter, also called Sarah, who had entered school in December 1765. "I've a little Son that I want You shou'd receive into Your School. If You wou'd, I shou'd except it as an Inesteemable Favour. And wholly give him up to You, to be altogether under Your wise Instruction, 'till he arrives to ye age of twenty one years." Sarah may have wanted her children to receive a Christian education to save their souls; she may have wanted them to acquire literacy in English to help them make their way in the world; and she may have hoped that school would afford them a refuge from hardship, hunger, and hostility. Like thousands of Native American parents who sent their children to boarding schools and colleges in the centuries that followed, she had one major request: "that You wou'd at proper seasons, allow him ye privilege of visiting me."[52]

Like Richard Henry Pratt, superintendent of Carlisle Indian School more than a century later, Wheelock firmly believed that the best way to educate Indian children was to "remove them entirely from all connection with their countrymen" and keep them "out of the reach of their Parents, and out of the way of *Indian* examples."[53] Allowing students to return home, even to visit sick or dying relatives, risked re-exposing them to Indian ways and jeopardizing the "progress" they had made in school. In the contest of cultures waged between European and Native American societies, Indian war parties frequently took captive English children with a view to adopting them and converting them into Indians. English soldiers rarely took Indian prisoners, but the Indian children at Wheelock's school, like those at later American boarding schools, surely felt themselves captives in the process of cultural conversion.

In June 1768, Wheelock sent Sarah Simon a letter that was by turns lecturing, whining, and punitive. With regard to her son James, he wrote: "if you intend to take him away from me, or encourage his going away as others have done after I have been at great Expense to educate him, or when he has half got his Education, I insist upon it that you let me know it now, before I spend any more money to be thrown away upon him." Wheelock claimed there were hundreds of others who would gladly take his place. "It grieves & breaks my Heart that while I am wearing my Life out to do good to the poor Indians, they themselves have no more Desire to help forward the great Design of their happiness here and Eternal Salvation in the World to come . . . those on whom I have bestowed much Pains & Cost pulling the other way and as fast as they can undoing all I have done." He prayed God would show them the way out of their misery. As for her daughter: "Sarah carries herself very well, but I think it not best that she should come home to visit you until this Fall."[54]

In April 1769, Sarah wrote a formal request to Wheelock ("Revend and Honrd Sir") asking that she be allowed to go home and visit her sick mother, "for I donot think she is long for this world." Sarah's letter revealed Wheelock's influence on her education and her understanding of the kind of language she needed to employ to win his approval. "Oh how I orto Blease and adore that grat and kind God that put in the hands some of his Pepple to take so much Care of the poor indions nee above all the rast. It Seems to me I could go any where or do anything if it would do any good to my poor Parishing Brethren." She signed herself "your Ever Dutyfull Sarvant."[55]

Two of widow Sarah's sons, Abraham and Daniel, entered school in 1768 or 1769 and moved with Wheelock from Lebanon, Connecticut, to Hanover, New Hampshire. Daniel was the only one of Wheelock's Indian students to receive a college degree in Wheelock's lifetime. He was the also first Native American to graduate from the new institution Wheelock established at Dartmouth College.[56]

*Chapter Two*

# SAMSON OCCOM AND THE INDIAN MONEY, 1765–75

❦ IN THE LETTERS he wrote to Eleazar Wheelock, Samson Occom routinely referred to himself as Wheelock expected he should, as "your worthless servant" and a "poor Indian." Yet, despite enduring the prejudices and conditions that stifled the lives of Indian people in eighteenth-century New England, Occom achieved prominence as a scholar and preacher. He crossed the Atlantic, drew crowds, and moved in high places. He was a tribal leader and later in life a tribal builder. He never set foot on the Dartmouth College campus, but his name is everywhere: Occom Pond, Occom Ridge, Occom Commons, the Samson Occom Chair in Native American Studies. Portraits of him hang in Baker Library and in the Native American Studies Library. If the College were given to honoring its luminaries with statuary, Occom would surely deserve a statue or bust to accompany those of Eleazar Wheelock, Daniel Webster, Chief Justice Salmon P. Chase, and Thaddeus Stevens. He was, in effect, Dartmouth's first development officer.

As Moor's Charity School grew, Wheelock needed even more money. Within a few years of opening the school, he was thinking about moving. It would be "much for the advantage of the school to remove it," he wrote in 1757, "perhaps some hundred miles."[1] As the number of students increased and space in Lebanon became tight, he began to make plans. In 1763, with Britain's victory in the French and Indian War secure, he wrote "A Proposal for Introducing Religion Learning, Agriculture, and Manufacture Among the Pagans of America" and submitted it to General Jeffery Amherst, the British commander-in-chief in North America, and to the Marquess of Lothian. He proposed

That a Tract of the late Conquered Land, 30 or 35 Miles Square, conveniently Situate in the Heart of the Indian Country, be granted in Favor of this Design, that every third

Township be given and so Secured to the Indians, and their Heirs, that it may not be in their Power to Sell it to the English — That a large Farm of Several Thousand Acres of and within sd Grant be given to this Indian School — That the School be an Academy for all parts of useful Learning, part of it a College for the Education of Missionaries School Masters, Interpreters &c, and part of it a School for reading and writing &c.

Such a project, said Wheelock, would "convince the Savages of the sincerity of our Intentions," as well as win their friendship and "render our cohabitation with them safe for us." British North America was preoccupied with the war against Pontiac at the time, and Amherst told Wheelock it was not in his authority to dispose of the lands Britain had conquered from France.[2] But the idea of building a new college in Indian country persisted, and the search for funding became urgent.

Wheelock looked across the Atlantic and looked to Samson Occom to help raise the money for a new school. The idea was not his. The English preacher George Whitefield, a regular transatlantic voyager, suggested it to Wheelock on a couple of occasions. So did Rev. Charles Jeffrey Smith in March 1764: "When the Indian War is a little abated would it not be best to send Mr. Occum with another Person home a begging?" he asked; "An Indian minister in England might get a Bushel of Money for the School."[3] Occom was the ideal choice: educated, intelligent, and a minister, he was a model of what Wheelock's schooling could accomplish — given the right level of funding. Nathaniel Whitaker, pastor of a church in Norwich, Connecticut, was selected to accompany Occom. Leaving his family once again, Occom set out on a two-year voyage. He and Whitaker sailed from Boston two days before Christmas, 1765. After a six-week ocean passage (about average for the time; the westward voyage took even longer), they traveled inland to London and arrived there the first week of February. They met up with George Whitefield, who introduced them to William Legge, the Earl of Dartmouth ("a Worthy Lord indeed," Occom noted in his diary), and took "unwearied Pains to Introduce us to the religious Nobility and others, and to the best of men in the City of London." Occom also got a taste of the less elegant aspects of life in eighteenth-century London. Taking a walk on his first Sunday evening in the city, he "Saw Such Confusion as I never Dreamt of — there was Some at Churches Singing & Preaching, in the Streets some Cursing, Swaring & Damning one another, others was hollowing, Whestling, talking gigling, & Laughing, & Coaches and footmen passing and repassing, Crossing and

The Reverend Mr. SAMSON OCCOM,

The first Indian Minister that ever was in Europe, & who accompanied the Revd. Nathanl. Whitaker D.D. in an application to Great Britain for Charities to support ye Revd. Dr. Whitlock's Indian Academy, & Missionaries among ye Native Savages of N. America.

Publish'd according to Act of Parliament, Septr. 20. 1768, by Henry Parker, at No. 82. in Cornhill, LONDON.

Samson Occom. *Courtesy Dartmouth College, Rauner Library.*

Cross-Crossing, and the poor Begars Praying, Crying, and Beging upon their knees."[4] He met King George III and the archbishops of Canterbury and York, saw the sights (Westminster Abbey, the Tower of London), made the social rounds, "and found many gentlemen well Disposd towards our Business."[5]

Britain had seen American Indians before—Pocahontas, a string of kidnap victims, Cherokee, Creek, Iroquois, and even Mohegan delegates all crossed the Atlantic before Occom.[6] But Occom was the first Indian minister to visit Britain and he was a hit. He began preaching, and he attracted large congregations, although he was disturbed to hear he was being mimicked on the London stage. He and Whitaker stayed in London until August, left on a four-month tour of the west of England, returned to London, and then headed north via Liverpool to Scotland, where they preached in Edinburgh, Glasgow, Aberdeen, and other towns. In all, Occom delivered more than 300 sermons. The bishops of England apparently were not impressed: "they never gave us one single brass farthing. It seems to me that they are very indifferent whether the poor Indians go to Heaven or Hell," Occom wrote after he returned home.[7] But others felt differently. "It was Right to send over Mr Occum, as a Specimen of the benefitt of ye School," one minister in Bristol wrote Wheelock; "As far as I hear he pleases in every Town & city—So much Simplicity appears in the man: So honest, guiless a Temper, with Seriousness in his public Service; So well he speaks in publick, & So well he acts in private among his friends & mankind, that he engages their hearts. May you be as successfull in training others to the ministry as you have been in him!"[8] Occom and Whitaker raised £9,497 in England and an additional £2,529 17s. 11d. in Scotland. It was "the largest amount collected through direct solicitation by any American institution in the colonial era."[9] Occom and Whitaker each received £100 for their services. Meanwhile, without Occom to provide for them, his wife and family were in dire straits and appealed to Wheelock for help, which he provided.[10]

Wheelock considered several sites for the new school, and a number of people made suggestions.[11] Nathaniel Whitaker suggested North Carolina rather than a northern location where the land was harder, and more expensive "& the Winters so long that they eat up the Summer."[12] Wheelock himself favored the Wyoming Valley around the northeast branch of the Susquehanna River in Pennsylvania. He was a member of the Susquehanna Company, a joint-stock company formed in 1753 by Connecticut land speculators who believed that Connecticut's colonial charter, which granted sea-to-sea rights, entitled the colony to the Susquehanna Valley. Once the French and Indian War was over, the Susquehanna Company was determined to settle the Wyoming Valley immediately, "to the Amount of a Thousand families and Upwards." Settlers from Connecticut moved into the area, building cabins and planting fields. But Pennsylvania contested Connecticut's claim to the region, the Delaware chief Teedyuscung and the Iroquois both protested against the invasion, and the British government tried to restrain the settlers, fearing they would provoke another Indian war. Wheelock hoped Sir William Johnson in his dealings with the Indians might make provision for setting up his school with three or four towns "of the better sort of people around it," somewhere in the vicinity of the Susquehanna River, and said he would gladly move there with the school, as would several other ministers, "men of known honesty and integrity and such as Love Indians." Gideon Hawley, writing from the Iroquois town of Onoquaga, wished Wheelock well with his school but doubted "whether you will live to see it on that land." The Indians knew from experience that English actions were self-serving and could "discern through all our hypocritical pretences to the contrary," he warned; "the more acquainted Indians are with white people, even professing Christians, the more prejudiced they are against our nation & the more averse to their getting a footing in their country." Sir William warned Wheelock against any kind of settlement in the Susquehanna country because the Indians "are greatly disgusted at the great Thirst which we all seem to shew for their Lands."[13] Whether or not Wheelock recognized himself in Hawley and Johnson's descriptions of hypocritical land grabbers, the region was volatile and the ground was contested.

In 1768, Johnson met with 3,000 Iroquois at Fort Stanwix (present-day Rome, New York) in a treaty council to negotiate moving westward the boundary between Indian and white settlement that had been established at the Appalachian Mountains by royal proclamation in 1763. Wheelock sent a couple of missionaries to this council to try and secure a tract of land in the Susquehanna country. Sir William said they "busied th[emselves] verry much on the pretended Score of Religion," hoping to persuade the Oneidas not to cede the Susquehanna country but to keep it "for the purposes of Religion." The missionaries' arguments in private with the Indians, "& the Extraordinary private Instructions of Mr. Wheelock of wch I am accidentally possessed would shew them [the missionaries] in a very odd Light," wrote Johnson. Wheelock tried to distance himself from these maneuverings by referring to the "Wild, distracted, stupid, head long Conduct of Mr. Jacob Johnson," one of the missionaries, but Sir William, who became the biggest landowner in the Mohawk Valley, knew a Yankee land speculator when he saw one.[14] Wheelock did receive the offer of a site in Pennsylvania in 1768, but by then he was already looking up the Connecticut River.

English colonial authorities had had their eyes on the upper Connecticut for some time. In 1752, Theodore Atkinson, secretary of the province of New Hampshire, had reported that plans were afoot to settle "*A Tract of the finest Land on the Continent, call'd by ye Indians Co-os.*" Coos, Cowass, or Koasek, meaning "where the white pines are" or "white pine place," was an important Abenaki community located on the oxbow of the Connecticut River near present-day Newbury, Vermont. Rich soils, game-filled forests, and plentiful harvests of trout and salmon made it an attractive place, and the Abenakis cleared and cultivated extensive cornfields. Cowass was also a crossroads of trails and waterways. The French established a Jesuit mission there early in the eighteenth century and Indians, French, and English all recognized the strategic importance of the site. "I really believe, if we do not settle it the French will, for 'tis the main passage made use of by the Indians from Canada to this country," said Atkinson. When the English spoke of Cowass, they meant more than the immediate area of the Abenaki village: "'tis the cream of the country, the Intervale land on both sides of the river for 30 or fifty miles successively in many places a mile wide, where at first you have little to do but Plow, it being generally clear like a salt marsh & but about 40 or 50 miles Distance from many of our new settlements."[15] The northern limit of English settlement at the time Atkinson wrote was Fort Number Four, located near present-day Charlestown, New Hampshire. Hearing that the English had plans to build a fort at Cowass, Abenakis went to Fort Number Four and announced in no uncertain terms that "for the English to settle Cowass was what they could not agree to. And as the English had no need of that land, but had enough without it, they must think the English had a mind for war, if they should go there." Faced with Abenaki resistance and the imminent threat of war with the French in Canada, the English shelved their plans for Cowass.[16]

But ten years later everything had changed. Britain's victory over France deprived the Abenakis of allies in their struggle to hold back the English and opened the valley to a flood of settlement. New Hampshire governor Benning Wentworth issued grants for about 50 townships east of the Connecticut River and another 150 on the west side in what is now Vermont. In 1761 alone, 78 new townships were granted, including Hanover, Lebanon, Hartford, and Norwich, in "the New Country Commonly known by the general Name of Cohos." Between 1760 and 1774, 100 new towns were settled in New Hampshire and 70 in Vermont. The non-Indian population of northern New England increased from perhaps 60,000 to 150,000 in fifteen years, and the number of settlers in the upper Connecticut Valley jumped from a few hundred to several thousand.[17] The region fit Sir William Johnson's criteria for the site of an Indian school: not too remote from the Six Nations, who "have a strong Aversion to sending their Children far off," but a reasonable distance east of the Hudson and "sufficiently out of the Way, so that their Parents can neither divert them from their Studies or corrupt them through bad Example." The lands offered by Governor Wentworth would do nicely.[18]

Wheelock favored a location in the Cowass region, and the English Board of Trustees approved it. In 1768, Wheelock appointed Rev. Ebenezer Cleaveland of Gloucester, Massachusetts, and one of his own parishioners, John Wright, to make a tour of the Cowass country and report on suitable sites. The infant towns in the upper valley—Charlestown, Hanover, Haverhill, Lyme, Orford, Piermont, Plainfield, Hartford, Hartland, Norwich, Thetford, and Newbury—competed to attract the school. Some offered handsome grants of land, others in-kind subscriptions. Wheelock chose Hanover: it was a day's travel closer to Connecticut than Haverhill or Newbury; it was centrally located on the river, convenient for transportation and for communication with Portsmouth, Lake Champlain and Canada, and "as near as any to the Indians."[19] It was also thinly settled, without established political cadres with whom he would have to deal. Hanover had originally been chartered to grantees from Connecticut in 1761 and was first settled in 1765. On December 13, 1769, Governor John Wentworth (who had succeeded Benning, his uncle, two years before) signed the charter for the new college. He assured the Board of Trustees that the College would do more to "civilize the Indians & spread Christianity among them than any other public or private Measures hitherto granted for Indian Instruction." He also believed that it would win the Indians over to Britain and do more to prevent Indian raids on the northern frontier "than the best Regiment of Troops that could be raised." In Wentworth's opinion, the new college was "the most noble, useful, & truly pious foundation now in America."[20]

The charter itself is worth a close look. After a lengthy preamble reviewing Wheelock's educational efforts for Indians, the success of the Occom-

Whitaker fund-raising tour, and the suitability of an upper valley location "for carrying on the great design among the Indians," the charter declared:

KNOW YE, THEREFORE that We, considering the premises and being willing to encourage the laudable and charitable design of spreading Christian knowledge among the savages of our American wilderness, and also that the best means of education be established in our province of New Hampshire, for the benefit of said province, do, of our special grace, certain knowledge and mere motion, by and with the advice of our counsel for said province, by these presents, will, ordain, grant and constitute that there be a college erected in our said province of New Hampshire by the name of Dartmouth College, for the education and instruction of youth of the Indian tribes in this land in reading, writing, and all parts of learning which shall appear necessary and expedient for civilizing and christianizing children of pagans, as well as in all liberal arts and sciences, and also of English youth and any others. And the trustees of said college may and shall be one body corporate and politic, in deed, action and name, and shall be called, named and distinguished by the name of the Trustees of Dartmouth College.[21]

The phrase "and also of English youth and any others" was significant. Although it might appear to have been added as an afterthought to the mission of Indian education, in fact, it was the other way around. Wheelock's first draft of the charter said Dartmouth was being founded to educate "Youths of *the English* and also of the Indian Tribes." Then, in historian James Axtell's words, "he remembered that several thousand British benefactors had given thousands of pounds to a charity school primarily for Indians, not white colonists, and he scratched out the reference to English youth and added it at the end of the passage as if to indicate their subordinate position in his grand design." The charter also stated, more explicitly, "that without the least impediment to the said design, the same school may be enlarged and improved to promote learning among the English."[22] As the SSPCK noted later, the charter made no mention of the fund under its care that was intended solely for "maintaining and educating Indian youths."[23]

In August 1770 Wheelock gave public notice in New Hampshire and Connecticut newspapers that "My Indian charity school . . . is now become a body corporate and politic, under the name of DARTMOUTH COLLEGE" and that he hoped "soon to be able to support by charity a large number, not only of Indian youths in Moor's charity school, which is connected and incorporated with the College, but also of English youths in the College, in order to their being fitted for missionaries among the Indians."[24] Indians would continue to attend Moor's Charity School, but Dartmouth students, it seemed, would be white. Wheelock had his college, but he was losing interest in his great design.

He had been suffering from poor health for some time. As his letter to Sarah Simon showed, he had also become increasingly frustrated by the cultural resistance and resilience of his Indian students — what he called backsliding and what later boarding school officials like Richard Henry Pratt referred to disparagingly as "returning to the blanket." Wheelock's Indian students did not appreciate the sacrifices he made for them, he complained. He was disillusioned with the students he'd had, and frustrated in his efforts to get others.

Things had been going badly with the Iroquois. In the spring of 1768, one of the Oneida boys at Wheelock's school "was taken With Vomiting Blood," and doctors feared he might bleed to death. Even when the bleeding stopped, he was left "in So low a state that his Life is now almost despaired of." An Oneida named William Minor, or "Little William," died at the school — "a pretty Little Boy," Wheelock said, and "the first Indian Scholar that has died at my House." Another, Mundius, was "raised from the Gates of Death" after a long illness, but his parents came and took him home that summer. The next year, Oneida parents pulled their children out of Wheelock's school after hearing rumors of mistreatment.[25] The situation was not much better in Mohawk country, where Molly Brant remained angry at Wheelock and Sir William Johnson grew cold to Wheelock's entreaties for assistance in recruiting Iroquois students. In 1768, Wheelock had written:

I apprehend it will be most for ye general good of ye design before us, and what indeed of necessity at present, yt ye Mohocks to whom I first sent Missrs & Schoolmasters, should be wholly neglected, as those places are reserved for, and are daily expected to be supplied with Missrs, from home. And many have learnt to despise any but such as come from ye great Minister almost as big as ye King. I hope soon to have a supply of my own pupils, & such as are promising — I find by experience yt English Youth must have ye lead at present.[26]

The "great Minister" was William Johnson, who had grown increasingly hostile to Wheelock's Congregationalism, his educational goals and methods, and his land speculation. Johnson was a member of the Church of England

and Anglicans became strident in their denunciations of "the stupid Bigots" Wheelock sent as missionaries into Indian country; one warned Johnson that "Wheelock's Cubs" were "wicked eno' to kindle a Civil War." Johnson withdrew his patronage of Wheelock's grand design.[27]

Wheelock insisted on sending his son Ralph to Iroquois country as an emissary and recruiting officer. It was not a good choice. The only surviving son from Wheelock's first marriage, Ralph suffered from epilepsy so severe that it seems to have led to dementia. Wheelock thought highly of his son's ability to deal with Indians, but in reality Ralph was totally unsuited to the job and tried to compensate for his inadequacies with bluster. He assumed a domineering attitude and was subject to fits of temper as well as seizures. On one occasion he berated Oneida chiefs for not jumping at his father's offer to send teachers and preachers: telling them "they must take the Consequences and go to Hell their own way," he stormed out of the council.[28] Needless to say, few Iroquois students came to the new school.

In August 1770, Wheelock, his wife and family, his black slaves, and about thirty students, some driving cattle, traveled up the eastern bank of the Connecticut River to Fort Number Four and then on to Hanover. The location was ideal, Wheelock thought: "the situation is on a beautiful plain, the soil fertile and easy of cultivation. The tract on which the college is fixed, lying mostly in one body, and convenient for improvement." But it was still "wilderness," and the Hanover Plain was covered in stands of white pine. He had brought laborers to erect buildings, and they set to work felling trees and building crude log huts. He had an eighteen-foot-square log cabin built for himself and huts for the students.[29] David McClure, who had graduated from Yale in 1769 and had taken charge of Moor's Charity School, moved with the school to Hanover, where he found "the appearance of all things was new & wild." He taught the school "in a large log house, near the center of the present green," and also tutored at the College, which he described that first year as "intended for a temporary affair, & run up in a hurry."[30] The first educational structure—the Old College—was built between 1769 and 1771; Commons (College Hall) was constructed between 1770 and 1774. As Dartmouth began its second year, Wheelock announced in the press that he had "the fairest prospect in a little time to be able to support an hundred Indian and English youths upon charity, and all with a view to the first and grand object of the Institution, viz., the spreading the blessed gospel of the Redeemer among the savages."[31]

Woodcut depicting Dartmouth's founding. *Courtesy Dartmouth College, Rauner Library.*

Unlike other colonial colleges, Dartmouth was not just a school for young gentlemen. The sons of the elite were not attracted to Wheelock's college in the woods, where students studied the Bible and the classics but were also expected to contribute to the upkeep of the school and prepare themselves to teach Indians to farm by performing manual labor, working in the fields, and cutting timber. Catalogues of the students at Dartmouth and Moor's Charity School in 1771 and 1772 listed several Indians "on charity" and preparing for admission to the college,[32] but there were no Indians in Dartmouth's first, tiny, graduating class; nor would there be for six years. Four students graduated at the first commencement in August 1771: John Wheelock and Samuel Gray, "independent students," and Levi Frisbie and Sylvanus Ripley, both "educated for missionaries among the remote Indians." David McClure, who attended, found it "pleasing to see the solitary gloom of the wilderness give place to the light of science, social order & religion." The next day the ministers present ordained David Avery, prior to "his immediate departure as a missionary to the Indians" to work alongside Samuel Kirkland in Oneida country.[33] Wheelock continued to take Indian children at Moor's Charity School and continued to insist — as he wrote to David Towsey, a Stockbridge Indian father who wanted to send his sons, aged three and seven, to be educated: "My heart's desire is if possible to spread the great redeemer's name thro' this whole land, that all the poor benighted nations may all become partakers of the great Salvation."[34] Wheelock took Towsey's older boy, Benjamin, and advised Towsey to wait until the younger one was ready for school. But he had changed his mind about training Indians to be missionaries, and he had no intention of making Dartmouth an Indian college.[35]

Samson Occom saw what was happening and he called Wheelock on it. Formerly Wheelock's devoted student, Occom was furious at Wheelock's misuse now of the funds Occom had worked so hard to pry out of English and Scottish hands. He may also have been displeased that the school he helped to found was better placed to educate Abenakis, who had sided with the French in recent wars, than this own Mohegan people, who had been allies of the English. These were dark days for Occom. His health was poor and he was struggling to support a large family. He evidently found solace in drink on at least one occasion and Wheelock magnified and publicized it as a fall into intemperance. Then, in February 1771, Occom's eldest son, eighteen-year-old Aaron, who had been in and out of Moor's Charity School, died, leaving a pregnant wife.[36] Occom's relations with Wheelock grew strained and finally snapped. Wheelock had written Occom in January, expressing great sorrow at his former pupil's "repeated" fall, and told him that unless his repentance was very public and evident to everyone, "your usefulness is near at an end where you are." Wheelock wanted him to leave Mohegan and go to Iroquois country. Switching to Dartmouth, Wheelock said: "I hope in a little Time you will have opportunity to see scores of your Tawney Brethren nourished by the Breasts of this Alma Mater." For Occom, it was finally too much. The letter he wrote to Wheelock merits quoting at length:

I am very jealous that instead of your Semenary Becoming alma Mater, she will be too alba [white] mater to Suckle the Tawnees, for She is already aDorn'd up too much like the Popish Virgin Mary. She'll be Naturally asham'd to Suckle the Tawnees for She is already equal in Power, Honor and Authority to any College in Europe. I think your College has too much Worked by Grandure for the Poor Indians, they'll never have much benefit of it, — In So Saying I Speak the general Sentiment of Indians and English too in these parts. . . . I verily thought once that your Institution was Intended Purely for the poor Indians with this thought I Cheerfully Ventur'd my Body & Soul, left my Country my poor young Family all my friends and Relations, to sail over the Boisterous Sea to England, to help forward your School, Hoping, that it may be a lasting Benefit to my poor Tawnee Brethren, With this View I went a Volunteer — I was quite Willing to become a Gazing Stock, Yea Even a Laughing Stock, in Strange Countries to Promote your Cause — We Loudly Proclaimed before Multitudes of People from Place to Place, that there was a most glorious Prospect of Spreading the gospel of the Lord Jesus to the furthest Savage Nations in the Wilderness, thro your Institution, We told them that there were So many Missionaries & So many Schoolmasters already sent out, and a greater Number woud soon follow. But when we got Home behold all the glory had decayed and now I am afraid, we shall be Deem'd as Liars and Deceivers in Europe, unless you gather Indians quickly to your College, in great Numbers. . . . Many gentlemen in England and in this Country too, Say if you had not had this Indian Buck you woud not [have] Collected a quarter of the Money you did, one gentleman in Particular in England Said to me, if he hadn't Seen my face he woudnt have given 5 happence but now I have 50£ freely — This one Consideration gives me great Quietness.[37]

If Wheelock saw any legitimacy in Occom's complaints, he never admitted it. Instead, he took umbrage at what he doubtless considered insubordination and ingratitude. He replied to Occom: "I thought my dear sir you had fully known my object to be the Indians which has been invariably the same from the first. They are also the first object in the charter." He justified the shift to educating English boys for missionary work as the policy that would ultimately be of most benefit to the Indians: "Dartmouth College is and invariably has been and will be as long as any Indians are left primarily designed for them, and the presence of white students only serves to make the project more effective." He hoped soon "to be able to support an hundred Indians and youths designed for Indian service on charity." Although "My heart is broken and spirits sometimes almost overwhelmed with the behavior of some I have taken unweired [unwearied] pains for," Wheelock was determined to continue, working for them as long as he lived, "and I believe in so doing I am unto God a sweet savor of Christ, though they all perish after all that can be done to save them."[38] Occom expressed interest in seeing the college Wheelock had built with the money he raised, but Wheelock did not encourage such a visit. Occom complained that Wheelock had stopped writing; Wheelock complained Occom had not treated him as a friend. Their correspondence petered out and "their 31-year relationship ended in mutual silence."[39]

Wheelock also had to do some explaining to Lord Dartmouth and other English trustees who expressed concerns similar to Occom's. Reminding Wheelock that the funding was for the express purpose of "creating, establishing, endowing and maintaining an Indian Charity School," they could only "look upon the charter you have obtained and your intention of building a college and educating English youth, as going beyond the line by which you and we are circumscribed."[40]

The few Indians who were at the College were far from happy. Daniel Simon complained that he had little time for studying because he was required to do so much work, which was not what he understood the purpose of the school to be: "What good will the Charity money do the Indians?" he asked; if they were expected to work to pay their way, they could just as well go somewhere else for their education. "Wo unto that poor Indian or white man that Should Ever Com to this School, without he is rich." Daniel was anxious to get on with his education and if he could not do it at Dartmouth, he told Wheelock, he'd go elsewhere. Daniel stayed, and graduated in 1777, but his was a common complaint.[41] Like all students everywhere, Daniel also sometimes found that rowdy fellow-students made studying difficult. In the winter of 1773, he, a Stockbridge Indian named Peter Pohquonnappeet, and two non-Indian students complained to Wheelock about "the Indians that Lives in the room against us" (who were probably Mohawks from Kahnawake) who interrupted their studies by "hollowing And making all manner of n[o]ise."[42]

Wheelock had not yet totally given up on the Iroquois. He sent David Avery to the Oneidas in 1772 to gauge their attitude toward his missionaries and sending their children to Dartmouth. The Oneidas had pulled their children out of Wheelock's school three years before and had no intention of letting them return. "Our father is really to be pitied!" said a headman named Thomas, referring to Wheelock. "He resides yonder at a great distance, in the woods as well as we, & knows nothing what is done & doing here among us Indians. There he sits & thinks — & longs to have all the Indians become an holy people — & does not conceive or imagine any great obstacles in the way, because his heart is so full of benevolence towards the Indians, & thinks that they must view his good designs in the same light as he does." Oneida headmen at the village of Kanowalohale (present-day Vernon, New York) were less charitable: "English schools we do not approve of here, as serviceable to our spiritual interest," they said; "& almost all those who have been instructed in English are a reproach to us. This we supposed our father was long ago sufficiently appraised of." In fact, the Oneidas were "despised by our brethren, on account of our christian profession. Time was when we were esteemed as honorable & important in the confederacy: but now we are looked upon as small things; or rather nothing at all." Ralph Wheelock's speech carried no weight with them, they said, and Eleazar Wheelock had not taken the time to get to know the Indians' minds before he sent out his missionaries: "And so his missions have turned out a mere sham, & all in vain." That year, Wheelock sent Ralph to Onondaga, the central council fire of the Iroquois League, in a final effort to win back the Iroquois. The Onondagas were even more forthright than the Oneidas in expressing their views about Wheelock's schooling. Shaking Ralph by the shoulder, they told him they knew only too well the methods the English used to teach Indian children. "Learn yourself to understand the word of God, before you undertake to teach & govern others," they said and then, which Wheelock must have hated to hear, "learn of the French ministers if you would understand, & know how to treat Indians. They dont speak roughly; nor do they for every little mistake take up a club & flog them."[43] In February 1772, two Narragansett former students, John Matthews and Abraham Simon, went from Hanover as emissaries to Tuscarora country. They returned in June bringing word that the Tuscaroras too "had determined to have no English schools among them."[44]

Dartmouth's missionary outreach remained ambitious but its recruiting efforts came up short. In May 1772, David McClure and Levi Frisbie "were ordained at Dartmouth College to the work of the Gospel Ministry." McClure preached in College Hall on the Sunday before their departure to the Indian nations of western Pennsylvania and "those distant & savage tribes beyond the Ohio [where] no missionary from New England had ever gone!" Wheelock asked God's blessing on this mission "& on all the labors of Missionaries to spread the knowledge of the true God & Saviour among the heathen." The sspck funded the mission.[45]

Frisbie fell ill at Fort Pitt (present-day Pittsburgh) and McClure carried on alone. His journey was a case study of what often happened when missionary assumptions and attitudes encountered Indian realities and responses. Reaching the Delaware villages in the Muskingum Valley in September 1772, McClure was hospitably received by the Delaware chiefs, Netawatwees (a.k.a. Newcomer) and Killbuck. They granted him an audience with the Delawares' tribal council. Through his interpreter, McClure spoke of his long journey and his mission, and offered to stay with the Delawares "a considerable time . . . to teach them the way to happiness & heaven."[46] The Delawares listened politely and said they would think about it. They thought about it for almost two weeks.

During that time, McClure made observations on Delaware government and culture, bemoaned their drinking habits, their vices, and the workings of clan vengeance, introduced them to the concept of the Sabbath, and tried to preach the Gospel. After McClure preached on the second Sabbath, the speaker of the Delaware council, whom McClure recognized as "a very sensible and thoughtful person," engaged him in a theological debate that anticipated Red Jacket's famous rebuttal of missionary endeavors half a century later:

you have told us that we must receive what is in the book (meaning the bible). We believe there is one Almighty *Monetho*, who made all things; he is the father of the Indians and of the White People. He loves one as well as the other. You say, he sent you that book a great while ago. He has not sent it to us. If he intended it for us, he would have let us know it, at the same time as he let you know it. We don't deny that the book is good and intended for you, and no doubt, when you want to know what you should do, you must look into that book; but the Great Monetho has given us knowledge here, (pointing to his forehead) & when we are at a loss what to do, we must *think*.

The other Delawares waited to hear McClure's answer. "It was a deistical objection, founded in the pride of erring reason," wrote McClure, "and more than I expected from an uncultivated heathen." He offered several arguments but the Delaware remained unreceptive and finally declared: "The white people, with whom we are acquainted, are worse or more wicked than we are, and we think it better to be such as we are than such as they are." Stuck for a rebuttal, McClure could only admit that the frontier traders they knew were indeed not Christians; "If you want to see christians you must go to Philadelphia," he said weakly, referring to the Quakers.[47]

A couple of days later, the speaker gave the council's decision, in what McClure aptly described as a laconic answer: "My brother, I am glad you have come among us, from such a great distance, & that we see each other, and rejoice that we have had an opportunity to hear you preach. Brother, you will now return home & when you get there give my love to them that sent you. I have done speaking."[48] In other words, thanks for stopping by. Convinced he was in "a frontier of depravity," where the whites were as savage as the Indians, McClure saw no prospect of bringing the gospel to the heathen and headed home. "I am sorry," he wrote Wheelock from Fort Pitt, "I can give you no more favorable Idea of those Poor Savages, who are running with madness the downward Road." McClure and Frisbie returned to Dartmouth in the fall of 1773 after a journey that took them sixteen months and 4,268 miles (by McClure's computation) but yielded no students.[49]

Less than a month later, Wheelock sent McClure and Sylvanus Ripley on a fund-raising tour of New Hampshire, Massachusetts, and Connecticut. The Old College was intended for temporary use until a more permanent structure could be built of brick or stone (Wheelock argued that is was not feasible to house Indian students in a combustible wooden building because of their propensity to be careless with fire!) and Wheelock wanted to see a new building before he died. The state legislature had granted only $500, and he knew "the gentlemen in England & Scotland" would be reluctant "to forward much of the money, (collected for the purpose of christianizing the Indians, and committed to their care) for the purpose of erecting a large & costly building." McClure's fund-raising tour was not very successful. Construction of Dartmouth Hall did not begin until 1784 (and it was not completed until 1791).[50] Nevertheless, McClure was a good servant of the College. He served on the Board of Trustees for twenty-three years and was awarded an honorary doctorate of divinity.[51]

With no Indians students to be expected from Iroquoia or west of the Appalachians, Wheelock turned to Canada. The Mohawk community at Kahnawake, near Montreal, the Abenaki community at St. Francis, now Odanak, on the St. Lawrence, and the Huron community at Lorette near Quebec had grown up around Catholic missions. Their warriors had fought as allies of the French and, in numerous raids against settlements in New England, had carried off English captives—usually women and children—whom they adopted into their societies. The most famous example was Eunice Williams, daughter of the minister at Deerfield, Massachusetts, who had been captured along with her family during a massive Indian and French raid on the town in 1704; she was adopted into a family at Kahnawake, married a Mohawk, and spent her life there, refusing all efforts to get her home.[52] Cultural crossings were not uncommon on the frontier. David McClure met English captives living with Indians when he was at Pittsburgh. Like Benjamin Franklin, Hector St. Jean De Crèvecoeur, and others who commented on the phenomenon, McClure tried to make sense of it:

There is an unknown charm in the Indian life, which surprizingly attaches white people; those especially who have been captivated in early life. Whether it is, that uncontrouled liberty, which is found among savages, or that freedom from all anxiety and care for futurity, which they appear to enjoy, or that love of ease, which is so agreeable to the indolence of human nature, or all these combined, the fact is established by numerous instances of english & french captives, who have resisted the most affectionate and inviting alurements to draw them, and chose to spend their days among their adopted Indian friends.[53]

As many as 1,600 people were taken captive from New England between 1677 and 1760. Scholars disagree about the numbers who "went Indian," but over the years the Indian communities on the St. Lawrence adopted and absorbed many English captives, and produced children of English ancestry.[54] Wheelock believed that Indians with "English blood" would make better students. Though they were born among the Indians, and shared their vices," he wrote, "they appear to be as sprightly, active, enterprising, benevolent towards all, and sensible of Kindnesses done them, as English Children commonly are."[55]

In 1771, "an Indian (named Michael) from Caghnawaga, near Montreal, happening to come to Hanover just at that time, was entertained with care, and sent home in high spirits, promising to commend the school to his tribe."[56] There is no evidence that Michael ever returned for an education himself, but he was clearly wined and dined in the expectation that he would send other Mohawk students from Kahnawake. In addition, Wheelock sent recruiters more than two hundred miles by canoe and forest trail to the villages on the St. Lawrence. In the summer of 1772, Sylvanus Ripley and Lieutenant Thomas Taylor of Claremont, New Hampshire, who "had long been a captive with the French and Indians in those parts, and was well acquainted with the customs of both," traveled to Canada "to obtain a number of likely Indian boys to receive an education here upon charity; or which I rather chuse if it may be the children of English captives, who were taken and naturalized by Indians and married among them." The two recruiters returned with ten children — eight from Kahnawake and two from Lorette (Lewis and Sebastian Vincent). Two of the Kahnawakes, John Phillips and Thomas Stacey, were sons of white captives. (John Phillips's father had been captured in New York as a boy, now went by the Mohawk name Sanorese, and had married a woman from St. Regis with whom he had eleven children. Thomas Stacey's father, John, had been captured as a boy in 1756, married a Kahnawake Mohawk woman, and now ran a trading post at Kahnawake.) One of the Kahnawakes seemed to Wheelock to be "near thirty Years old." Wheelock thought the young men from Lorette were "endowed with a greatness of mind, and a thirst for learning," but things did not go well with the Kahnawakes: "after I had cloathed them decently, they soon began to discover the Indian Temper, grew impatient of Order and Government in the School, shew'd a great Inclination to be hunting and rambling in the Woods." Four of the Kahnawakes were dismissed within a year. Wheelock himself went recruiting to Canada, as did Levi Frisbie in 1773.[57]

When Thomas Kendall traveled to Kahnawake in 1773 "to give them the offer of sending their Children to the Colege with me to learn to read & write," he had to overcome Catholic influence and Indian hesitancy. "It appears that the Deavils Castle must be stormed before it can be taken," he wrote, "for they have two Priests in this Village." The Indians held a council to consider his proposal: "they Seem to be a People of surprising understanding of things & never set about any thing before they have wayed the matter in their own minds." Kendall had to be careful not to appear too eager, but he found encouraging prospects in the Indian boys he worked with: "I have my hands full mending their pens & seting their Coppys & hearing them read," he wrote, "all the while I endeavour to appear as indifferent about their com-

ing to learn as I can[,] knowing that if I appear over fond they will be back-
ward. They learn very fast both to read & write."[58]

Wheelock also dispatched Thomas Walcutt to St. Francis. Walcutt, who
was born in Boston in 1758, had been sent by his widowed mother, Elizabeth, to Moor's Charity School when he was twelve with the intention that he
should become a missionary. David McClure took young Thomas under his
wing and thought him a personable and promising youth. The "rising College
is well fixed, settled & under comfortable Circumstances for so new a Country," McClure assured Elizabeth. Wheelock was untiring in his efforts to do
something for "the tawny Inhabitants of America," and Thomas could be "an
instrument of everlasting good to his fellow Men & a light to enlighten the
Gentiles & spread the honor of his Name among the heathen."[59]

Unfortunately, Thomas was not a good student. Wheelock told his mother
that although he had talent and the makings of a scholar, "he is so fickle,
heedless, & inclined to trifling, that I fear he will be ruined if he should continue with me." What was more, Thomas was "very cunning and artful to
excuse himself and very apt to forget his promises of amendment." He needed
a steady hand, and Wheelock recommended apprenticing him to a farmer
until he was sixteen or seventeen, at which point "Providence permitting, I
will take him again upon trial."[60] A stream of correspondence ensued, with
Elizabeth imploring her wayward son to buckle down and grow up; he should
make the most of his opportunities, think about the family's reputation, and
consider how much good he could do if he improved his learning "and god
gives you grace for the poor ignorant indians." Thomas's elder brother, Benjamin, wrote saying much the same. Thomas was not a good correspondent
at the best of times and on the few occasions he did write home his letters
looked hurried and distracted, with multiple scorings out, which further dis-
mayed his mother who urged him to write clearly and more often. She was
concerned about his soul, she said. She also sent him half a dollar and some
ribbon for his neck and hair.[61]

It looked for a time as if Wheelock would expel Thomas, but Thomas redou-
bled his efforts in a bid to be admitted to Dartmouth. In September 1773, he
told his mother that he had completed his year's studies and "entered the College on condition that I improve the vacation in studying," which meant he
would not be coming home to Boston in the fall unless he postponed entering the College for another year.[62] He mentioned that there was some talk
of his going to Canada the next year with James Dean to learn Indian lan-

guages; then he crossed it out—he doubted anything would come of it. In fact, Dean set out for Canada with Kendall in May 1774; Thomas went with Levi Frisbie in June.[63] Anticipating a mother's concerns as her son set out to live far away among the Indians, Frisbie wrote to reassure Elizabeth. Thomas would be guaranteed an education when he returned because he would know Indian languages and be better equipped for missionary work. Frisbie could not say for sure when Thomas would come back, "but undoubtedly when he has gained a competent knowledge of some one Indian Tongue, which considering his Youth and Memory will not take him a long time." There was no doubt that this was the best thing for Thomas: "I think Providence seems to point out such a Method and I hope you will be enabled to rest the Matter entirely with God, and give your Mind No anxiety about it." Frisbie promised to do his utmost to befriend Thomas.[64] With Boston in prerevolutionary upheaval and a son leaving for Indian country, Elizabeth hurried off a letter: "keep your collar Close and your Lungs warm," she told Thomas, who was never a very healthy young man.[65]

In September, Thomas wrote to his mother from St. Francis. Setting out from Dartmouth in mid-June, he had walked about seventy miles to Crown Point, then carried on down Lake Champlain to Montreal. After trying a couple of Indian towns, it had been decided he should go to St. Francis. He was now living there, comfortably "in English fashion," he assured his mother. James Dean had recruited some boys in the village and would soon be heading back to Dartmouth. Thomas hoped to be home next August after he had learned Abenaki. "I am Very Well Contented with my Condition and Hope my dear Mother Wont Give Herself any Uneasy Thoughts about me but Commit me to the Hands of God that is able to Take Care of me as Well Here as if I were in the Poor Afflicted Town of Boston."[66]

When Dean returned to Canada in March 1775 he carried a packet of letters for Thomas. Classmates urged him to do God's work. Narragansett Daniel Simon told him his heart was with him and that things were going on as usual at Dartmouth.[67] Things were not going on as usual for the Walcutt family, however. Thomas's mother and his sister, Lucy, had moved to Hanover from Boston, where "things are Very Dark." Elizabeth was working as caretaker of the Indian boys at Moor's Charity School: "Mr. Dean Can inform you how I am imployed here taking Care of the Boys in the Character of a mother and they Learn very well," she wrote. She looked forward to seeing Thomas soon and hoped he had learned the language and done God's work among the Indians. "Present my Respectful Regards to his majesty gill and Lady and tell them that their Son with the other Boys Lives with me and I am their mama and give my Love to all their parents."[68] "His majesty gill" was Joseph Louis Gill, the chief at St. Francis. Gill was the son of two English captives from Massachusetts who had been adopted into Abenaki society and converted to Catholicism. Gill's first wife was killed when Robert Rogers's New Hampshire Rangers had attacked and burned St. Francis in 1759. Nevertheless, Gill sent his son and nephews to Dartmouth with Dean. Eleazar Wheelock's letter, written the same day as Elizabeth's, was decidedly upbeat and obviously intended for Abenaki parents. "The Boys from St. Francis are all well and behave very well," he said; "they love the School and make good proficiency." They were quite contented and had not said a word about going home, except for a couple who said they wanted to bring more Abenaki boys to Dartmouth. After Elizabeth and Lucy arrived, "your Mother undertook to be a mother to them—and she has taken the best care of them to Comb their Heads, mend their Cloaths &c.&c. they love her as they do their Eyes." Jacob Fowler, Occom's brother-in-law and a former pupil of Wheelock, was teaching at the school. Teachers and students shared the same lodging: Fowler and his wife in a room at one end; the Indian boys in the middle, and Elizabeth and Lucy Walcutt in a room at the other end. "You may tell the Boys Parents of this & that their Children want for nothing we can do for them," Wheelock wrote. "Our State is very happy indeed here—Love, peace and Joy reign Triumphant." Wheelock urged Thomas to bring more boys back with him if there were any likely prospects.[69]

In the spring of 1772, Wheelock had only five Indian students in Moor's Charity School, all of them from New England; by 1773, he had fifteen or sixteen, and by the end of 1774, "upwards of twenty," mostly from Canada. The gathering clouds of revolution threatened to interrupt future missions, but McClure remained optimistic "that the numerous Tribes of Savages will yet reap lasting benefit from that pious & charitable Institution."[70] As anthropologist and linguist Gordon Day noted, it was the beginning of a long relationship: "for the next 80 years boys from St. Francis made up over half of all the Indians attending Dartmouth and preparatory schools with Dartmouth funds."[71]

In the summer of 1774, New Hampshire historian Jeremy Belknap visited Dartmouth. He dined with Wheelock and after dinner took a walk down to the river, where he "observed a tree where the bark was cut off, the figure of an Indian painted, which was done by one of the Indian scholars." He visited all the Indian students, "most of whom could speak good English," although one little boy "was so shy that he would not be seen." Belknap also attended the examination of Joseph Johnson, "an ingenious, sensible, serious young man," who was Occom's son-in-law.[72] Johnson was examined by six ministers during commencement and granted a license to preach the Gospel, "with a principal View to the Benefit of his own Nation." He preached in College Hall and then headed off to Mohawk country, but before he left he sent his wife, Tabitha, 5 dollars by his friend Daniel Simon, "for your relief, and Comfort, and a Token of my Sincere regards, and love for you, and a Sign to let you know that the lord hath verily prospered me."[73] With Johnson licensed to preach and Jacob Fowler teaching Indian students, there was still a Mohegan connection, and an Occom family connection, if not much of a Mohegan student presence at Dartmouth.

A summary of expenses for the years 1767–75 indicated (rounded to the nearest pound) £1929 spent on missionaries, £834 on schoolmasters, £4,258 on Indian Youths, £3,000 on English Youths, and £3,200 on labor and materials.[74] But the proportion of Indian to white youths was shifting dramatically. When donors voiced concerns about the diversion of funds from Indian education to English youth, Wheelock responded that he would run the Indian school and Dartmouth College as parallel institutions, but in practice he drew on funding for the former to develop the latter. By 1775, he had spent all of the money Occom raised in England, mainly in building Dartmouth College. The sspck kept a tighter grip on its funds, however, and held Wheelock to a strict accounting so that the money designated for Indian education went to Indian education. They did not approve of shifting his recruiting efforts northward to bring boys from Canada, "a measure which is but little conducive to the great purpose 'of evangelizing the Heathen.'"[75]

Correspondence between Dartmouth and the sspck on the issue of the funds continued intermittently for the best part of a hundred years. Frustrated by the difficulties of recruiting and retaining Indian students, successive Dartmouth presidents suggested other uses for the money—to educate pious young men for the ministry, to fund professorships, to pay teachers' salaries, or for the general upkeep of the College. But the sspck would have none of it and insisted that the fund be used for its intended purposes.

Scottish money, raised by Samson Occom and controlled by the sspck, kept Dartmouth in the business of educating Indians.

*Chapter Three*

# DARTMOUTH, INDIANS, AND THE
# AMERICAN REVOLUTION,
## 1775–1800

ᛦ DARTMOUTH was the last colonial college to be established and it was founded in calamitous times. When the American Revolution broke out, wrote David McClure and Elijah Parish, "the frontier situation of the College exposed it to the terrors of war, and especially to the Indians, an enemy most to be dreaded."[1] Hanover in 1775 had a population of just 434.[2] The residents of the town and their neighbors in the upper Connecticut Valley feared that history would repeat itself: that the British and their Indian allies would descend from Canada just as the French and their Indian allies had done throughout so much of New England's history. In the Declaration of Independence, Thomas Jefferson accused Britain of unleashing savage allies on defenseless settlers. Dartmouth lay in a direct path from Canada to Massachusetts, on a well-traveled war route. The infant college, like the infant towns in the upper valley, looked nervously northward for much of the war. Wheelock repeatedly portrayed Dartmouth and the neighboring settlements as "Easie prey" for "a northern army of Savages." He requested that his students be supplied with firearms, urged the Continental Congress to help support his Indian school, and repeatedly depicted the presence of Indian students at Dartmouth as the best security against Indian attack.[3] The attack never came, but the Revolution affected the lives of Indian students, whether living in Hanover or back in their home communities.

The Revolution split Wheelock's community of students. Joseph Brant and Samuel Kirkland had been friends at school in Lebanon, Connecticut, where they first met in the summer of 1761 when Brant was eighteen, Kirkland nineteen. Brant taught Kirkland Mohawk; Kirkland helped Brant with his English. But both split with Wheelock and followed different paths. After he left school, Brant returned to Mohawk country and to the orbit of Sir William Johnson. As tensions escalated between Johnson and Wheelock and between

Britain and its American colonies, Brant reaffirmed his ties to the Johnson family, the Crown, and the Church of England. Kirkland went as missionary to the Oneidas at Kanonwalohale. The Oneidas rejected Wheelock's form of education and Kirkland too drifted away from Wheelock, expressing dissatisfaction with his former mentor's methods and priorities. He also squared off against William Johnson in the contest for Iroquois hearts, minds, and souls. Unlike Brant, Kirkland adhered to the Congregationalist religion and the patriot cause. With the outbreak of the Revolution, Brant and Kirkland became bitter enemies. Each exerted his influence in the tug-of-war for Indian allegiance: Brant helped to bring the Mohawks out for the king's cause; Kirkland generated divisions within the Oneidas but swayed the tribe to support the colonists. Between them, they helped fracture the ancient unity of the Iroquois League in what, to many Indians, looked like an English civil war.[4]

The Continental Congress relied on Kirkland in its dealings with the Iroquois — and on another of Wheelock's students, Dartmouth alumnus James Dean. Born in Connecticut in 1748, Dean had grown up at the village of Oquaga or Onoquaga, probably taken there by his missionary step-uncle, and had been adopted by the Oneidas. According to one account, he was "a perfect Indian boy, in language, manners and dress" by the time he was thirteen. Wheelock admitted Dean to Dartmouth at no charge and covered all his expenses (2 pence for a skein of sewing thread, for example), in return for his valuable skills. As Wheelock explained in a notation in Dean's ledger account: "Mr James Dean was admitted to receive an Education in Dartmouth College only upon the fair prospect of his being uncomonly qualified to do eminent Services for the Redeemer among the Indians, and upon Condition of his serving me as Interpreter as I should find Occation for him and to instruct such of my Schoolers as should desire to be instructed in the Indian Tongue."[5] He graduated in 1773 and made a couple of missionary and recruiting expeditions, including that to the Indian communities on the St. Lawrence River in the spring of 1775. Adopting the Iroquois metaphor for strengthening or renewing an alliance, Wheelock anticipated that reaching out to the Canadian tribes would "brighten the chain of friendship between them & this school" and help secure the frontier from an invasion from the North. Dean was

a thorough Master of the Language of the Six Nations and can also speak the Huron Language. [H]e is a young Gentleman of Learning, Virtue & great Prudence, was early

Naturalized among the Indians, well understands their customs, is much esteemed by them as an orator, & has great Interest in their affections, and is in my opinion the fittest man I know on Earth to be employed, if there should be occasion for one among the western and northern Tribes.

No man had more influence among the Iroquois, thought Wheelock, with the possible exception of Sir William Johnson.[6] When Dean returned from Canada, Wheelock sent him on to the Continental Congress in Philadelphia and had him write a report to impress upon the Congress the important role Dartmouth could play in the gathering storm. The Continental Congress granted $500 to defray the expense of Dean's mission to Canada and support the school.[7]

The Continental Congress also dispatched Dean to Albany to serve under the commissioners of Indian affairs of the Northern Department. On Christmas Day, 1775, Dean wrote Wheelock, relating his travels since leaving Dartmouth. In the fall he had gone to Onondaga, and he had spent two months in the Indian country. He had then been in Philadelphia, but British agents were active in Iroquois country and now he was heading back there for the winter to counteract their efforts "& communicate intelligence."[8] Together with Kirkland, Dean used his knowledge of the language and his influence to win the Oneidas to the American cause. Kirkland served as chaplain, and Dean served as an interpreter and guide in the early stages of General John Sullivan's devastating campaign in Iroquois country in 1779. The next year Dean accompanied Oneidas who fled to Schenectady seeking refuge from Loyalist and Mohawk attacks.

The retreat of the American army from Canada in 1776 seemed to leave the northern frontier open to attack by the British and their Indian allies, but the upper Connecticut Valley escaped relatively unscathed from the kind of frontier warfare that ravaged upstate New York during the Revolution. The conflict in the upper valley mostly involved scouting parties ranging the north woods. It is often suggested that this was largely attributable to the influence of Eleazar Wheelock and his "Indian school." Not only did Wheelock count Joseph Brant, now a prominent war leader in the British-Indian alliance, among his alumni, but he also made a point of recruiting sons of the chiefs of "the most Respectible Tribes in Canada." He had ten children from Kahnawake and St. Francis at the school when the Revolution broke out, "eight of whom are descendants from English Captives." Wheelock considered them "as Hostages," and was confident that their parents would "send for them before they will proceed to Hostilities." Military men concurred.[9] Keeping the Indian students at Dartmouth now assumed vital strategic importance, which Wheelock stressed in his petitions to Congress and which Congress acknowledged when it appropriated money to help support them, "as it may be a means of reconciling the friendship of the Canadian Indians, or at least of preventing hostilities from them in some measure." With funding from Britain cut off during the war years, Wheelock continued to solicit financial assistance from the government for his Indian students.[10]

But he was unable to keep all the students in school. The sudden departure of four Abenaki students in 1777—the same year that General Burgoyne's invasion threatened to cut off New England—caused alarm. Joseph Louis Gill had sent his son, Anthony, and three nephews, Benedict, Joseph, and Montuit, to the school, but that October, Wheelock wrote in his diary, "Anthony & Benedict discover[ed] an ugly Temper." Anthony dropped out. Wheelock sent him home with a letter of explanation for his father: "I have faithfully done the best I could for him, and the School Masters have taken much pains with him—but he dont love his books, but loves play & idleness much better. I hope you will know better than I do what to do with him & for him." He assured Gill he would do his best for any other boys the chief might send him, but he warned that they "should be well instructed in the business of farming before they come, or else be told they must learn it here." Some of the Abenaki students had evidently resisted the agricultural component of Wheelock's educational program, and told him "they had not come here to work." But Wheelock insisted it was vital in a changing world: "for if they should not be able in future life to get their living by the business of a learned profession, and wild game should be all gone from the country, as they likely will be within a few years, your sons will be in a very unhappy state if they should not know how to get their living by farming." Benedict, he said, was struggling with English, reading, and writing, but Joseph and Montuit were doing well: "Joseph entered college last August and bids fair to make a good schollar. Montuit will be fit to enter college as soon as he is old enough. I hope these two will be wise learned and useful men, and do much good in the world if their fathers are wise enough to let them go through their learning and not take them away to spoil them as some have done." But Benedict and Montuit went home to St. Francis with Anthony in the first week of November. Wheelock gave them each a Bible, catechism, and spelling book.[11] Francis Joseph Annance, son of Joseph Louis Gill's sister, spent two years at Dartmouth, until 1780, and often appears in the records as "the Great Francis."

In his repeated memorials to Congress, Wheelock stressed the need to keep the Canadian Indian students at his school and to keep his school on its feet. He persevered in his efforts right up to the end of his life. In his last will and testament, dated April 2, 1779, he named his son John to be his successor as "President of my Indian Charity School and Dartmouth College, with and into which said School is now incorporated." The same day, he wrote a letter thanking Congress for its grant of $925 "as a donation towards the former support of the Canadian Indian Youth, that were members of this School" and humbly requesting that they do so again.[12] It appears to have been his final letter. Three weeks later, aged sixty-nine, Wheelock was dead.

By now, there were only five Indian students in residence, with another about to enter, but President John Wheelock urged Congress to continue supporting the upkeep of students from Kahnawake and St. Francis as a small price to pay for strengthening the attachment of those tribes to the new United States.[13] With British garrisons at both Kahnawake and St. Francis keeping an eye on the inhabitants, and British agents telling all Indians that the Americans intended to take their lands and destroy them, Dartmouth may well have added some weight to the American side in the diplomatic tug-of-war.

But Dartmouth's indebtedness to Indians for its survival during these dangerous years went beyond the reluctance of Indian fathers to burn the school their sons were attending. Samson Occom wished that the British and Americans would leave the Indians alone and not drag them into the war; "what have they to do with your Quarrels?" he asked John Thornton, one of Dartmouth's English benefactors. At the same time, he hoped the breach between the colonies and the mother country would "not intirely Stagnate the Streams which have run so long to refresh the Souls of these poor perishing Indians with Divine knowledge" — in other words, not cut off funding from England. The "poor Heathens," he noted with deliberate irony, were amazed to see Christian brothers killing one another![14] But the pressures exerted by both sides meant that neutrality was not a viable option for Indians: Britons and Americans alike assumed that Indians who were not for you were against you and should be treated accordingly. Eventually, recognizing that the Americans posed the greater threat to their lands and cultures, most Indians who fought in the war of the Revolution fought with the British.[15]

Except in New England. Indians in Massachusetts and Connecticut, surrounded by colonial neighbors, rallied to the American cause and served steadfastly despite suffering heavy losses. Former students of Eleazar Wheelock—Daniel Mossuck, Emanuel Simon, James Niles, and others—enlisted. Indians from the mission town of Stockbridge in western Massachusetts took up arms for the patriot cause almost soon as the Revolution broke out. Eight Stockbridges attended Moor's Charity School and Dartmouth College between 1771 and 1780 and several were enrolled on the eve of the Revolution.[16] Lewis Vincent, a Huron from Lorette who entered the College in 1772, and "James Indian" volunteered for service in New Hampshire companies in the first months of the war. John Wheelock was appointed captain of a Hanover company in 1776–77 and commissioned as a major in the service of New York, although his battalion was disbanded without seeing action after he failed to raise the requisite three companies. Lewis Vincent enlisted in Wheelock's battalion, as did John Stockbridge (Konkapot) and "Peter Indian," both students in Moor's Charity School.[17] (Presumably this was the same Peter Indian who was involved with "Joseph Indian"—probably Joseph Mecheekampauh from Stockbridge—and another student named Ebenezer Brown in breaking a window at the College in February 1773.)[18]

The situation farther north was more ambiguous. Like the settlers in the Connecticut Valley, Abenakis at St. Francis wanted to avoid a recurrence of what had happened in the French and Indian War, when Robert Rogers's Rangers had burned their village. They had little love for the British—after all, they had fought against them for eighty years—but they had to live with the reality of British power in Canada and weigh that against the prospect that the Americans might stage a successful invasion of Canada. The Revolution generated disagreement, division, and shifting allegiances in St. Francis, as it did in many American and Native American communities.[19]

While the Continental Army battled British regulars to the south, Abenakis provided scouts and the first line of defense for the northern settlements.[20] In July 1775, the New Hampshire Committee of Safety ordered Colonel Timothy Bedel of the New Hampshire militia to take measures to defend the upper valley and "to use your utmost Endeavours to gain & keep the Friendship of the Indians." Bedel had attended Moor's Charity School, and he had the expertise and connections to enlist Indian allies. He was said to have a good reputation and influence among the Mohawks at Kahnawake and the Abenakis at St. Francis. He tried to convert his influence into allies with minimal financial resources, and in the face of substantial difficulties he achieved some success. In February 1776, as he prepared to march for Canada with his regiment, he asked Eleazar Wheelock for a chaplain who understood Mohawk or Abenaki.[21] The next month, he reported to the Committee of Safety that he had "been at great expences on account of the Indians who have been very sick: two of them are dead and sent to Dartmouth College to be buried and the rest marched off yesterday in good spirits." He sent word into Indian country that the Americans were ready to trade with them at Cowass. The plan was to attract Abenakis to the area as a protective buffer: "if the Indians trade with us we need no Soldiers," Bedel reasoned. Abenakis and Mohawks from Kahnawake came to the Haverhill area, some looking for security themselves. The Americans even considered building a fort at Cowass, but the defense of the downriver settlements depended on the militia and the Abenakis, not on fortifications. Bedel employed the Indians as scouts, ranging the north woods on the lookout for signs of enemy activity.

In the summer of 1778 Joseph Louis Gill came to Haverhill, asking what the Americans intended to do for his people, "as he says we have many friends that way." In November, Gill told Bedel the St. Francis Abenakis were "all willing to Join the United States." But the Indians around Haverhill suffered from lack of blankets and clothes. "I have here about 30 fighting Indians and double the number of Women & Children all Naked and daily coming in," Bedel wrote at the end of 1778; "coud they be supplied with Blankets & Indian Stockings they would be a very good Guard to this Quarter, but at present they are not fit for service." Bedel continued to request supplies, to no avail. Congress awarded Gill a commission as major in the American army, but as the likelihood of an American invasion of Canada diminished, Gill understood that he needed to mend fences with the British and at least make a show of supporting the Crown. He now assured the British that they could rely on Abenaki support. The British did not entirely trust him, but Abenaki strategy was consistent: to protect their land and community in perilous times. The Abenakis did not play a dramatic role in the Revolution; they fought no major actions, and they frustrated the British and Americans alike. Scouting for the Americans at Haverhill and scouting for the British from St. Francis, Abenakis may have encountered Abenakis in the woods more times than the records reveal; and if so, they likely sat together and smoked rather than exchanging gunfire. The Abenakis kept the fighting at arm's length and avoided the kind of losses they had suffered in the French and Indian War and that other Indian communities in New York, the Ohio Valley, and the South suffered during the Revolution.[22]

Both John Wheelock and John Stockbridge served with Bedel.[23] Some Dartmouth students proved useful as scouts and interpreters, especially Lewis Vincent. Wheelock described him as one of "the Most promising Young Indians I have ever Yet Seen, and the most likely to answer the great and good Ends of an Education." He also observed "no undue appetite" in Lewis for "Strong Drink."[24] In April 1775, however, the month the Revolution broke out at Lexington and Concord, Massachusetts, Lewis was involved in a case of excessive drinking. New Hampshire law made it illegal "to sit Drinking or Tipling after Ten a Clock at Night," to remain in a tavern more than two hours, or to drink to excess. Vincent, together with another student and the college cook, went to an inn at ten in the morning, drank egg toddy, and then consumed half a dozen bottles of wine during the course of the day. All three of them got pretty intoxicated. The innkeeper and the cook were fined; the students were acquitted, Lewis "being but late emergent from a State of Paganism & as yet unacquainted with the Language, Laws & Customs of the English."[25] Otherwise Vincent seems to have been a good student; he, John Phillips, Thomas Stacey and some other students sent Wheelock a formal request that he preach a sermon to them.[26] During the war he served as an interpreter, emissary, and scout. Wheelock said he spoke Huron, Mohawk, French, and English well, and he was sent to the Mi'kmaqs in Nova Scotia and the Penobscots in Maine. He presumably knew Bedel from school, and he served as a scout with Bedel's rangers.[27]

John Sauck or Sauk from Kahnawake also attended Moor's Charity School. In July 1775, Wheelock wrote a certificate for him to travel to Canada and stated that he had not "Interested himself on Either Side of the Public Controversy of the present day." By the spring of 1781, however, "John Socks" was providing information to the British and perhaps even scouting for them. According to one British officer, Sauck "speaks, reads, and writes good English and received his education at Dartmouth College, on Connecticut River.[28] Sauck attended Dartmouth for four months in 1775–76. He wrote at least one letter in Mohawk.[29]

Abenaki and Kahnawake assistance, or more likely their insistence on keeping their involvement in the war minimal, helped ensure that Dartmouth College did not get caught in a vicious cycle of raids and counterraids as happened in the Mohawk Valley. The British-Indian threat from the north was real, and the Hanover militia turned out in August 1780, when "word came that the enemy were killing the people on the White River" (an Indian war party had struck the towns of Barnard and Bethel and carried off four captives), and in October, when a force of British and Indians attacked Royalton, just twenty-five miles away in present-day Vermont, and took more captives. The Royalton raiding party included at least one former student of Eleazar Wheelock, and a white captive turned Mohawk who had a son at Wheelock's school. One of the captives seized in the raid was saved from being tomahawked by an Indian whom he recognized as a boyhood friend from Moor's Charity School when it was in Lebanon, Connecticut. The white Mohawk was Sanorese, who had sent one son, Thomas Phillips, to Wheelock in 1773; had a son, John, at Moor's Charity School in 1777; and may have had another son named Talbot there at the time of the raid. The documents mention that one of the captives was released with a letter to "Capt. Phillip's son at the college," although the contents of the letter are unknown.[30] Despite such scares, the settlers' worst fears did not materialize and Dartmouth survived the Revolution intact.

Dartmouth faced other threats, potentially more terrible than Indian raids. When Sylvanus Ripley made his recruiting trip to the Indian villages on the St. Lawrence in the summer of 1772, he "passed thro' the small-pox, which he took by inoculation, as it was judged unsafe for him to travel that country without it."[31] On one occasion Timothy Bedel sat in council at Kahnawake despite being ill with smallpox. Smallpox was nothing new in either the St. Lawrence Valley or the Connecticut, and it was only one of many deadly diseases that plagued Indian country. An epidemic ravaged coastal New England in 1616–19, sweeping Native populations away "by heapes" and leaving lands open for English Pilgrims to occupy. A disease that might have been smallpox hit Indians living south of the Merrimack River in 1631. In 1633 smallpox swept along the St. Lawrence, down the Connecticut Valley, through New England, and west to the Great Lakes. Governor William Bradford of Plymouth Colony said that one Indian village in the Connecticut Valley suffered a mortality rate of 95 percent in this epidemic. Such death rates were not uncommon when smallpox hit a population for the first time. Smallpox struck Indian communities in the Northeast again and again during the rest of the seventeenth century. It hit the Abenakis again in 1729–33 and in

1755–58.[32] By the time Wheelock founded Dartmouth College, the Indian populations from which he wished to recruit his students had been reduced to a fraction of their former size. Though much less virulent among colonial populations than in Indian country, smallpox remained a dread disease for Europeans as well. In the one hundred years before the American Revolution, smallpox was absent from the American colonies for as long as five years on only two occasions.[33]

The disease attacked during the Revolution as well.[34] Cases cropped up in Boston and neighboring towns in 1774. As armies assembled in crowded and unsanitary conditions and refugees fled the fighting, they provided an ideal environment for the spread of smallpox. It plagued Boston, Philadelphia, Charleston, and other eastern cities. Josiah Bartlett, New Hampshire's delegate to the Second Continental Congress in Philadelphia, worried about bringing it home to his family and had himself inoculated. Preventing smallpox from spreading to his army as it besieged Boston was a major concern for George Washington, though he himself was immune, having had the disease as a child. In March 1776, Ripley, by now a chaplain with the American army invading Canada, wrote home: "I fear the consequences of the small Pox, which begins to rage in our Army, and bids fair to have a general spread."[35] Smallpox soon became "a more terrible enemy" than the British, and when the disease-ridden army limped back from Canada it brought the epidemic with it.[36] Washington had his army inoculated in 1777, but the disease continued to flare up, adding to the miseries of war for soldiers and civilians alike.[37]

The imminent threat of smallpox raised the controversial question of inoculation among the students of Dartmouth College and the townspeople of Hanover. Prior to Edward Jenner's discovery of the cowpox vaccination in 1796, inoculation offered the best chance of protection from the dread disease. But it was risky (as Abigail Adams well knew when she agonized in letters to her husband about inoculating her children.) Eleazar Wheelock feared it might actually spread rather than contain the disease, and he proclaimed a series of "Laws respecting the Small Pox," mainly to quarantine students who had been inoculated. Despite Wheelock's concerns and regulations, about twenty students went to nearby Lebanon, New Hampshire, to get themselves inoculated. Then "six or seven of the Indian Boys went to the same place & had it." Fear of the pox was far greater than fear of the College president. When cases of smallpox appeared in the area, the students asked the town for a house at the Mills (present-day Mink Brook, where there was a saw and grist mill) to serve for inoculation and quarantine. The town of Hanover was sympathetic, but Wheelock was infuriated by what he considered the town's interference and usurpation of his authority, so much so that he even talked of moving his College to New York.[38]

Things could have been much worse. Smallpox struck the Onondagas in the winter of 1776–77, the Oneidas in December 1780, and Senecas in the winter of 1781–82. The death tolls in the East paled in comparison with the horrors in the West. Smallpox killed an estimated 18,000 people in Mexico City between September and December 1779.[39] From there it spread in all directions: to northern Mexico, Guatemala, Colombia, Ecuador, Baja California, and New Mexico. By the time of the American Revolution, the infusion of new goods and the diffusion of horses had generated new levels of movement and interaction and extended old networks of commerce and communication throughout the West. The epidemic swept along well-traveled trade routes, spreading across two-thirds of the continent in two to three years and killing thousands of Indians. Smallpox kept coming in the early nineteenth century, eroding the Indians' populations and capacity for resistance just as the new nation created out of the Revolution was beginning to expand westward. Dartmouth men who ventured into the American West entered a world that had changed dramatically before Americans ever set foot in it.[40]

As it turned out, Dartmouth and the Indian students escaped relatively lightly from the smallpox, just as they escaped the worst of the fighting. Other illnesses took their usual toll, however. Wheelock's diary records that on January 23, 1776, an eighteen-year-old student, Levi Washburn, died of throat distemper (diphtheria) and Joseph Johnson preached a funeral sermon. Paul, an Indian who was part of a delegation from the northern tribes that had visited the New Hampshire Provincial Assembly in Exeter, died on the way home and was buried at Dartmouth on February 23. Wheelock preached and Lewis Vincent interpreted.[41] An Indian minister preaching at the funeral of a dead white boy and a white minister preaching at the funeral of a dead Indian in the same place and in the space of a month was not a common occurrence in early America.

❦

The Revolution caught up with Thomas Walcutt and his family. He returned to Hanover from St. Francis in June 1775, with a certificate for safe passage that Governor Carleton of Quebec had issued to him after he took an oath of allegiance to the king.[42] Thomas apparently entered the freshman class at Dartmouth: in December he and some classmates wrote to their tutor asking him to ease up on the lessons so they could keep up without damaging their health![43] That spring his brother Benjamin sent him word from Mount Independence, near Fort Ticonderoga on Lake Champlain, about a position as clerk in the hospital that paid 5 shillings a day; Thomas had better get there as fast as he could to take the chance and make a man of himself, he said.[44] His mother and sister returned to Boston, but Lucy said "it is a very sickly & Dying time here." When one of Thomas's brothers died and another was taken prisoner, it was almost too much for his mother to bear. Thomas, now at the hospital in Albany, continued to write home infrequently. His mother urged him to stay at the hospital, "as you know you are not abel to Endure the fatigues of a private Soldier." Poor health kept Thomas from regimental service, and he spent most of the war as steward and ward master at the hospital.[45]

In payment for his services, at the end of the war Thomas received one share in the Ohio Company. Rapid settlement of the West following the Revolution made this a likely prospect. In 1787, when "Ohio fever" was high, Thomas said his whole fortune was tied up in the Ohio Company. He traveled to Ohio, visited the company's town at Marietta, and viewed the prospects for economic advancement. But his western land venture proved unsuccessful, and he had to sell it off bit by bit for taxes.[46] Instead of making his fortune, he spent forty years copying documents as a clerk at the Massachusetts State House. He retained an interest in Indian languages and their preservation. He collected books and manuscripts, donated a large collection of books to the Dartmouth Library, and became a founding member of the Massachusetts Historical Society.[47] He died in poverty at McLean Asylum for the Insane in 1840, aged eighty-two.

In the midst of the Revolutionary War, Dartmouth College graduated its first Native American student: Daniel Simon, who received his degree in 1777. The next year he went to the Indian community at Stockbridge, Massachusetts, where he taught school and did some preaching in the neighboring towns. By the end of the Revolution, he was serving as an Indian missionary in Cranbury, New Jersey.[48] Little is known of Simon's time at Stockbridge, but he had moved into a community that was itself in transition if not in turmoil, as some of its members prepared to relocate to New York.

Even as the Revolution brought devastation to many Indian communities, Indian people regrouped to rebuild and to build new communities. Samson Occom dreamed of establishing a new Indian community, separate and removed from New England and its Yankee vices. By the end of the Revolution, he was more disenchanted than ever with white society and with Dartmouth. "This war," he wrote in 1783, "has been the most Distructive to poor Indians of any wars that ever happened in my Day." Kirkland had alienated the Indians against all missionaries when he served as Sullivan's chaplain and "went with an Army against the poor Indians." It was a dark time for Indian people. And Occom was still bitter, perhaps more bitter than ever, about Dartmouth:

And Docr Wheelock's Indian Acadameia or Schools are become altogether unprofitable to the poor Indians — In short he has done little or no good to the Indians with all that Money we Collected in England, Since we got home, that Money never Educated but one Indian and once Mollatoe, that is, part Negro and part Indian and there has not been one Indian in that Institution this some Time, all that money has done, is, it has made Doctor's family very grand in the World.

Things were no better with Wheelock's son at the helm. John Wheelock had to sell lands to keep the struggling college on its feet, but in Occom's mind he continued to sell out the Indians:

Mr. John Wheelock is now President of that College, and I believe he has but very little regard for the poor Indians, he may Speak or Write with Seeming Concern for the Indians under a Cloak, to get Some Thing for himself, or for the White People, for the College is become a grand College for the White people, you know and all England knows that we went through England, beging for poor Helpless Indians; not for able White People, — In very deed I have nothing to do to help that Institution; If I had Twenty Sons I woud not send one there to be educated I would not do it that Honour. . . . In a word, that Institution is at an End with the Poor Indians, they never Will or Can reap any Benefit from it.

As far as Occom was concerned, Dartmouth was "all a Sham."[49]

Occom became convinced that Indians must have Indian teachers: "They have very great and reveted Prejudice against the White People, and they have too much good reason for it," he said.[50] Before the Revolution, he had developed a plan to establish an independent, self-governing New England Christian Indian community, with its own teachers and ministers. His son-in-law, Joseph Johnson, went with Samuel Kirkland to request land from the Oneidas for this purpose. In keeping with the Iroquois tradition of "extending the rafters" of their longhouse and affording the shelter of their league to newcomers, the Oneidas granted a tract of land in their east central New York homeland. Occom and Johnson recruited volunteers from seven New England Indian communities — at Charlestown, Groton, Stonington, Farmington, Niantic, Montauk, and Mohegan — to form a new settlement near the present town of Kirkland, New York. Some moved there in the spring of 1775. The Revolution interrupted the process; when British troops advanced along the Mohawk Valley, the migrant Indians took refuge at Stockbridge. But the movement resumed after the war. By 1785, 200 Indian people lived at their new town of Eeyamquittoowauconnuck, or Brothertown. They constructed their community on the model of a New England town government and formed, in Occom's words "a Body Politick."[51] Many of the individuals involved in the movement were former students of Eleazar Wheelock — Occom, David and Jacob Fowler, Joseph Johnson, Abraham and Emanuel Simon, James Niles, John Matthews, Benjamin Towsey, Daniel Mossuck, Samuel Tallman, John and Mary Secutor, and Peter Pohquonnappeet, who graduated from Dartmouth in 1780 — but they used their education and their network to pursue their own agenda, and build a new Christian Indian community that was independent of white society.[52] Occom's wife, Mary, stayed at Mohegan, and Occom traveled back and forth between his old home and the new community he had helped to create.

Stockbridge Indians, who had fought alongside the Americans in the Revolution, as they found their township was taken over by American neighbors, moved also to New York and established New Stockbridge six miles from Brothertown. Many Stockbridges preferred Occom to their own minister, John Sergeant, Jr.[53] In the fall of 1787, members of the Brothertown and New Stockbridge communities invited Occom to live there and serve as their teacher and minister of their church. Occom cut back on his preaching itinerary, but there was more traveling to do. In the winter of 1788, Occom, David Fowler, and Peter Pohquonnappeet went on a fund-raising tour of Pennsylvania and New Jersey, soliciting assistance for their people: "the late unhappy wars have Stript us almost Naked of everything," they said; "we are truely like the man that fell among Theives, that was Stript, Wounded, and left dead in the highway."[54]

Things did not go smoothly at Brothertown. No sooner had the migrants settled there than they became involved in disputes with the Oneidas over the legal disposition of the lands they had been granted. In 1774, the Oneidas had given the New England Christian Indians title without reservations. Now, Americans in New York were pressuring the Oneidas to cede yet more land to them. The Oneidas, perhaps feeling the Brothertown community had let them down by not assisting them in the Revolution, reduced the land allocated to the Brothertown Indians and tried to get them to surrender it entirely and "live at large with them on their Land." At the Treaty of Fort Schuyler in 1788, the Oneidas ceded almost all their lands to the Americans, except for a reservation three miles long and two miles wide, a reservation for the New Stockbridge Indians, and a reservation for the Brothertown Indians. Land troubles continued as some Brothertowns made leases of land and timber to incoming white settlers, which Occom steadfastly opposed. Occom's leadership at Brothertown proved controversial and divisive: His rivalry with Sergeant split the church, and his insistence that Brothertown be a self-governing and autonomous Indian community earned him enemies.[55] Factionalism at New Stockbridge increased when Peter Pohquonnappeet was chosen as leader of the party opposed to Mahican chief Hendrick Aupaumet. Although direct evidence, and the exact date of Pohquonnappeet's death, is lacking, Levi Konkapot, Jr., in the 1850s, reported that it was said that some of Pohquonnappeet's enemies became "jealous of his growing power, influence, respectability and fame" and "secret orders were issued to put an end to his life by poison."[56]

The two letters that survive from the last six months of Occom's life show him keeping up the fight for Indian autonomy and Indian education. One, to Governor George Clinton of New York, concerns land disputes and factionalism at Brothertown. The other, to an unknown minister, ends: "I have an Evening School for the young People, and a Number come, I am instructing to read & speak English proper, and come on well."[57] Occom died on July 14, 1792; like Eleazar Wheelock he lived to be sixty-nine. Three hundred Native people from Oneida, Brothertown, and New Stockbridge attended his funeral. Samuel Kirkland preached at the service.[58]

Peter Pohquonnappeet and Lewis Vincent were the last Indians to graduate from Dartmouth for many years. After the war, Vincent, class of 1781, worked "assisting the Reverend Mr. Stuart in school keeping in the City of Montreal." In February 1784, he wrote John Wheelock: He would never forget the kindness and charity he received from Wheelock and his family, and with no saying how long his present situation would last, he asked him to send word of any employment opportunities "in that country for there are none in this."[59]

In 1782 John Wheelock went to Europe to try and raise money for the College. He carried with him a large (approximately 20 × 27 inches) letter of introduction written on vellum (sheepskin) to the people and potentates of Europe, signed by George Washington and various generals and state governors, the U.S. secretary of state, and the French minister. He traveled to France, the Netherlands, and London, where he met the Earl of Dartmouth and other former benefactors. The letter of introduction reviewed the history of the College, including the fund-raising efforts of Occom and Whitaker, and reminded Europeans that an institution "intended in the first place, for the purpose of civilizing the wild, wandering Tribes of Indians in North America, and next for promoting religion, virtue, and literature among people of all denominations" was worth funding.[60] But Europeans were not impressed by a second Wheelock playing the Indian card a second time, and the fund-raising trip was unsuccessful. The number of Indian students at the school dropped to three in 1782 and then to one in 1783. By 1785, there were no Indian students at Dartmouth, and there were none for fifteen years: John Wheelock decided to enroll no more Native students in Moor's Charity School until his father's debts were met.[61]

In 1785, however, he petitioned the General Assembly of Vermont, then sitting across the river in Norwich, for a grant of land "for the institution, embracing Dartmouth College and Moor's Charity School." The independent Vermont legislature (Vermont did not join the Union until 1791) granted Wheelock a vacant township of 23,000 acres, which became Wheelock, Vermont. The revenues from the town were to be divided equally between Moor's Charity School and Dartmouth. In 1791, in anticipation of income from the Vermont grant, a building was erected for Moor's Charity School. Wheelock also initiated a new round of correspondence with the Boston board of commissioners of the sspck with a view to continuing the work of Indian education, whether with Indian or non-Indian teachers.[62] In 1806, the Vermont legislature voted to sue Dartmouth for failing to honor the obligation it had assumed when it accepted the town of Wheelock as a gift. Income from the town could not be divided between the College and Moor's Charity School if, as it seemed to the legislators, the latter no longer existed. In response, the New Hampshire House of Representatives in 1807 reaffirmed the relationship between the two entities: "it has always been considered that Dartmouth College and Moor's Charity School are different branches of the same institution and that the president of said College ever has been and ever should be president of said School."[63] Both institutions had survived the Revolution and entered the new century, but funding remained precarious. So did the commitment to the education of Indians. By 1800, Dartmouth had graduated only three.

*Chapter Four*

# DARTMOUTH MEN IN INDIAN COUNTRY, 1775–1820

THE HANDFUL of Native students who attended the College did not represent the full scope of Dartmouth's involvement in Indian affairs in the early years of the new nation. Dartmouth began with the intention of sending missionaries and teachers to Indian communities, but Dartmouth men also went into Indian country as explorers, Indian agents, and land speculators. Several played key roles in the campaign to transform Indian ways of life, in dispossessing Indians of their homelands, and in reshaping the Native American West.

A year before Eleazar Wheelock died, one of his former students, John Ledyard, became the first American citizen to reach the Northwest Coast of America. A Dartmouth dropout, Ledyard had a hand in changing the lives of thousands of Indian people and pushing the new United States to the far side of the continent and to the Pacific. He was born in Connecticut in 1751, the son of a sea captain who died of malaria in the Caribbean; he arrived at Dartmouth in its second year of operation. "He was received into the Freshman class upon charity to prepare for service as a missionary among the Indians."[1] He didn't stay long—little more than a year. Wheelock's school was not for him; he craved a life of adventure. He had arrived in a two-wheeled carriage, causing quit a stir in backwoods Hanover; he left in a dugout canoe he carved himself and paddled 140 miles down the Connecticut River to Hartford. Then he knocked around for three years: first he tried to become a divinity student; after that he worked as a seaman, which took him to England. In June 1776, just a month before America declared its independence, he enlisted on Captain James Cook's third and final voyage around the world, "the greatest voyage in the age of sail." Sailing under British colors, he spent fifty months at sea and was the first American to travel to Alaska, Hawaii, and the Pacific Northwest.

Ledyard met Native peoples in Hawaii, British Columbia, Tonga, Tahiti, and New Zealand. He described those on the Northwest Coast as "the same kind of people that inhabit the opposite side of the continent," presumably a comparison with the Indian people he had met in New England.[2] He impressed Cook, as he would Thomas Jefferson, with his knowledge of Indian languages and customs and "fostered the strong impression that he had actually lived with the Native Americans for several months during his time at Dartmouth." He slept with Native women, wrote about Native customs, government, clothing, religion, and lifeways, and displayed more respect for Native peoples and cultures than was common among European and American sailors at the time. But he also viewed Native peoples with many of the prejudices of his age and society. After the brutal killing of Captain Cook by Hawaiian Islanders, Ledyard participated in the sailors' vicious retaliation that left nearly 100 Hawaiians dead and 1,000 houses burned.

Later, Ledyard met Thomas Jefferson in Paris. Sharing a mutual interest in languages, he gave the future president a long memorandum comparing the English vocabulary with those of the Ojibwa, Sioux, and Nootka. Together they came up with the idea that Ledyard should walk around the world and hike across America from the West Coast to the East (the same journey in reverse that Lewis and Clark would complete twenty years later). Heading east, Ledyard made it as far as Siberia, where he came to believe that the Tartars and the Native Americans were the same people. He noted that Russian colonization had similar effects on the indigenous people there to those that American colonization had on the Indians, as traders and missionaries pushed into their territory: "The cloak of civilization sits as ill upon them as on our American Tartars," he wrote. Catherine the Great of Russia had him arrested on suspicion of spying and sent him back to Poland. Next, he set out to travel across northern Africa. He fell ill and died in Cairo in January 1789. He was thirty-seven.[3]

Had Ledyard made it back to the Pacific Northwest, he would have found it much changed, for after Cook's third voyage, the world had rushed in on the Indian peoples there.

Russians had already arrived on the Pacific Coast when Ledyard was there, and he had met some. After Vitus Bering, a Dane sailing in the service of the tsar, had reached the Aleutian Islands in 1741, Russian traders had exploited the Native peoples of the Aleutian chain and coastal Alaska to acquire the thick and lustrous pelts of the playful sea otters that abounded in the cold waters of the North Pacific. Spanish expeditions had sailed up the coast to see what the Russians were up to, and by the time of the American Revolution many Northwest Coast Indians were adept traders. But it was Cook's third voyage that really opened up the sea otter trade, and it was Ledyard who brought the United States into that trade. Although Cook was primarily concerned with finding the fabled Northwest Passage that sailors believed would provide a direct water route from the East Coast of America to the Orient, his expedition revealed the enormous potential of the sea otter trade. After Cook was killed in Hawaii, his crew carried on to China, where sea otter pelts were in great demand as markers of status. The crew sold their skins and made, Ledyard said, "an astonishing profit." He wanted to get back to Nootka himself to make his fortune and he wanted the United States to get in on the action. In 1783 he published an account of the voyage, heavily plagiarized from other accounts, to promote American involvement in the trade. It was the first book copyrighted in the United States. It sold well. "Skins which did not cost the purchaser sixpence sterling sold in China for 100 dollars," Ledyard announced. He addressed a memorial to the Connecticut Assembly assuring them that his book would be "usefull to America in general but particularly to the northern States by opening a most valuable trade across the north pacific Ocean to China & the east Indies." Predicting a return of 1,000 percent, he formed a company with Philadelphia financier Robert Morris and some pretty shady business partners with the goal of trading for furs on the Northwest Coast, selling them in China, and returning to the United States laden with cargos of tea and silk.[4]

In the end, Ledyard failed to get the backing to lead his own expedition to the Pacific, and he turned his attention to other adventures. But by the time he died in Egypt, his publicizing efforts had galvanized Americans into action. A vast commerce embracing three continents sprang up. Ships from England and New England loaded up with manufactured goods, then sailed around the tip of South America and up the Pacific Coast, and landed at Indian villages on the shores of Washington, Oregon, British Columbia, and Alaska. The Indians paddled out to the ships in cedar canoes, bringing sea otter pelts to exchange for guns, metal tools, woolen blankets, and rum. With their holds stuffed with pelts, the ships sailed to Hawaii, where they often spent the winter, and then on to Chinese ports, where the captains sold their otter skins at huge profits and bought silks, spices, and tea, items that commanded high prices back home. At one time or another, British, Spanish,

Portuguese, Russian, and even French and Swedish vessels vied for the Indians' trade, but by 1800 American ships dominated the coast to such an extent that one historian called it a "trade suburb of Boston." When Lewis and Clark reached the Pacific in 1805, they found the Native inhabitants were already familiar with Americans. Ledyard's dream of a thriving American commerce on the Pacific Rim had come true.[5]

But that dream produced nightmares for the Indian peoples of the Pacific Northwest. The maritime traders brought new goods and new materials, which the Indians readily adopted, adapted, and incorporated into their cultures, and local chiefs enjoyed brief power and prosperity as they played rival traders and competing nations off against each other. But the sea otter was hunted to the brink of extinction and the ships that carried cloth and copper also carried guns, alcohol, syphilis, and smallpox. Lewis and Clark saw abandoned villages and Indians with pockmarked faces who swore like sailors.

Land attracted more Dartmouth men to Indian country than furs did. Some of Eleazar Wheelock's students and Dartmouth alumni continued his practice of keeping an eye on land development as well as on Indian education. As the young republic expanded, its leaders faced a dilemma: how could they take Indian lands and still claim to act with humanitarian concern for the Indian peoples? They persuaded themselves they could do both at once. Indians must change if they were to survive. The keys to survival were education, Christianity, and agriculture. But Indians were not likely to become farmers so long as they had plenty of hunting territory. Consequently, the best way to convince Indians to abandon their "savage" way of life as hunters and adopt a more "civilized" life as farmers was to deprive them of hunting territory. If Indians could make the transition, they could find a place in a republic of Christian farmers. Articulated at the national level by Thomas Jefferson and others and implemented at the local level by Indian agents and missionaries, the work of "civilizing" Indians went hand in hand with dispossessing them.[6]

Independence from Britain gave Americans the opportunity to build a nation on principles of liberty and equality. But who would be the citizens of this new society? What roles would be accorded to women, to African Americans, to Indians? The fact that most tribes had fought alongside the British in the war for independence persuaded many Americans that Indians deserved no place in the new nation and should not even be permitted to remain on their lands within territory now claimed by the United States. In a string of postwar treaties, American commissioners with troops at their backs dictated terms to Indians, telling them they were a defeated people, that their lands belonged to the United States by right of conquest, and that they would be allowed to remain on their homelands only if they surrendered most of their territory to the United States. Indian lands were the fruits of American victory and the bases for national expansion.[7]

The Oneidas were promised, and expected, preferential treatment by their former allies after the war. At the Treaty of Fort Stanwix in 1784, the United States confiscated lands from the other Iroquois tribes who had supported the British but assured the Oneidas and Tuscaroras that their lands would be safe. Samuel Kirkland was present at this treaty and James Dean, alias Kalaghwadirhon, translated. But American memories were short and American land hunger was insatiable. Dean and Kirkland now applied their language skills and influence to separating the Oneidas from their lands, and the tribe was soon signing away millions of acres. At the Treaty of Herkimer in 1785, New York pressured the Oneidas into selling a large tract of land along the New York–Pennsylvania border. Kirkland was present, as was David Fowler. Peter Pohquonnappeet represented the Stockbridge Indians. James Dean interpreted, and the Oneidas granted him two square miles of land "in Consequence of his long and faithful services." Dean was the official interpreter at every New York–Oneida land cession from 1785 to 1818 (he and Kirkland also interpreted in U.S. negotiations with the tribes northwest of the Ohio River in 1793). He was in on some infamous land transactions. "Whenever push came to shove," concludes historian Alan Taylor, Dean and Kirkland "proved better friends of the state than to the Oneidas." Both were up to their necks in land deals. They assisted John Livingston's New York Genesee Company of Adventurers in obtaining, for an annual rent of $1,000, a 999-year lease of Iroquois homeland as a way of getting around a state law that prohibited private purchases of Indian lands. Dean was a shareholder in the Genesee Company. Despite having promised the Oneidas he would never take any of their land, Kirkland acquired thousands of acres for himself and his family.[8]

In August 1792, a month after presiding at Occom's funeral, Kirkland traveled to Dartmouth to attend his son George's graduation. By then he was busy with plans to found the Hamilton-Oneida Academy, a school modeled on Wheelock's and intended for Indian and white students. He invited Onondiyo (alias Captain John), a young Oneida chief, to accompany him to "form a better Judgement of the effects learning would produce upon the human mind." Onondiyo made a good impression at Dartmouth. President John Wheelock invited him to speak at the commencement exercises. "Father," Onondiyo addressed Wheelock, "I have often heard of this great School, being set up in this place which but a little while ago was a wilderness, shaded with the tall pines, & now it has become like a feild of light." Turning to the "young sachems" who were the graduating class, he told them "this is the place for enlightening the mind" and urged them to "never deviate from the strait path" as they went forth into the world. Onondiyo's speech was greeted with shouts of applause, but George Kirkland evidently did not pay it much heed. After graduating he headed home, got into the land speculating business, fell into serious debt, and went bankrupt, adding to his father's increasing financial worries. (In an effort to recover his fortunes, George entered the West Indies trade and then, in 1806, joined Francisco de Miranda's ill-fated attempt to overthrow Spanish rule in Venezuela. He died of fever in Port-au-Prince, Haiti at age thirty-nine.)[9]

Samuel Kirkland and James Dean continued to mediate between the Oneidas and the government. In 1794, the United States made a treaty with the Oneidas, Tuscaroras, and Stockbridges, providing the tribes with compensation for their losses in the Revolution. In return for $5,000, a saw and grist mill, and $1,000 for a new church to replace the one burned in the war, the Indians relinquished any further claims. Dean interpreted, and Kirkland and John Sergeant were present as witnesses. John Konkapot, an alumnus of Moor's Charity School, attended as part of the Stockbridge delegation.[10] Kirkland built his academy, but like Dartmouth it deviated from its original mission and became an institution for white students. Kirkland died in February 1808. He had spent forty-three of his sixty-six years in Iroquois country. James Dean translated the funeral sermon for the Indians who attended.

Dean, as New York governor DeWitt Clinton put it, "coaxed" the Oneidas out of huge expanses of land. He consolidated his fortune by developing these lands and bringing families from New England to settle them. This man who had grown up among the Oneidas, promoted their allegiance to the United States, and then helped strip them of their lands went on to become a Federalist judge, a state assemblyman, and a respected citizen in central New York society.[11] The "white Indian" who attended Dartmouth with all expenses paid from charity funds had parlayed his role as a culture broker into securing a prominent place in white society.

Meanwhile, a contemporary of Dean secured a place in Indian country. Davenport Phelps, a grandson of Eleazar Wheelock, graduated from Dartmouth in 1775. He served in the Revolution as quartermaster in Bedel's regiment in the Canadian campaign of 1776, and was captured by the British and imprisoned in Montreal. After the war he married his cousin, Wheelock's granddaughter and, following a stint in law and business, moved to Niagara, Canada, where he secured a grant of 84,000 acres. There his new neighbor Joseph Brant urged him to become a missionary and used his considerable connections in both Canada and the United States to help get him ordained as an Episcopalian minister. In 1801, Phelps began "his real life's work" as an itinerant missionary. "Traveling from little frontier towns to remote Indian villages," according to one source, "he lived among the red men, learned to understand them, and won their confidence." He founded churches and, in the tradition of his grandfather, trained Indians to carry on missionary work themselves. He served in Onondaga and Seneca country until his death in 1813.[12]

Another grandson of Eleazar Wheelock had a hand in the defeat of the last great Indian war of resistance east of the Mississippi. Eleazar Ripley Wheelock, class of 1800, fought against Tecumseh in October 1813 at the Battle of the Thames, where the Shawnee war chief and his vision of an independent Indian state both perished. Promoted to brigadier-general, Ripley also fought against the British and Indians at the Battle of Lundy's Lane in 1814.[13]

Dartmouth also produced Indian agents and missionaries who spread to Indian country in the South. John Wheelock proposed to the SSPCK that a mission to the Cherokees would be an appropriate use of funds and made plans to send representatives to Tennessee to recruit promising Cherokee students. But the Society, mindful of how Wheelock senior had spent the money raised in England, was suspicious and rejected the scheme.[14] Wheelock sent Rev. Lyman Potter of Norwich, Vermont, on a mission to the Cherokees in 1799. Lyman was a Yale man, but his two sons graduated from Dartmouth in 1799 and 1802, and he himself earned an A.M. degree at Dartmouth in 1780.[15] John Sevier, governor of Tennessee, furnished Potter with a letter of introduction to the chiefs and warriors of the Cherokee nation, and described him as "a person distinguished for his piety, sobriety, & moral conduct." If the Cherokees wished "to engage a suitable person to instruct and teach your young people in the useful branches of Education, Religion, and the finer Arts," they could not do better than Potter.[16] However, some of the Dartmouth trustees, unhappy with John Wheelock's presidency, alleged that Potter's mission was nothing more than an expedient to appease the sspck and pursue self-interested designs:

The President had then no Indians on hand, on whom he could lavish the Scotch fund; and could conveniently spare an hundred dollars. It was necessary to do something about the Indians, . . . which might to the society wear the appearance of great zeal to spread the Gospel among the natives. Such an opportunity was not to be neglected; the President immediately proposed that Mr. Potter should take a mission, for which he would pay him $100. Mr. Potter went to the western part of Pennsylvania, to Ohio, and Tennessee; preached a few sermons occasionally, spent three or fours days among the Indians, made his purchase, was gone about four months, and returned.

His expenses were charged to the sspck, and he was immediately appointed to the Board of Trustees. Wheelock's defenders pointed out that Potter performed his services to the satisfaction of the sspck, and they denounced the trustees' insinuations of fraudulent transactions as patent falsehoods.[17] Soon after, Potter quit his position as minister in Norwich and moved west with his family, taking up land in what became known as the Western Reserve, at Steubenville, Ohio, "the very outpost of settlement and civilization."[18] He continued to promote the twin goals of missionary work and settlement in Ohio.[19] His son Lyman, class of 1799, died in Mississippi.

In 1794 President Washington appointed Silas Dinsmoor (class of 1791) as agent to the Cherokees. After graduating from Dartmouth, Dinsmoor taught at Atkinson Academy and in June 1794 was appointed first lieutenant in the Army Corps of Engineers, which position he resigned a month later to accept Washington's appointment. At the request of Secretary of War Henry Knox (conduct of Indian affairs was the responsibility of the War Department at the time; the Bureau of Indian Affairs (bia) was not transferred to the Department of the Interior until 1849), he took charge of a deputation of Cherokees then visiting Philadelphia, sailed with them to Charlestown, South Carolina, and accompanied them home. He remained with the Cherokees for five years.

Silas Dinsmoor. *Courtesy Dartmouth College, Rauner Library.*

His duties were to reduce hostilities between the Cherokees and their white neighbors on the frontier and to instruct the Cherokees "in the raising of stock, the cultivation of land, and the arts." This involved imposing a new gender order as well as a new economic order in a society where traditionally the men hunted and the women performed—in the eyes of Dinsmoor and his contemporaries—menial tasks. He ordered spinning wheels for Cherokee women.[20] According to Dinsmoor's son, the old Cherokee chief Bloody Knife at first opposed the new agent and his program but was eventually won over and became his father's friend.[21]

Dinsmoor's duties also included convening the Cherokees to meet "at the shortest notice" with American treaty commissioners in 1798 and obtaining provisions for the treaty council, the goal of which, as the secretary of war gently phrased it, was "to dispose the minds of the Cherokees to make a sale of such part of their land as will give a more convenient form to the State of Tennessee." "You must, moreover, be convinced," President John Adams wrote to the Cherokees in 1798, "that the United States can have your good only in view in keeping Mr. Dinsmoor in your Nation."[22] Adams dismissed Dinsmoor in 1799, and in 1800–1801 he served as purser on the *U.S.S. George Washington* in the Mediterranean, which was dispatched against the Barbary pirates.

When Thomas Jefferson entered the White House, he recalled Dinsmoor to the Indian service. In 1802 he was appointed temporary agent to the Choctaws in southern Mississippi, a post he held for twelve years.[23] Secretary of war Henry Dearborn reminded Dinsmoor of his duties as an Indian agent: "the cultivation of peace and harmony between the U. States, and the Indian Nations generally; the detection of any improper conduct in the Indians, or the Citizens of the U. States, or other relating to the Indians, or their lands, and the introduction of the Arts of husbandry, and domestic manufactures, as means of producing, and diffusing the blessings attached to a well regulated civil Society." Dinsmoor was to "use all the prudent means in your power" to achieve these objectives.[24]

The United States was in too much of a hurry to let the process of transforming Indians proceed gradually. In 1803, American emissaries in Paris purchased the Louisiana Territory, buying some 827,000 square miles between the Mississippi and the Rocky Mountains for a mere $15 million, and the United States doubled its size overnight. Many Americans saw the West as barren and virtually empty, useless for American farmers but good enough for Indian hunters. Removing Indians from the East was now a practical possibility.

And Jefferson knew how to do it. Writing to Governor William Henry Harrison of Indiana territory in 1803, he explained that it was U.S. policy to live in peace with the Indians, to guide them to an agricultural way of life, and to strip them of their lands, which became less valuable to them as the pressure of American settlers depleted the game. "To promote this disposition to exchange lands, which they have to spare and we want, we shall push our trading houses, and be glad to see them run in debt, because we observe that when these debts get beyond what the individuals can pay, they become willing to lop them off by a cession of lands." In this way, the president understood, American settlements would gradually engulf the Indians, "and they will in time either incorporate with us as citizens of the United States, or remove beyond the Mississippi." The United States was now so powerful that the Indians "must see we have only to shut our hand to crush them." If any

Indians were so foolhardy as to take up the hatchet, the United States would seize their land and drive them across the Mississippi.[25]

Silas Dinsmoor's son believed that his father "considered himself in honor bound to look after the interests of the tribe over which he was placed, as well as over the interests of the United States."[26] Doing both simultaneously was possible under Jefferson's construction of Indian policy: depriving Indians of land forced them to become civilized, or to move out of harm's way. Dinsmoor became an instrument of both aspects of Jeffersonian Indian policy: civilization and dispossession. He enjoyed a reputation as a man "of good will, ability, and stalwart integrity."[27] Yet he also served as a treaty commissioner, working to separate Indians from their lands. In 1805, Dearborn appointed Dinsmoor and Tennessee land speculator James Robertson as commissioners to deal with the Chickasaws and Choctaws. Dinsmoor ordered "a long list of gourmet foods, premium cigars, fine whiskies, and the best wines" to help smooth the negotiations.[28] In July, he and Robertson concluded a treaty with the Chickasaws. The opening article was Jeffersonian Indian policy in action: "Whereas the Chickasaw nation of Indians have been for some time embarrassed by heavy debts due to their merchants and traders, and being destitute of funds to effect improvements in their country, they have agreed and do hereby cede to the United States . . ." What the Chickasaws ceded was a huge tract of land stretching from Kentucky to Alabama, in return for $20,000 and the payment of their debts, plus annuities to key chiefs.[29] In November, at the Treaty of Mount Dexter, in exchange for $50,0000 plus an annuity in goods of $3,000, Dinsmoor and Robertson obtained from the Choctaws more than 4 million fertile acres in south central Mississippi. Panton, Leslie and Company actually received $48,000 of the $50,000, in settlement of debts the Choctaws had run up in the deerskin trade. The company brought lawsuits against Dinsmoor for nonpayment of some of the debts, and Jefferson felt the Choctaws should have been paid more; nevertheless, the Mount Dexter treaty "accomplished the purpose behind Jefferson's policy of allowing the Indians to bankrupt themselves out of all their territory."[30]

According to his son, Dinsmoor also worked to protect Choctaw lands, at a time when Andrew Jackson, a renowned Indian fighter and expansionist, was intent on driving the Choctaws out. "The Indians were in possession of excellent land, and some speculative white men wanted to get hold of it. Andrew Jackson was in their interests, but the agent watched the corners so closely as to be a thorn in their sides." Dinsmoor also ran afoul of Jackson by

insisting that anyone going into the Indian nations, including Jackson himself, carry passports in compliance with treaty provisions. Jackson apparently
tried to have Dinsmoor removed and even threatened to burn his home. On
another occasion, Dinsmoor was wounded in a duel "fought with pistols
while at the dinner table," which must have been an interesting squabble.[31] In
1820, Jackson bullied and threatened Choctaw chiefs into making a treaty at
Doak's Stand, ceding lands in Mississippi to the United States and accepting
lands in the West in return. Dinsmoor was no longer the Choctaws' agent, but
he turned up at the treaty council in the hope that it might include a provision of land to indemnify him for personal property he had lost when he was
agent. The Choctaw chiefs submitted a petition in support of his claim, but
Jackson refused Dinsmoor's request as unwarranted.[32]

Meanwhile, controversy stirred around another Dartmouth graduate with
an interest in Indians: Solomon Spaulding, who served in the Revolution in
his youth. He graduated with his class in 1785, studied divinity, preached for a
few years, and then gave up the ministry because of ill health. He speculated
unsuccessfully in Ohio lands and lived in Ohio until the War of 1812. He carried out excavations of the great earth mounds that ancient Indian inhabitants had constructed in the area, and, imagining them to have been built
by the lost tribes of Israel, wrote a romance or novel, entitled *Manuscript
Found*, about the origins of American Indians. The manuscript was submitted to a printer in Pittsburgh but was never published. Some people argued
that after Spaulding's death in 1816 Joseph Smith acquired the manuscript and
plagiarized it to produce the Book of Mormon. The controversy continues to
this day.[33]

For one reason or another, most Americans came to believe that Indians
belonged west of the Mississippi. The land there was barren: suitable for hunters but useless for farmers. Making their way across Montana via the Missouri
River in 1805, Meriwether Lewis and William Clark had called the country
"the deserts of America" and doubted any of it could ever be settled.[34] But a
Dartmouth man was largely responsible for fixing the image of the West as
"the Great American Desert."

Stephen H. Long was born in Hopkinton, New Hampshire, and graduated from Dartmouth in 1809. He entered the army in 1814 and transferred

to the Corps of Topographical Engineers in 1816. After exploring the Fox and Wisconsin rivers on the upper Mississippi in 1817–18, Long was assigned to command a government expedition to the Rocky Mountains. In 1819, he traveled with a party of scientists and soldiers by steamboat from Pittsburgh to St. Louis and then up the Missouri River. The expedition was dogged with problems and got no further than Council Bluffs, north of present-day Omaha, Nebraska. Long returned the next year with nineteen men and followed the Platte River to the Rockies. The expedition botanist and geologist, Dr. Edwin James, a graduate of Middlebury College, wrote an account of the journey, published in 1823.

Echoing Thomas Jefferson's instructions to Lewis and Clark, secretary of war John C. Calhoun's orders to Long included the clause: "You will conciliate the Indians by kindness and presents and will ascertain, as far as practicable, the number and character of the various tribes, with the extent of country claimed by each."[35] The expedition had ample opportunity to gather information about Indians, and James's account contains lengthy descriptions of the ways of life, tribal customs, and intertribal relations of the various peoples encountered along the way. The party met several families of Shawnees from the village of Apple Creek ten miles from Cape Girardeau in Missouri. James noted the women wore silver armbands and earrings, for which the Shawnees were famous. These people had preceded the Americans into the West. During the Revolution, the Shawnees in Ohio had split, and about half the nation had migrated west to Missouri rather than stay and face perpetual conflict with the Americans invading their lands. James said little about the Shawnees' reaction to seeing Americans , but they, ever on the move ahead of the advancing American frontier, must have viewed Long and his companions with misgivings.[36]

Around St. Louis, the expedition saw many earth mounds "and other remains of the labours of nations of Indians that inhabited this region many ages since." They were at the site of Cahokia, the great pre-Columbian metropolis, trade, and ceremonial center that had been inhabited hundreds of years earlier by as many as 20,000 people. Overgrown with bushes and briars, the great mound inspired James to reflect on the fleeting nature of human power and aspirations: "We feel the insignificance and the want of permanence in every thing human," he wrote. In keeping with the attitudes of the time, the visitors to this ancient Indian city did not think twice about digging open graves and examining human remains in the interest of scientific investigation.

(Cahokia remained overgrown by trees until the second half of the twentieth century; UNESCO designated it a World Heritage Site in 1982.)[37]

Heading west, Long's expedition passed through the lands of the Osages, Kansas, Otos, Iowas, Missouris, and Omahas. They met with tribal delegations, giving James plenty of opportunity to make observations on different tribes and individual chiefs. They held a council with 400 Omahas and their chief, Big Elk, and were visited by Teton Sioux, who had challenged Lewis and Clark when they ascended the Missouri River sixteen years earlier. James described the Sioux as "fine looking men" who dressed in their finery to meet the Americans.[38] Arriving in Pawnee country, Long led his men into the village of the Grand Pawnees in ranks and with banners flying but met an anticlimactic reception. No chiefs or warriors came to greet them. A group of women and children crowded around, gave them some boiled corn, and left. It turned out that the village leaders were engaged in a medicine ceremony and would not be interrupted. Later, Long and his men "smoked with their chief, *Tar-ra-re-ca-wa-o* or *Long-hair*," but their attention was caught by a young chief "about twenty-three years of age, of the finest form, tall, mus-

Stephen Long's Council with the Pawnees of the Grand, Loup, and Republican Bands, October 10, 1819. From an original watercolor by Samuel Seymour, artist with Long's expedition. *Courtesy Dartmouth College, Rauner Library (Account of an Expedition from Pittsburgh to the Rocky Mountains under the Command of Stephen H. Long, opp. p. 252; Rauner Presses I36ja).*

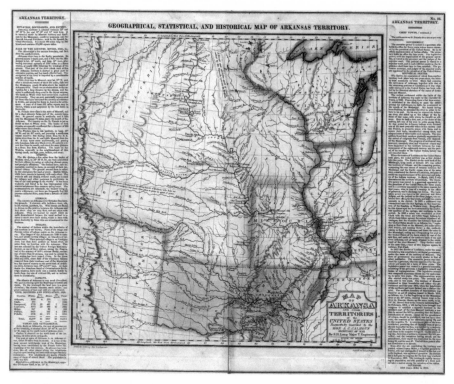

Stephen Long, *Map of the Arkansas and other territories of the United States . . . 1822.*
*Courtesy Dartmouth College, Rauner Library (Alumni qL655m, p. 139).*

cular, exceedingly graceful, and of a most prepossessing countenance. His head dress of war eagles' feathers, descended in a double series upon his back like wings." Upon inquiry they learned that this was Petalesharo, whom they already knew by reputation as "the most intrepid warrior of the nation," destined "to be the future leader of his people."[39]

They followed the south fork of the Platte, passing Long's Peak, which they named in the leader's honor, and climbed several mountains. Long sent Captain William Bell down the Arkansas River while he returned to Fort Smith via the Canadian, which he at first mistook for the Red River. They met Cheyennes, Arapahos, Kiowas, Comanches, Osages, Caddos, and western Cherokees. By the time the expedition returned to Cape Girardeau, it had completed a huge loop and, using only rudimentary equipment, produced the first scientific survey of the southern plains. For New Englanders like James and Long, "plains landscapes were both foreign and strangely unsettling," and it is not surprising that they described them in negative terms and had a difficult time envisioning them populated with Yankee farmers. "In regard to this extensive section of country," wrote James, "we do not hesitate in giving the opinion, that it is almost wholly unfit for cultivation, and of course uninhabitable by a people depending upon agriculture for their subsistence. . . . The whole of this region seems peculiarly adapted as a range for buffaloes, wild goats, and other wild game, incalculable multitudes of which, find ample pasturage and subsistence upon it."[40] Incorporating geographical information about the upper Missouri and Yellowstone rivers from William Clark's map of 1814, Long produced a manuscript map of the West in 1821. Across the western plains between the Platte and Canadian river he wrote in bold letters: "GREAT DESERT."[41]

Long led another government expedition—to determine the source of the Minnesota River—in 1823, a journey that took him up the Red River of the north to Lake Winnipeg, and he surveyed the border region between the United States and Canada. However, even though Zebulon Pike had said much the same about the West ten years earlier, none of Long's other achievements had such an enduring impact as the two words he wrote on his map. Convinced that the West was arid and inhospitable, the War Department recommended that it be used for resettling the eastern tribes who were being targeted for removal.

❦

While the work of civilizing and dispossessing Indians went ahead full steam in Indian country, the work of educating Indians at Dartmouth sputtered along, although it never quite sputtered out. In 1800 Jacob and Joseph, sons of Joseph Brant, were admitted to Moor's Charity School. The SSPCK supported them, and they stayed about a year and a half, but when they returned home the school was "destitute of Indians." A few Indians attended every year until the War of 1812 severed communication with Indian country, but their presence was dwarfed by that of the thirty to sixty white students.[42]

Visitors to Dartmouth in the first decade of the nineteenth century were aware of its original mission but saw little evidence of Indian education. Timothy Dwight, former president of Yale, had heard Occom preach twice: "His discourses, though not proofs of superior talents, were decent, and his utterances in some degree eloquent," he grudgingly acknowledged. "The original design of educating Indians and missionaries to the Indians has been frustrated," Dwight wrote. Only a couple of Indians had graduated, and the trickle of missionaries had dried up. But no blame attached to Dr. Wheelock "or any others entrusted with this concern." Dwight explained at some length:

An Indian student cannot be obtained ordinarily without extreme difficulty. What is at least as unfortunate, his habits are in a great measure fixed before he can be brought to a place of education, and more resemble those of a deer or a fox than those of a civilized youth. In the literal sense, he must be tamed, and to tame him is scarcely possible. He may possess the average talents, or even those which are superior. He may learn (for some of them do learn) easily whatever is prescribed to him as a task. Still he is a perfect devotee to idleness and wandering, impatient of subordination, hostile to the regularity of life, and enslaved to his gun and his dog. To engraft literature and science on such a stock demands a degree of skill, patience, and perseverance not often found in the mind of man. Few employments have been more helpless than this.

Given the wars that had raged from the Revolution until General Anthony Wayne defeated the Indians of Ohio at the Battle of Fallen Timbers in 1794, it was hardly surprising "that missions to the natives should for a long period be wholly interrupted." As far as Dwight was concerned, Indian character flaws and Indian hostilities were responsible for Dartmouth's failure to carry out its founding mission. Despite the Indians' intransigence, he affirmed, if the original donors were alive they would have the satisfaction of knowing that Dartmouth "has yet been a source of extensive benefit to mankind."[43]

Edward Augustus Kendall found only one student "of Indian extraction" at Dartmouth in 1808, and three Indians among the thirty-eight students attending Moor's Charity School, which, having failed in its original mission, now catered almost exclusively to teaching the children of neighboring communities. The Dartmouth student and two of the three Indian students at Moor's School were Abenakis from St. Francis. "Of the first design, that of affording schooling to Indian children," wrote Kendall, "no trace remains, except in the application of the annual sum of four hundred dollars, the produce of a fund held in trust by the Scotch Missionary Society, and which would be forfeited if applied to any other purpose." Tuition costs were rather lower than today: students paid $20 a year, in addition to $12 for the use of half a room, and $1.50 a week in board.[44]

Almost all of the Indians who did come to Hanover in the first half of the nineteenth century came from northern tribes, and most from St. Francis.

Some were children; most were in their early teens. Most attended Moor's Charity School, some attended affiliated academies, and all were supported from the sspck fund.[45] For instance, Louis Annance, age nine (?), John Taubausanda, age twelve, Joseph Taukerman, age nine, and Paul Joseph Gill, age twelve, all came from St. Francis in 1803. Taubausanda left in 1804, Taukerman the year after. Gill was accounted a "star pupil" and enrolled in the college class of 1810 but was dismissed in his senior year as "wholly bent to vice." Joseph Stanislaus attended from 1804 to 1807 and William Gill from 1806 to 1808.[46] Francis Noel Annance came to Hanover in 1808. Louis and Francis Noel were brothers, sons of Francis Joseph Annance ("the Great Francis"), who had attended Moor's Charity School and Dartmouth.[47]

Louis Annance left in 1809, joined other Abenakis fighting alongside the British in the War of 1812, and then became a Mason and a well-known guide in Maine. Francis Noel left in 1813, a year before he was supposed to graduate, and led the Abenaki contingent in the war. Simon Annance left Moor's Charity School in 1816 because of ill health.[48] After the war, Francis went to work in the Canadian fur trade, employment that took him deep into Indian country in the far West. He joined the North West Company, and after it amalgamated with the Hudson Bay Company in 1821 he became an interpreter and clerk for the new operation. He spent most of his service west of the Rocky Mountains in the Columbia Department. Hudson Bay Company governor George Simpson described him in 1832 as "About 40 Years of Age. 13 Years in the Service. A half breed of the Abiniki Tribe near Quebec; well Educated & has been a Schoolmaster. Is firm with Indians, speaks several of their Languages, walks well, is a good Shot and qualified to lead the life of an Indian whose disposition he possesses in a great degree. Is not worthy of belief even upon Oath and altogether a bad character although a useful man. Can have no prospects of advancement." Simpson was known for his blunt words and strong prejudices, but he was right on the last point: Despite his education, his fluency in French and several Indian languages, and his skills as a woodsman, hunter, and trapper, Annance was unable to rise to the rank of chief trader or factor. He was appointed postmaster, "the highest office available to mixed-blood men," and sent to Fort Simpson, a remote post on the Mackenzie River. There he had an affair with the Native wife of chief factor John Stuart, which did his reputation no good. When Annance's contract expired in 1835, Simpson dismissed him as "a most troublesome useless servant." Annance retired to Montreal and in 1845 returned to St. Francis, where he took up the post of schoolmaster.[49]

An "Account of Dartmouth College in America," published in the *Christian Observer* in 1814, acknowledged that the College's record of success in converting Indians appeared "to have been much less than the zealous minds of Dr. Wheelock and his English friends at one time confidently expected."[50] In 1819, Congress established an annual "civilization fund" of $10,000, and from that time forward financial support for education became a central component of federal Indian policy. But the pressure to remove Indians from their homelands soon outstripped the efforts to "civilize" them.

*Chapter Five*

# DARTMOUTH IN THE AGE OF INDIAN REMOVAL, 1820–50

🦌 IN THE SPRING of 1835, fifteen Abenakis encamped in Windsor, Vermont, attracting the attention of a local newspaper: "They are part of the tribe of the Missisques, who live a wandering life on the eastern shore of Lake Champlain, and are on a journey to Hanover, N.H. for the purpose of entering a member of the family in Dartmouth College." The "patriarch" of the family band was seventy-three; the prospective student, named "Say-so-saph Sa-ba-tese Al-anum," was seventeen. Overtaken by winter, they had pitched their tents and erected two wigwams on the bank of the Connecticut River and supported themselves by making and selling "Indian articles."[1] It is not clear if the young man made it to Dartmouth, but an Abenaki family setting off to take their son to college in the 1830s merits attention, as it did then.

Increasingly, Americans believed that Indians were not long for the world that Americans were creating. In New England, according to Jedediah Morse's *Report on Indian Affairs*, submitted to the secretary of war in 1822, a "few feeble remnants" teetered on the brink of extinction. James Fenimore Cooper's novel *Last of the Mohicans* (1826) pictured Indians as a tragic race, inevitably disappearing before a relentless white tide. Town histories regularly reported the passing of the "last" Indian in the neighborhood.[2] Dartmouth president Nathan Lord shared the sentiments of his time and place. He wrote to the SSPCK in April 1832 suggesting that the money in the "Scotch Fund," originally earmarked for Indian education, be diverted to other purposes. The goal of the fund was noble, but things had changed and Indian population had declined. "They have *been* melting away, have lost, at least in New England, all that was once commanding & attractive in their character, and the few now remaining are sunk in helpless desperation." Since New England Indians could no longer be educated, Dartmouth must look to Canada or the West to find suitable students who must then be transported at greater expense. And, at the rate Indian population was falling, "probably, at no distant time, all traces of Indian existence in the U.S. will be obliterated."[3] For the president of Dartmouth, Indians seemed a lost cause.

Moreover, things did not bode well for Indian students at his institution, where, according to the *Dartmouth Catalogue* of 1831–32, "The Faculty wish it to be understood that the College is a desirable place, not for the intractable and perverse, but for the regular, the gentlemanly, and good, for those whose object is intellectual and moral improvement."[4] Indians seldom seemed to fit that description. Lord found them an irritation: "The care of this Indian appropriation is greater than can easily be conceived by any person unaccustomed to it," he complained. Over and above his normal duties as president of the College, he had to supervise every aspect of the Indians' education — correspondence, counseling, contracts, and accounting for every expense charged to the Scotch Fund. It was time-consuming and frustrating work, and the president received no additional compensation for his extra duties: "as Indian agent he has nothing."[5] Nevertheless, despite predictions that Indians were disappearing, a national policy that sought to clear them out of the East, and a faculty and administration that were less than welcoming, Indians did attend both Moor's Charity School and Dartmouth College, and several students made a mark, both on the College and on their Native communities.

At the same time, the country continued to wrestle with the question of what place American Indians occupied in the new nation. Acquiring Indian lands between the Appalachians and the Mississippi was a clear goal of the United States from the end of the Revolution to the 1850s, and the Indian Removal Act in 1830 made ethnic cleansing in that area of the country a national policy. Dartmouth graduates played significant roles in the politics of Indian removal, and Native and non-Native alumni alike took positions on both sides of the issue.

The Cherokees were prime targets for removal. The Cherokee homelands originally extended into five southeastern states, but war and treaties repeatedly diminished their territory. Some Cherokees moved west voluntarily early in the nineteenth century, and most of those who remained were confined to Georgia. But they still possessed valuable lands, and their success in adjusting to American ways of life only made their non-Indian neighbors more covetous. In 1817, Andrew Jackson made a treaty that he expected would secure wholesale removal of the Cherokee Nation to Arkansas. The American Board of Commissioners for Foreign Missions (ABCFM) came to the Cherokees' aid.

The Board had decided to extend its operations to the Cherokees in 1816 and built its first mission station among the Cherokees at Brainerd, Georgia, the next year. Jackson's treaty threatened the mission work as well as the Cherokees. In 1819 the ABCFM dispatched Dr. Samuel A. Worcester to Washington to assist the Cherokee delegation in its negotiations with the secretary of war. Worcester (whom many historians have confused with his more famous namesake and nephew, the litigant in *Worcester v. Georgia*), was born in Hollis, New Hampshire, in 1770 and graduated from Dartmouth in 1795. In 1804 he was appointed professor of theology at the College and six years later became the first corresponding secretary of the ABCFM. He arrived in Washington late in the negotiations but appears to have assisted in the final wording of the treaty. By its terms, the Cherokees lost several million acres of land in North Carolina, Georgia, Tennessee, and Alabama, but they hoped it would safeguard them from further threat of removal. Future Cherokee chief John Ross said Worcester was "very active in promoting much good towards our welfare and future happiness." The next year Worcester made a missionary tour through Choctaw and Cherokee country, but his health was failing. He died at Brainerd Mission, in June 1821, aged fifty. He was buried in the mission cemetery; his son later took his remains back home to Salem, Massachusetts.[6]

The ABCFM sent Alfred Finney, class of 1815, to establish a mission school for the 2,000 or 3,000 Cherokees who had previously moved west to Arkansas Territory. (Another graduate of the same class, Maurice Cary, served as a missionary in Iowa Territory.)[7] The western Cherokee chief Tahlonteskee had requested the mission earlier when he visited Brainerd. Finney and his wife left Randolph, Vermont, and traveled to Brainerd, where they rendezvoused with his brother-in-law, Rev. Cephas Washburn. Finney and Washburn then set off for Arkansas, traveling along the Natchez Trail through the Chickasaw Nation. Arkansas in 1820 was "a perfect *terra incognita*," said Washburn. Not knowing the route, they traveled with an Indian trader taking pelts to market on a packhorse. They endured a "toilsome journey," braving quicksand, floods, snakes, swarms of mosquitoes, and recurrent bouts of ague and fever. Losing his hat when his wagon became mired in quicksand, Finney was "compelled to adopt the fashion of the country" and wear a Cherokee-style turban. On the west side of Illinois Bayou, near present-day Russellville, Arkansas, they built Dwight Mission, naming it after the former president of Yale. It was one of the first Protestant missions founded west of the Mississippi. The western Cherokees were not yet hard pressed by the white population (although they were at war with the Osages, who regarded them as intruders) but Finney knew what the future held: "men of every description are coming in thick and fast around them," he wrote to Jeremiah Evarts of the ABCFM in 1824. Rather than "let hords *of indolent savage & unprincipled white men* line the borders of the Cherokee country," corrupting the Indians and poisoning their minds, it would be better to move from Dwight. Finney was ready and willing to go with them: "The desire of my heart, growing stronger every day is to live and die on Mission ground," he said. But when the western Cherokees were removed to Oklahoma in 1829 he was transferred instead to the Salisan River mission station, where he died that same year, aged thirty-nine.[8] Roderick Lathrop Dodge, who graduated from Dartmouth Medical School in 1834, was appointed by the ABCFM to serve as medical missionary to the Creek and Cherokee Indians west of Arkansas, before he became assistant surgeon at Fort Gibson in Indian Territory. His son was born at the Dwight mission in 1842. Dodge senior later became mayor of Little Rock.[9] Another ABCFM missionary, Rev. Alfred E. Wright, and his wife, Harriet, accompanied a group of Choctaws in their exodus to Oklahoma in 1832 and established Wheelock Academy and Wheelock Church, both named in honor of Dartmouth's first president. Ten years later the Choctaw Nation adopted the school into its school system as Wheelock Seminary, a school for girls. Fire destroyed the academy in 1869, but the Choctaws rebuilt Wheelock as a boarding school for girls in the 1880s, and it continued to operate until 1955.[10]

Dartmouth men played significant roles in the removal era debates over the rights of the eastern tribes. Dartmouth's most famous alumnus, Daniel Webster (class of 1801), was a celebrated orator and one of the nation's foremost attorneys, after he successfully represented his alma mater in *Dartmouth College v. Woodward* in 1818. He argued in favor of Indian rights, but Indian rights were not his primary concern. In the landmark 1823 Supreme Court case *Johnson v. McIntosh*, Webster served as co-counsel for the United Illinois and Wabash Land Companies, who were suing to retain 43,000 square miles of fertile farmland they had purchased from the Piankeshaw Indians in Illinois and Indiana. Webster argued that Indians had rights to the soil and could legally sell land to individuals: "all, or nearly all, the lands in the United States, is holden under purchases from the Indian nations," said Webster, "and the only question in this case must be, whether it be competent to individuals to make such purchases, or whether that be the exclusive prerogative of government." The Court agreed that Indians were indeed rightful occupiers of the soil with a just and legal claim to retain possession of it, but their power to sell to whomever they pleased was "denied by the original fundamental principle that discovery gave exclusive title to those who made it." The United States had inherited that title from Great Britain, and only the U.S. government had the right to purchase the land from the Indians. Webster's land speculating clients lost their case.[11]

The election of Andrew Jackson in 1828 put the most forceful advocate of removal into the White House. Jefferson had regarded Indians as culturally inferior but capable of improvement; Jackson portrayed them as racially inferior. Their cultural resilience and resistance proved that they were incapable of changing with the times. They must make way for civilized white people who would put their land to good use.[12] In May 1830, Congress passed the Indian Removal Act, authorizing the president to negotiate treaties of removal with all Indian tribes living east of the Mississippi. The Senate passed the bill twenty-eight to nineteen; the vote in the House was 102 to 97. The voting involved political and moral issues and did not break down along pro- and anti-Indian lines so much as along party lines. Some who voted against the bill did so out of opposition to Jackson rather than sympathy for the Indians; some who voted in favor of the bill did so in reluctant conviction that removal represented the Indians' best, and perhaps only, chance of survival. Despite his reputation as an Indian fighter, Davy Crockett of Tennessee voted against the bill. Daniel Webster worked with Henry Clay and other anti-Jacksonian politicians to defeat the bill, but he was more interested in impugning Jackson than in championing Indians. Like many politicians and businessmen, Webster profited by investing in lands obtained from Indians in the North but took up the Cherokee cause in the South. Dartmouth alumni voted on both sides. In the Senate, Levi Woodbury of New Hampshire (class of 1809) voted in favor of the bill; Samuel Bell of New Hampshire (class of 1793) and Dudley Chase of Vermont (1791) joined Webster in voting against it. In the House, Henry Hubbard of New Hampshire (1803) and Rufus McIntire of Maine (1809) voted in favor; George Grennell (1808) and Joseph Richardson (1802), both of Massachusetts, and Jonathan Hunt of Vermont (1807) voted against. The bill authorized the president to make removal treaties, but those treaties still had to be approved by a two-thirds majority in the Senate, where Webster vigorously opposed their ratification.[13]

Levi Woodbury was a loyal Jackson Democrat. The president rewarded him by appointing him secretary of the navy in 1831 and then secretary of the treasury in 1834. Since the General Land Office was housed in the Treasury Department, Woodbury had general supervision over the survey and sale of millions of acres of Indian land that became "public domain" and flooded the market as a result of Indian removals. District land offices increased in number and in volume of business. The General Land Office was a source of extensive political patronage and the secretary of the treasury played a key role in dispensing it, making appointments to administer the public domain. Speculation in real estate and corruption in the land office business were rampant. Jacksonian appointees as district land officers expected to make a profit as a reward for their services to the president and the party. Woodbury's tenure "coincided with the flood tide of the land office business" in 1834–37, and he was "curiously relaxed in enforcing the rules" that required receivers to deposit public monies promptly. Land officers defaulted for more than $750,000 during Jackson's presidency.[14]

Webster and other anti-Jacksonians helped to organize the Cherokees' legal defense. Time was running out for the Cherokees. After gold was discovered in Cherokee country in 1827, prospectors flooded in. The Georgia legislature passed a resolution asserting its sovereignty over Cherokee lands within the state's borders. Georgia demanded that the federal government begin negotiations to compel the Cherokees to cede their land, and carried out a systematic campaign of harassment and intimidation, culminating in an assault on Cherokee government. In 1830, Georgia created a police force—the Georgia Guard—to patrol Cherokee country. Over the next few years the Guard harassed Cherokee people, arrested Chief John Ross and seized his papers, and confiscated the printing press of the tribal newspaper, the *Cherokee Phoenix*. Webster and his colleagues persuaded former U.S. attorney general William Wirt to take up the Cherokees' cause, arguing that the tribe had a right to maintain its independence in Georgia and that a decision in favor of the Indians would embarrass the president politically.[15] With Wirt's assistance, the Cherokees won their case. The Supreme Court ruled in *Worcester v. Georgia* in 1832 that the Cherokee Nation was a distinct community with its own territory in which state laws had no force.

Nevertheless, Georgia continued to harass the Cherokees to drive them to the treaty table. In 1835, United States commissioners signed the Treaty of New Echota with a minority of Cherokees who agreed to give up their remaining homelands and move west. John Ross and the majority denounced the treaty and Webster spoke out against it in the Senate, but it carried by thirty-one to fifteen, securing by just one vote the two-thirds majority needed for ratification. Jackson signed the treaty in 1836, and two years later federal troops forced the Cherokees out at gunpoint. Thousands died on this "Trail of Tears" to the West. Most of the Choctaws, Creeks, Chickasaws, and Seminoles had already gone, although some managed to hide out in their traditional lands.

In the North, Shawnees, Potawatomis, Sauks, and other tribes experienced their own trails of death. "Christian Indians" as well as "civilized tribes" were uprooted and relocated. Within ten years of Samson Occom's death, white settlers outnumbered Indians five to one on the Brothertown lands. In 1818, led by Mahican-Stockbridge chief Hendrick Aupaumut, the Brothertown Indians joined the Oneidas and Stockbridges in plans to remove to Wisconsin, and three years later the Stockbridges relocated to the Fox River. For some years, the only minister to the New York tribes who removed to Wisconsin was "the erratic Eleazar Williams," who served as a missionary to the Oneidas and played an influential role in getting them to remove to Green Bay. Williams, a descendant of Eunice Williams, the famous Deerfield captive, was born into the Mohawk community at Kahnawake. His father put him in the care of a Massachusetts clergyman, a relative, with a view to getting the boy an education, and in November 1807, when Eleazar was nineteen, the clergyman sent him to Moor's Charity School.[16] He appears to have stayed only a week. In the words of a biographer, "we know only of his arrival, where he slept and took his meals, and of his departure." We also know that he was supported by the Scotch Fund. Williams himself said that his short visit to Hanover was for his health, but it is possible that his abrupt departure stemmed from his mortification at being placed in a school for Indians. Mixed ancestry was not uncommon at Kahnawake, but Williams seems to have tried repeatedly to shed his Indian identity as an obstacle to a career as a clergyman and the status he craved. He did become an Episcopalian minister. He also concocted a heroic role for himself in the War of 1812, ran up debts, fabricated histories about himself, and to cap his career as a charlatan, even claimed to be the "Lost Dauphin," the rightful heir to the throne of France![17]

After the Stockbridges' missionary, Rev. Jesse Miner, died in 1829, the ABCFM sent in his place Rev. Cutting Marsh. Born in Danville, Vermont, in 1800, Marsh graduated from Dartmouth in 1826 and from Andover Theological Seminary in 1829. When he arrived at the Stockbridge settlement in Statesburg, Wisconsin, in 1830 he found the inhabitants in dire straits. Measles and other diseases had recently carried off many children, and removal had produced poverty and dissipation. Some Stockbridge people "had grown very cold in religion & others had greatly backslidden. They were now left like sheep without a shepherd."[18] Marsh accompanied them when they moved again in 1834 to the east shore of Lake Winnebago. But he felt he was "in the midst of a gross darkness," surrounded by heathen tribes who had never heard of Jesus and who struggled against "superstition, degradation and drunkenness." Marsh believed that "the only thing which can arrest this work of extinction is the gospel." He was frustrated by his own inability to do more to save them, and eventually became disillusioned by the "indolence," political strife, and defects in Indian character that he identified as obstacles to their salvation.[19]

Marsh had not been in Wisconsin long when his mission felt the reverberations of the so-called Black Hawk War.[20] The Sauk Indians were removed from their homelands in the Rock River Valley of Illinois. When Black Hawk led his band back across the Mississippi in the spring of 1832 after wintering in Iowa, the Illinois militia was called up to repel the "invasion" and a vicious three-month war exploded. Among those caught up in the conflict was Stephen Mack, a Vermonter who graduated from Moor's Charity School in 1816, followed his father into the Great Lakes fur business, and married an Indian woman, Hononegah. Sauk warriors burned his trading post on the Rock River and took him prisoner. But, Mack wrote to his sister, Winnebagos (Ho-Chunk) "claimed me as their friend and trader" and saved his life. Escaping to Fort Dearborn, near Chicago, Mack joined a company of mounted riflemen, eager to see the Indians punished. "I can by no means approve of the tardy operations of our chief officers, for it gives time to the nimble footed Indians to ravage our frontier settlements and bathe their hands in the blood of helpless women and unsuspecting infants," he wrote to his sister. The war ended when American forces caught Black Hawk's people at the Bad Axe River and a gunboat strafed them with grapeshot as they tried to escape across the Mississippi. At least 150 people were killed, many in cold blood, many of them "helpless women and unsuspecting infants." With the Sauk removal brutally confirmed, Mack returned to the Rock River and built a new home and then a tavern, where he lived until his death in 1850.[21]

Cutting Marsh undertook a mission to the Sauk and Fox in 1835, but the Sauks were adamant that "they did not want missionaries." Marsh wrote observations about their population, condition, government, customs, and religious beliefs, and acknowledged that although Black Hawk had acted rashly, he had "had just cause" for the dissatisfaction that led to the conflict.[22]

Marsh was a steadfast critic of removal policy and likened it to "transplanting aged trees, which if not destroyed by so doing, hardly ever acquire sufficient thrift to rise above it and soon show marks of a premature old age." American land hunger would generate repeated treaties and removals, and "the poor natives will be eventually utterly extinguished from the face of the earth, unless they will avail themselves of the privileges and blessings of civilisation and the gospel and become a component part of the American nation." He attended the treaties that the Stockbridges made with the United States. Responding to historian Lyman C. Draper's inquiries after he retired in 1856, Marsh concluded: "I cannot review the scenes with which I have been conversant, and the whole history of the transactions of Government agents with the New York Indians, as they have related to them, time and again, without the deepest pain. I am ashamed of my country."[23]

Marsh had a stubborn streak. He became embroiled in tribal politics and adopted rigid positions that aggravated the divisiveness. When the Stockbridges split over the question of further removal, he denounced the Emigrant Party—a splinter group that separated from his church and relocated to Kansas in 1839 for about ten years—from his pulpit. In the 1840s, he got involved in the dispute between the "Indian party" and the "citizen party." In 1845, "an educated Indian missionary" named Jeremiah Slingerland arrived as missionary for the ABCFM. Claiming Mahican descent on his mother's side, Slingerland, a Stockbridge, had attended Moor's Charity School from 1841–43, after which he had gone on to Bangor Theological Seminary and served as missionary to the Penobscots at Old Town, Maine. When he arrived in Wisconsin, he moved in with Marsh and his family and worked as a schoolteacher and assistant minister. But Slingerland too became embroiled in Stockbridge politics; he joined the Indian party and alienated Marsh. When Marsh left the Stockbridges in 1848, he advised the ABCFM to neither ordain Slingerland nor fund him. The ABCFM withdrew from the Stockbridge mission, and the SSPCK transferred its funding to Marsh's fellow Dartmouth alumnus Rev. Asher Wright at Cattaraugus. Slingerland continued to preach—sometimes to white as well as Indian congregations—and he was finally ordained in 1866. With his wife Sarah, he taught school on the Stockbridge Reservation through the 1870s. He served on the tribal council and was elected tribal sachem.[24]

☙

Indian students who attended Dartmouth College and Moor's Charity School were swimming against the current in an era when Indian people were being pushed west to extinction rather than invited east for education. But Abenakis and a few Iroquois continued to come. Peter Paul Osunkhirhine (also spelled Osunkerhine and often written Wzokhilain) reputedly walked 300 miles from St. Francis to get to Moor's Charity School in 1822. Born in 1799 in New York where his parents were hunting, Osunkhirhine was raised at St. Francis. By his own account, "Since I was thirteen years of age I was following hunting life in the wilderness both in Lower and Upper Canada and in the State of New York until I went to school to Hanover when I was two and twenty." He was supported at Moor's Charity School "from Scotland funds for Indians, in clothing and boarding and all, except in the beginning of my studies I helped my self for six months by working for my board between school hours in Newport, N.H." (He had previously attended Newport Academy.)[25] He was sent home after a year owing to a dispute between Dartmouth and the sspck about submission of bills. In 1826 the sspck resumed payment and Osunkhirhine returned that September, along with another Abenaki, twenty-year-old James Annance. A year later, both seemed to be making good progress. President Nathan Lord said Osunkhirhine was doing well in his course of English studies and that there was "some reason to hope that he has recently become pious." James was "not pious" but was a young man of promising talents and an amiable disposition and was "strictly moral & has many serious thoughts on the subject of religion."[26] In 1829, Lord informed the sspck that Moor's Charity School would likely have to be closed temporarily to take care of repairs and replenish funds but suggested that its Indian students might still be supported by the Scotch Fund, either by "having private tuition on this ground, or being placed in some neighboring Academy under my care & direction, till the school here could be resumed." Otherwise, he said, the two Indians under his care at the school—James Annance and another Abenaki named Joseph Masta (a half-brother of Osunkhirhine), who had arrived in 1827 when he was sixteen—"would be disappointed & almost heart broken if now thrown back upon their tribe."[27] In 1829 the trustees suspended operations at Moor's Charity School for a time so its income could accumulate and be applied to paying debts and improving facilities.[28]

James Annance went on to attend Dartmouth but did not graduate. In the fall of 1831, President Lord advanced him $15 and gave him leave "for sundry reasons" to visit his friends in Canada. The following spring, he had still not come back to school. "I conclude that he does not incline to return," wrote Lord, "& that he will be another instance of Indian fickleness & lawlessness, which have always been proverbial on this ground."[29] After he left Hanover, Annance "lived in part, by guiding parties through the wilderness on the borders of New Hampshire and Canada." In the summer of 1841, when the Boston historian Francis Parkman was exploring the White Mountains, he tried to hire "an Indian named Anantz" who was known to be "by far the best hunter in this part of the country." Annance, said Parkman, "was an educated man, moreover, having passed through Dartmouth College, and celebrated through the country for his skill, faithfulness, and courage." Unfortunately, Annance was away in Vermont and Parkman had to get another guide. James Annance may not have shared Parkman's esteem for a Dartmouth education; he reputedly said that Dartmouth "spoiled a great many good Indians and made very poor white men."[30]

Peter Paul Osunkhirhine (who sometimes used his stepfather's surname and was often known at Dartmouth as Peter Masta) said he "never went to College" and "never went to theological seminary," but he did carry out Dartmouth's mission. He attended the Congregational Church of Christ in Hanover, converted to Christianity in 1827, and left Hanover in June 1829, having established a reputation as "a pious, intelligent, judicious, diligent & faithful man." He headed back to St. Francis, where he hoped to establish a school. The community was in dire straits. President John Wheelock had described it in 1811 as comprising "the remains of the Abenaquies, who formerly extended through the region" east of Lake Champlain and south of the St. Lawrence River. The population was in decline—505 in 1808, 320 in the 1820s—and under pressure to give up their remaining lands. "Seeing my own people in the same awful state as I was in before I was converted," Osunkhirhine was determined to change things.[31]

There was much work to do and many obstacles to overcome. The Society for Propagating Christian Knowledge in Canada was low on funds, and Osunkhirhine applied to the government of Lower Canada for funding. However, Osunkhirhine was a Congregationalist and the local Roman Catholic priest intervened; in Osunkhirhine's words, "he came to destroy my school" when the men were away hunting, "by preaching, scolding and forbidding the women to send their children to my school," and withheld absolution from parents who allowed their children to attend. The priest insisted that the government allow Osunkhirhine to teach at the village only if he said nothing about religion. Osunkhirhine asked President Lord if he could help him find alternative funding, and Lord recommended him to the ABCFM in Boston. The ABCFM felt the SSPCK should support the school, putting Osunkhirhine back to square one. The SSPCK Board in Boston employed Osunkhirhine as schoolmaster with his tribe for nine or ten months, but the society directors in Edinburgh, though "gratified to find that he is making use of the education he received, for the benefit of his native tribe of Indians," decided that "the fund being exclusively for educating Indians at Moor's school, the society had no power to apply that fund to any other purpose whatever."[32]

Osunkhirhine stuck to his task, however, and got his school. He petitioned the government to reinstate him as schoolmaster, got the chiefs at St. Francis to support his petition, and persuaded the priest to agree to the school and to his teaching religion in general so long as the children were not being led to any particular sect. He was reappointed at the usual salary of $7 a month — "not enough to support a teacher in this country of dearth," he said — and soon had thirty boys and girls attending school regularly, as well as some who came "now and then." As he informed Lord, the Abenakis also expected him to use his education for Abenaki purposes: "since I received my reappointment as Government Schoolmaster, the Chiefs have directed me not only to act as a teacher, but also as writer and Interpreter by keeping a regular correspondence for them with officers for Indian Affairs in Montreal and Quebec."[33]

In 1835, the ABCFM appointed Osunkhirhine missionary to the Abenakis at St. Francis. He described his village as "altogether a very wicked place," mired in poverty. He blamed its problems on the Catholic religion, the Abenakis' lack of "industry," and their intemperance. People struggled to subsist on "a small and poor tract of land," and many families had to leave the village "to gain their living" during the winter. Osunkhirhine urged them to give up their hunting and wandering lifestyle and pay more attention to farming as the only way to "get along."[34] In 1838, he founded the first Protestant Church at St. Francis. He also kept his eye open for likely candidates for Moor's Charity School. When President Lord visited St. Francis to see Osunkhirhine's school and "examine the state of the mission" for himself, he was "highly gratified by all I saw & heard." As a preacher, teacher, and Christian pastor, Osunkhirhine represented "one of the few instances in which the charity of the school has been usefully bestowed." Lord made arrangements to enroll one of Osunkhirhine's sons, "a remarkable fine boy," and a sixteen-year-old "full blood" in Moor's Charity School. He also took another teenager, Archy Annance, on probation. Unfortunately, Osunkhirhine's son died before he could come to the school, "to the great grief of his parents & the discouragement of the mission."[35]

Osunkhirhine published books for use in Indian schools — a spelling book, a reader in Abenaki including the Ten Commandments, an Abenaki cate- chism — and translated the Gospel. In the early 1870s, a donation of books to the library of the Vermont Historical Society included "three small volumes in the Abenaki tongue" that "were prepared for his tribe, the St. Francis, by Rev. Peter Paul Osunkhirhine, who was educated for a missionary among his tribe at Moor's charity School." The volumes were "the Gospel of Mark, a Spelling and Reading Book, and the decalogue, with comments on each com- mandment." "These are the only books in that language, and Mr. Osunkhir- hine assures us they are the only ones there will ever be, for the reason that the children who are now taught at all, are taught the English language, and to read in English books." By this time, Osunkhirhine was stationed at Sala- manca in Cattaraugus County, New York, ministering to the Senecas. From there he had sent the Society several sheets of hymns in Abenaki that he had "printed by himself at St. Francis, many years ago, using a little printing estab- lishment of his own."[36] Osunkhirhine's school — "the Dartmouth school," as it was often called — survived at St. Francis well into the twentieth century. Henry Masta, whose grandfather married Osunkhirhine's widow, attended the school as a boy and taught there in the 1920s. The school was evidence of "the good work the [*sic*] Dartmouth College had done through Peter Osun- khirhine," and "the seeds that were then sown had yielded a hundredfold," Masta wrote to Dartmouth English professor Eric Kelly. "We owe a debt to Dartmouth College which we can never repay."[37]

In 1836, Lord had two Abenaki boys, John Stanislaus and Lewis Benedict, both about seven years old, "under his care." Stanislaus had come in 1833, when he was just four. Lord intended to place them in Moor's Charity School when they were ready. John Stanislaus's father, also named John, had been there but Lord had sent him back to Canada: "He was too old to be fitted for a teacher." Nevertheless, he had learned to read, write, and cipher and showed evidence of converting to God, and Lord anticipated he would be able to assist Osunkhirhine in his school.[38] When Lord visited St. Francis in 1837 he selected John Masta, half-brother of Osunkhirhine, as a good pros- pect, and Masta began "elementary study" in 1838–39 at age sixteen. "If God shall spare him, I think he will become an important auxiliary to his brother," wrote Lord.[39] In the early 1840s Masta, John Stanislaus, Lewis Benedict, and another Abenaki named Elijah Tahamont (often spelled Tahamout in the records) were all being supported at Moor's Charity School by the Scotch Fund.[40] Stanislaus and Benedict lodged with the family of Mr. Stone, "a very estimable christian citizen."[41]

In his reports to the sspck, Lord said Lewis Benedict was well behaved and bright but not religious. He described Elijah Tahamont as well disposed but dull. He had "unexceptionable moral character & studious habits" but "was not promising as a scholar. He will not do for the College." Any "untutored Indian of whatever powers" at his age had trouble "adjusting the mind to the unaccustomed discipline of elementary studies & the habits of civilized life," he said, and Tahamont had limited abilities. By 1847, Tahamont had been "as long at the school as I think useful" and Lord was ready to dismiss him. He might turn his education "to good account among his people," helping Osunkhirhine and his church, but Lord did not expect him to do much otherwise. (Elijah's son, of the same name, became an Abenaki chief and gained some fame as Dark Cloud, a silent film actor and model for the western artist Frederick Remington).[42]

Benedict, Archy Annance, and John Stanislaus all left. Lord provided Benedict with money to return to St. Francis but suspected he would "not be content with Indian life." Annance and Stanislaus "were tempted to return to their people & former habits of life by the influence of several of their tribe, who set up their wigwams & visited for a few weeks" during the summer. Stanislaus's parents would not return to Canada without him, and he went home with them, despite Lord's entreaties. Now sixteen or seventeen, Stanislaus had apparently spent all but the first three years of his life under Lord's care and tutelage; but, Lord sighed, "This boy will now be an Indian forever." Annance "went clandestinely, taken away by some of his people in the night & without my knowledge." He heard nothing from Annance and Stanislaus after they "were tempted away from my care. I fear they will be worthless." Lord maintained that he let Benedict and Stanislaus go because there seemed no point in prolonging their education at sspck expense, as they showed no evidence of a religious character.[43]

John Masta stayed, and pursued his English studies. His conduct was irreproachable and his study habits exemplary, but Lord "never thought him sufficiently intelligent for a college course" or a suitable candidate for admission to Dartmouth. He predicted he "will be respectable in the branches of common education & will be qualified for any of the ordinary pursuits of life."[44] But after he left school, Masta studied medicine in Canada and at the Vermont Medical Institute in Woodstock and was accepted to Dartmouth Medical School. He wrote a thesis on pneumonia and graduated in 1850. He had never excelled in any of his studies, said Lord, but he left "with a good name, & fair promise." He predicted he "would make "a competent practitioner." He was right: Masta became a respected physician in Barton, Vermont, where he died young in 1862.[45] His brother Joseph also became a doctor, in Nashua, New Hampshire.[46] In 1856, Lord informed the sspck that he had dismissed another Abenaki as not fit for charity funding. He had taken John Lawless, a brother-in-law of Osunkhirhine, on trial but he did not live up to expectations; "his mind was not lively & he was easily distracted." Lord concluded: "very few of the Indians, of any Tribe, can be taken advantageously through the College course."[47]

Despite Iroquois rejections of Wheelock's overtures in the 1770s, a connection survived between Dartmouth and Iroquois country. Peter Noadiah Hooker Augustine, an Oneida, entered Moor's Charity School in November 1826 after three years at the Foreign Mission School at Cornwall, Connecticut. He was supported by sspck funds, became a member of the Church of Christ, and planned to become a missionary for the abcfm when he finished his education. He made the transition from Moor's Charity School to the College. In 1829, aged twenty-one, he was a freshman and President Lord had high hopes for him: "If he shall be able to prosecute his studies, he will doubtless become very useful to his country men." But Augustine suffered from poor health and did not finish college.[48]

Dartmouth men also figured prominently in Seneca country, during tumultuous years when the Senecas were struggling for their lands, rights, and government. The Senecas suffered devastation and dislocation during the Revolution when General John Sullivan destroyed most of their towns and Senecas fled to the British fort at Niagara and to the western reaches of New York. In the years between the Revolution and the Civil War, New York politicians, transportation interests, and land speculators conspired to convert Iroquois homelands into American real estate. Canals, railroads, the massive influx of settlers, and the rapid growth of cities like Buffalo transformed what had once been Iroquoia.[49] In 1826 the Senecas signed a treaty selling almost 87,000 acres of reservation lands to the Ogden Land Company for $48,260 —

about 55 cents per acre. The treaty was of doubtful legal validity at best — supposedly held under the authority of the United States, it was never ratified by the U.S. Senate or proclaimed by the president — and there were allegations of bribery and corruption.[50]

One of the interpreters at the treaty was Dr. Jacob Jemison, one of two Senecas whom Rev. Elijah F. Willey had brought to attend Moor's Charity School in 1815, the other being James Stevenson. Both were reported to be "amiable[,] well disposed youth," "very desirous to acquire that knowledge which may qualify them for usefulness," "sober minded," and ready to listen "to all the important truths of religion."[51] Jacob was a grandson of Mary Jemison, who was captured as a teenager during the French and Indian War, adopted into a Seneca clan, and spent the rest of her life living as a Seneca. When she related her autobiography, first published in 1824, Mary, then eighty years old, said that Jacob "went to Dartmouth college, in the spring of 1816 [*sic* — she seems to be off in her date], for the purpose of receiving a good education, where it was said that he was an industrious scholar, and made great proficiency in the study of the different branches to which he attended." College records support Mary's assessment, referring to the two Senecas as "regular in conduct and attention" and making good progress. In fact, the board of examiners in the summer of 1816 "were particularly pleased with the appearance of the two Indian Youth of the Senecas tribe, Jacob Jemison & James Stephenson." A little more than a year earlier they had been "entirely ignorant of reading, writing & arithmetic"; now they could read and spell easily and write with style. But the funds for their support seem to have expired. After two years, Jemison returned home and studied medicine at Buffalo."[52]

In August 1817, when the missionary Timothy Alden visited Buffalo Creek, Jemison acted as interpreter between Alden and the chiefs. "He had lately returned from Dartmouth college," wrote Alden, "and is considered as one of the best interpreters to be found among the Senecas." Another missionary, Rev. Thompson Harris, was less impressed. When he delivered his first sermon in 1821, he was "a little pained by the occasional laughs of one of the natives," whom he called Jacob Jamieson [*sic*]. "His acquaintance with men and books being more extensive than the rest of his nation, his influence is considerable." Like the Seneca chief Red Jacket, Jemison opposed the missionaries' plans to establish residential schools among the Senecas. Harris's initial impression was that he was a "rather dangerous person," though subsequent conversations tempered that opinion. Jemison believed that his people could not be educated in their present location; they should remove to "some distant country out of the reach of molestation and then send their children back to those who are well qualified to teach them," as, presumably, he had been sent to Dartmouth.[53] Jemison frequently translated Red Jacket's speeches and Seneca petitions.[54] He was appointed U.S. interpreter in 1826, certainly testament to his linguistic skills but perhaps also having something to do with the fact that he was known to favor Seneca removal and advocated selling land. When he served as interpreter at the 1826 treaty, he was on the payroll of the Ogden Land Company and primarily served its interests.[55] Two years later, Jemison resigned to become a surgeon's mate in the U.S. navy. His ship was sent to the Mediterranean to fight the Algerian pirates. According to a later account in the *New York Times,* he fell in love with a sheik's daughter, but the marriage was forbidden (even though the young woman stowed away on board his ship!). In 1836, at age forty, he died of a fever and was buried at sea.[56]

Meanwhile, the Senecas came under even more pressure. In 1838, sixteen Seneca chiefs signed the Treaty of Buffalo Creek, "one of the major frauds in American Indian history."[57] Coerced by threats, bribery, and alcohol, they agreed to sell their remaining lands in New York to the Ogden Land Company, give up their four reservations, and move to Kansas. Commissioner Ransom H. Gillet induced more chiefs to sign their agreement after the treaty council, but the Senecas waged a relentless struggle to overturn the treaty.

A non-Indian from Dartmouth was one of the Senecas' staunchest allies in their campaign. Born in Hanover in 1803, Asher Wright attended Dartmouth in 1826–27 and then apparently left for Andover Theological Seminary. He returned briefly in 1829, when he was registered in the Medical School, but he graduated from seminary and was ordained in 1831. The ABCFM sent him to replace Thompson Harris as their missionary at Buffalo Creek. His wife, Laura Shelton Wright, whom he married in 1833, joined him in his life's work. They learned Seneca and together devised a phonetic writing system, collected vocabulary, made linguistic studies, and edited a newspaper in the Seneca language. As Iroquois scholar William Fenton observed, Wright was ahead of his times: "It took the U.S. Indian Service a century to get around to bilingual teaching."[58] In addition to defending Seneca rights and Seneca lands, Wright was also instrumental in sending Maris Bryant Pierce to Dartmouth.

Maris Bryant Pierce, or Hadyanodoh (Swift Runner), was born in 1811 on the Allegany Seneca reservation. He attended a local Quaker primary school and then studied at Fredonia Academy and Homer Academy in New York and Thetford Academy in Vermont. When he was twenty-five he converted to the Presbyterian church, and in 1836 he enrolled at Dartmouth, sponsored by the sspck and supported by its funds. His transcript for his freshman year indicates "a rather pedestrian performance," but he improved steadily and grew in President Lord's estimation. He was, said Lord, an "intelligent, pious, stable, and a good scholar" and "a man of considerable character" who completed his degree "very honorably." He was the first Indian to receive a degree since 1781 and only the fourth to graduate from Dartmouth College.[59] He succeeded despite the fact that he spent much of his time and energy trying to preserve what was left of Seneca land and to prevent Seneca removal. He used his education to defy predictions of Indian extinction and to combat the government's policies of removal.

Pierce had signed the Treaty of Buffalo Creek, but he claimed the senior chiefs pressured him into it, and almost immediately he began to protest the treaty.[60] Taking advantage of the Dartmouth calendar, which, then as now, allowed students flexibility and times when they did not need to be in residence,[61] Pierce traveled to western New York to keep up with developments and to help wage a campaign to overturn the treaty. In his junior year he represented his nation as a delegate in Washington.[62] He gave speeches to educate white audiences about Iroquois culture and the devastating effects that removal would have on his people. One of those speeches—given at the Buffalo Baptist Church on August 28, 1838—appeared in print and has survived. In his "Address on the Present Condition and Prospects of the Aboriginal Inhabitants of North America," Pierce spoke for the Senecas in particular and Indian people in general. He denounced the greed and hypocrisy of white men who portrayed Indians as savages in order to steal their land and destroy their culture; he rejected the arguments used to justify removal and dismissed as "stupid folly" the notion that leaving their fertile lands and moving to the wild lands of the West would somehow improve the Senecas' condition. He appealed to all Americans of good conscience to oppose the land speculators who were robbing his people of the last of their homeland and to join in petitioning the U.S. Senate not to ratify the treaty.[63]

Pierce joined other Seneca chiefs in sending a letter to President Martin Van Buren protesting the Treaty of Buffalo Creek, in hiring legal counsel, and in traveling to Washington to present their case to the secretary of war. He also continued to give public speeches to try and win support for the Seneca cause. As revealed in his "Book of Memorandum, 1840," his senior year at Dartmouth involved study and travel, attending and giving lectures both on and off campus, and participating in college activities and social events, but it was overshadowed by the threat of Seneca removal. In spite of all his efforts, the Senate ratified the Treaty of Buffalo Creek and the president proclaimed it early that year. It was an election year. Sitting in his room in Wentworth Hall, Pierce reflected on the fact that "North American Indians have a great deal to do with the Presidential elections . . . though many of them are not conscious of it." Colonel Richard Johnson would not have been elected vice president had it not been for his claim to have killed Tecumseh; Andrew Jackson rode to the White House on a military reputation earned defeating the Indians in the Creek War and the British at the Battle of New Orleans; and William Henry Harrison was hailed for his victories over the Indians at Tippecanoe in 1811 and over the British and Indians at the Thames in 1813. In another entry, written after prayers in the College chapel on a cold and windy Sunday at 5:30 in the morning, Pierce expressed his concern that "The religion in the college is not very apparent." Attendance at prayer meetings was good, but there was a sense of indifference that troubled him. As graduation approached in July and it was time to go home, Pierce wondered: "Where shall I go? Where is my home, that I can call it my own—to the west? No. Where I was born[?] Shall it be my native home and remain inviolate[?] I hope it was so, but alas it is not so. Our people are in the state of a great dilemma, to go or stay." Humanity said they should stay in the land of their fathers, but the U.S. government said they must go. Selected as one of the students to deliver an address at commencement, Pierce gave his speech the title "The Destiny of the Aborigines of America."[64]

As an example of the kind of students President Lord's school attracted and produced, Pierce was instrumental in convincing the SSPCK to continue its funding. By the 1830s, the Society "had come to the conclusion that the education of native Indians at that school was all but hopeless." In 1839, it dispatched its secretary, John Tawse, and its law-agent, George Lyon, from Edinburgh to investigate the state of Indian education at Moor's Charity School and Dartmouth. They came with low expectations, but the visit to Hanover changed their minds. President Lord impressed them as a man dedicated to the work of civilizing Indians, and the three Indian students who were beneficiaries of SSPCK funding—John Masta, Jonathan Edwards Dwight, a Choctaw, and Maris Bryant Pierce—also impressed them. They devoted six pages

Maris Bryant Pierce. © *Buffalo and Erie County Historical Society, New York.*
*Used by permission.*

of their report to Pierce, quoting passages from his speech at Buffalo. Citing
the example of Osunkhirhine as well, Tawse and Lyon recommended that the
SSPCK continue its funding and extend it for any Indian student who showed
"more than ordinary talents" and carried on his education at Dartmouth "for
the purpose of civilising and instructing his countrymen.[65] Tawse described
Pierce as "altogether as interesting a young man as ever I saw, and I trust from
his talents, his sound principles, and the knowledge he has acquired, he will
prove a great blessing to the Nation of Indians to which he belongs, and to

whom, I suppose by this time he has returned." Having visited the Senecas during his tour of America and been impressed with the level of "civilization" they had achieved, Tawse was anxious to know their fate after his return to Scotland. He was appalled at the cruelty and injustice of U.S. removal policy and asked his correspondents in America whether the Senecas had been forced to remove yet, adding "That they will ultimately be compelled to do so I suppose there can be no doubt."[66]

After graduation, Pierce worked for two years in the law offices of Tillinghast and Smith in Buffalo, "the better to do business for his people."[67] He also worked as an interpreter for the Senecas as they tried to renegotiate the Treaty of Buffalo Creek. An amended treaty was signed in 1842; it fell far short of meeting Seneca expectations but did preserve for them a foothold in their homeland. They regained the Allegany and Cattaraugus reservations but not Buffalo Creek and Tonawanda (although the Tonawanda Senecas were "allowed" to buy back a small portion of their reservation in 1856). In 1843, Pierce married the daughter of a British army officer and they lived at Buffalo Creek until the reservation was abandoned in 1845, when they moved to Cattaraugus, where they spent the rest of their lives. Asher and Laura Wright also moved to Cattaraugus. Pierce continued to fight for Indian rights and to represent his people in dealings with the government and the land companies. He remained a strong advocate of education and Christianity as the path forward for the Senecas, even as they retained the best of their traditions, and in 1848 he played a significant role in the political revolution in which the Senecas replaced hereditary life chiefs with elected chiefs and created the Seneca Nation. Wright recorded Seneca political structures and translated the new constitution of 1848. In 1855, the Wrights opened the Thomas Asylum for Orphan and Destitute Indian Children, which became the Thomas Indian School. The Senecas were living on patches of their original homeland, but they survived, and in the opinion of one historian, "Maris Pierce is the person most responsible for the Senecas remaining in New York."[68] He died in 1874. Asher Wright died a few months later, in April 1875, after forty-four years as missionary and teacher to the Senecas.

Another prospect came to Dartmouth with more than his share of worldly experience and hard knocks, and left promptly. In 1850, Lord, against his better judgment he said later, accepted an Ojibwa named John Tecumseh Henry. His father was the Canadian Ojibwa chief and former Methodist minister George Henry, who, using his Native name, Maungwaudus, organized a troupe, mainly members of his own family, to give traveling exhibitions of Indian customs, including demonstrations in scalping. "By all accounts a slick operator," Maungwaudus and his troupe toured the northern states and in 1844 crossed the Atlantic to England. They briefly joined artist George Catlin and his traveling exhibit in Paris and performed there and in Brussels before returning to London, and back to America in 1848. But the trip was a tragedy: Maungwaudus's wife and three of his children died in Europe.[69] John Henry survived, and his father visited Dartmouth and asked President Lord to admit him to his school. Lord took him for a few months on probation. In the spring of 1850, Maungwaudus, "dressed and decorated in the Indian style," attracted the attention of the *Hartford Daily Courant*, which reported: "He is now on his way to visit his son, who is receiving his education at Dartmouth College, N.H. with the intention of placing, if possible, another son at the same institution." But things did not work out with the first son. "I incline to the opinion that none but Christian Indians should ordinarily be placed on this charity," Lord wrote to the SSPCK. "The young man proved unstable. His fickleness & irresoluteness at length discouraged me, & I dismissed him." He thought the instruction Henry received would make him "better able to take care of himself in life." But "the good seemed not to me equal to the cost, in view of better candidates."[70]

In 1853, Lord wrote to the SSPCK arguing yet again that the Scottish funds be spent on young men "of somewhat mature years & religious character," regardless of whether or not they were Indian. "The Indians are not eminently capable," he said. "They cannot vie with the Saxons & Normans about them. They can never save the world. But they may save each other, & much that we bestow upon them will be laid up in heaven." With a couple of exceptions, the Indians students were not promising. Peter Paul Osunkhirhine was "still good & true," and his pastoral work with "that little remnant," the Abenakis of Canada, deserved sympathy and support.

The other exception came from a very different place, in the form of Joseph Folsom, a Choctaw from Oklahoma.[71] For the first time, Dartmouth was recruiting Indian students from beyond the Mississippi.

*Chapter Six*

# STUDENTS FROM INDIAN TERRITORY,
## 1850–85

⚘ BY THE MIDDLE of the nineteenth century, the United States had relocated thousands of Indian people across the Mississippi to what became known as the Indian Territory. Initially conceived of as a block of territory that would cover much of the West and serve as a kind of permanent Indian reserve, Indian Territory came in time to refer specifically to land in what is now the state of Oklahoma. Dissatisfied with the students from Canada, and with few Indian populations to draw from east of the Mississippi, Dartmouth presidents now looked to the Indian Territory to recruit the students they needed if they were to continue to draw money from the Scotch Fund. The students who came to Dartmouth were usually the sons of parents who had migrated under the government's removal policies. They were a new type of student, usually young men rather than children or teenagers, sometimes graduates of their own nation's seminaries, and they pursued their education as a tool for helping to reconstruct their nations.[1]

The first student from the so-called Five Civilized Tribes — the Cherokees, Creeks, Choctaws, Chickasaws, and Seminoles — in Indian Territory was a Choctaw named Jonathan (sometimes given as Joseph) Edwards Dwight, who in 1838 "ventured east alone" at a time when most southern Indians were being forced west. He came to Moor's Charity School on the recommendation of the ABCFM, studying to be a teacher. President Lord described him as "a worthy young man." He went on to become a preacher in the Choctaw Nation.[2]

Another Choctaw, Joseph Pitchlynn Folsom, wrote a sketch of his early life and his attendance at Moor's Charity School and Dartmouth. Born in Toosukla, Mississippi, in 1823, Folsom was the only boy among six children. His grandfather was white, he said, but his mother and grandmother were both full-blood Choctaws. His mother died before the Choctaws were removed west. (Most Choctaws left their Mississippi homeland after they signed the Treaty of Dancing Rabbit Creek in September 1830.)[3] He worked with his father on the farm and herded cattle. At fourteen he began to attend school at Wheelock Academy, but only during part of the year. Later his father allowed him to attend school full-time, by working for his board. Reverend Alfred Wright and his wife selected Folsom to go to Dartmouth to attend Moor's Charity School. He took steamboats down the Red River to New Orleans, up the Mississippi and Ohio to Cincinnati, and then to Pittsburgh; from Pittsburgh, he made his way "on canal boats, railroads, steamboat, stages and sometimes by private conveyances." In Boston, he fell ill with mumps but was eager to escape the "noise and din of the busy city life" and took the train to Concord, New Hampshire. After a bumpy ride on a crowded stagecoach from Concord, and still weak from the mumps, he arrived in Hanover on a July evening in 1844 and had to be helped from the stage to the inn.[4]

He spent the next ten years in Hanover. He roomed initially with John Masta and Elijah Tahamont at the house of Mr. Stone, where they were well cared for, "the family being religious & remarkably well ordered."[5] President Lord was impressed with both the Choctaws: "Our own Indians are better than the Canadians," he said.[6] At Moor's Charity School, Folsom studied Latin and Greek. He felt that young Indians needed to study English as the key to the sciences if they were "to become useful to their people." He came up against a rule that no student should receive funding at Moor's Charity School for more than four years, and he protested it. The system seemed designed for Indians to fail, he said. In the end he stayed six years there, with funding. "Utmost kindness and cordial sympathy for me was manifested throughout," he wrote, although his teachers made it clear that, as he phrased it, "the education less than Collegiate one would be best for me to have."[7]

Folsom proved them wrong and entered Dartmouth in 1850. Funding remained an issue: could the sspck continue to draw on its funds to support him in college? Again, Lord lobbied on his behalf: Folsom had completed three-quarters of his college course, Lord informed the sspck in the spring of 1853; "It would break his heart to be now stopped."[8] Folsom graduated with his class in 1854, the first Choctaw to do so. Lord thought he would not distinguish himself as a scholar but would make a respectable one. He was "intelligent, judicious, & capable," totally dependable, and "conducted himself with great propriety; a truly Christian man." For his part, Folsom wrote,

Joseph Pitchlynn Folsom. *Courtesy Dartmouth College, Rauner Library (neg. 3210).*

"it is proper and just to state here that President Lord was a believer of the final preservation and perpetuation of large remnants of the American Indians who will be yet members of the government of [the] United States. He believes that it will be brought about by the religion of Christ and education alone." Folsom spoke at commencement on "The Indian of fiction and of history" and, according to press reports, "interested the audience more than any other speaker, not that his oration was of a higher order than those of his associates, but his color, his figure, his theme and his earnest plea for his race, all excited sympathy." He left Hanover with "pleasant recollections."[9]

Folsom went on to study law and was for many years a member of the Choctaw Council. He compiled a digest of Choctaw legislation, served as a delegate to the Okmulgee intertribal council in the 1870s, and was one of the committee members who drafted what became known as the Okmulgee Constitution. He traveled to Washington in 1881 to oppose the grant of a charter to the St. Louis and San Francisco Railroad Company across Choctaw land, and in 1884 came in second in the elections for principal chief. According to his class report, Folsom died in 1889, "beloved by the entire Choctaw race." The report quoted Wilson N. Jones, who, like Folsom, had stood for the office of principal chief. Folsom, he said, "served his people faithfully, manly, honestly. He was ever on the alert for any improvement which could in the least contribute to the betterment of our people. He collected and codified our laws, opened up our neighborhood schools, planted a higher order of civilization, and taught our people self-respect and sobriety. We mourn his death."[10]

Like Folsom, Simon James, another Choctaw, impressed Lord as an earnest and conscientious young Christian: Lord described the two young men (they were both in their twenties) as "among the best specimens of Indian character I have had under my care" and assured the sspck that "our charity is well bestowed on them."[11] James attended Moor's Charity School and then Kimball Union Academy to better prepare him for Dartmouth. Apparently, Simon's relatives were able to support him at the academy.[12] He entered Dartmouth in 1855 but did not stay. Lord said he returned home to Indian Territory because of his health and did not come back. "I am persuaded that very few of the Indians, of any tribe, can be taken advantageously through the College course," wrote the disappointed president.[13]

James Ward was born in Cherokee country in Georgia in 1826 and presumably moved west with his family along the Trail of Tears. He attended Dwight Indian Mission and entered Dartmouth as a member of the class of 1855, which would furnish many men for the Civil War. President Lord rated Ward "more highly gifted" than Folsom or James. He was sound-minded, quick-witted, energetic, and an exemplary Christian; in short, he would "compare favorably with any Saxon."[14] But Ward left school in 1853 and returned home to Indian Territory. By then Lord was just as happy to see him go; he had lost interest in his studies and there had been some problems with temper and insubordination, Lord said.[15] Charles Stewart or Steward, another Choctaw from Indian Territory, arrived around the time Ward left. Lord described him as a "perfect Indian" (that is, a full blood) and a promising prospect. Stewart "honorably concluded" his course of study by 1856 and left.[16] Jeremiah Evarts Foreman, named after Jeremiah Evarts of the ABCFM, who had been a steadfast opponent of removal, graduated from the Cherokee National Male Seminary in February 1856 and attended Moor's Charity School, though he appears on

Albert Barnes. *Courtesy Dartmouth College, Rauner Library.*

some lists as a member of the Dartmouth class of 1859. Lord had great hopes for him. But he was called home by his father late in the fall of 1857 and did not return, although he does appear on one list for 1858 as a special student. Lord rated him a good scholar but with "more ingenuity than application," and some of "the characteristic fickleness of his people.'" He was not inclined to be a teacher, preferring more active pursuits. Lord thought the education he had received would serve him well enough for that kind of life.[17]

Two more Cherokees enrolled at Dartmouth in 1857: Albert Barnes, aged twenty-three, and DeWitt Duncan, aged twenty-seven. They were the first Cherokees to graduate from Dartmouth, and Lord informed the sspck in April 1861 that "the Indian fund has never, in my judgment, been so well applied as to the education of these two young men." Albert Barnes was evidently not a great scholar but he was diligent, "his Christian and moral character" was "above reproach," and he was well liked by students and professors. He graduated from the Chandler School in July 1861.[18]

De Witt Duncan. *Courtesy Dartmouth College, Rauner Library.*

DeWitt Clinton Duncan was born in the eastern Cherokee Nation in Georgia. His father, John, was said to be "half Cherokee" and his mother, Elizabeth Abercrombie Duncan, a white woman. The family migrated west with the Cherokees in 1839. Duncan attended mission and Cherokee Nation schools before Dartmouth. Lord put him under a private tutor for a few weeks' review of his studies at the Cherokee seminary, and he was soon ready to enter the Academic Department. In his freshman year he became ill with "the common fever of this latitude" and, Lord reported to the sspck explaining the additional expenses incurred that year, "lay between life and death" for several weeks. Duncan was taken to "our excellent hospital, where, by assiduous care, & God's blessing, he was restored." By his sophomore year, Duncan was fulfilling all his promise and establishing a reputation as a scholar and a Christian: "He stands among the best of our students, in all respects, and so far justifies all the expenditure bestowed upon his education," Lord reported. In fact, in Lord's estimation, Duncan "excelled all those who have been under my care during my term of thirty-four years." A classmate recalled him as "as fine a specimen of man, physically, mentally, and morally, as I have ever known in a prolonged life."[19] He was elected to Phi Beta Kappa and graduated at age thirty-two, the year the Civil War broke out.

Unlike Simon James and John Ward, Duncan did not return immediately to Indian Territory. He taught at one of the neighboring academies and after the war settled at Charles City, Iowa, where he taught, practiced law, and became the town mayor. He also remained active in Cherokee affairs and in the 1880s began writing for Cherokee newspapers, the *Indian Chieftain* at Vinita and the *Cherokee Advocate* at Tahlequah. Something of a poet, he wrote "The Red Man's Burden," a poem in response to Rudyard Kipling's poem "The White Man's Burden." He moved to Oklahoma in 1890; served the Cherokee Nation as attorney; taught English, Latin, and Greek at the Cherokee Male Seminary; and translated the Cherokee laws. He wrote dozens of letters under the pen name Too-qua-stee, primarily condemning the U.S. assault on Cherokee sovereignty that culminated in the dissolution of the Cherokee government when Oklahoma achieved statehood in 1907. Duncan died of Bright's disease in 1909.[20]

Indian Territory was a volatile place during the Civil War. The conflict divided tribes as it did the nation. Confederate agents solicited Indian assistance, many Indians espoused the Confederate cause, and bands of guerillas from both sides operated in the region.[21] Jeremiah Evarts Foreman served under the Cherokee general Stand Watie in the Confederate army. Married to a Creek woman in 1862, he withdrew from the army because of poor health and died before the end of the war and before the birth of his twin sons, only one of whom survived birth.[22] Foreman's cousin, Albert Barnes, espoused the Union cause but served as superintendent of education for the federal government rather than as a soldier.[23] After Simon James returned home from Dartmouth, "about all that can be learned of him is that during the Civil War he was captain of a company of Indians in the Confederate service, and was killed by one of his own men while attempting to quell a riot, at Fort Arbuckle, Chickasaw Nation, Indian territory, Feb. 22 1862. He was married." Another source indicates that he had become a dentist.[24]

The war claimed another "Dartmouth Indian" casualty the same year. After he returned home to Indian Territory, James Ward was a member of the Methodist church, taught in a Cherokee school, and in 1857 entered the service of the Moravian church as a teacher and missionary, stationed at New

Spring Place. He was married and had four children. On September 2, 1862, "a band of 30 or 40 horsemen belonging to the Federal side, partly Cherokee Indians, partly white men, appeared at the station." According to several accounts, Ward was "shot from his horse." His killers held his wife captive for a time but then released her. New Spring Place was severely damaged and "once more the Cherokee mission was wrecked."[25]

The war severed Dartmouth's communications with Indian Territory. No one arrived to take the place of Barnes and Dwight, and Lord said he would have to look to Canada again for recruits if "the present distracted state of the country" continued.[26]

In fact, several Senecas came to Hanover in the Civil War years. Reverend Asher Wright kept an eye out for promising young Senecas to send to Dartmouth, and sixteen-year-old Edward Wright Pierce, the son of Maris Pierce, arrived in 1863. He studied at Thetford Academy and the Chandler School, and Lord had high hopes for him as "a bright, intelligent and active young man." But Lord was forced to resign after he expressed his proslavery views in a pamphlet published in 1863. and when Pierce asked to leave before the end of the fall term of 1864, the new president, Rev. Asa D. Smith, granted his request. "His taste was for business," and it seemed questionable whether he would derive any great benefit from continuing his education, Smith explained to the sspck. "I shall hope to hear of his doing well in the world," he added.[27] When Chester C. Lay and Daniel Twoguns, both Senecas from Cattaraugus, arrived, however, Smith judged they were not prepared to enter the Scientific School and put them under a private tutor for a term in the hope they could be "fitted" for college. Instead they were sent home for further training. Even if they did not return to Dartmouth, said Smith, what had been done for them would not be wasted: "Some rays of light have, through them, been cast into the wilderness."[28]

But President Smith's heart was not in educating Indians. He continued what was by now a Dartmouth tradition — corresponding with the sspck about the possible diversion of the Indian funds to pay for other expenses. "The whole business, as you already understand, has become a somewhat onerous one," he wrote on New Year's Eve of 1872. "We have no Indians near us. If they are received here at all, they must come from a great distance. We have no distinct school for them." When Indian students did come, they required a lot of attention. "I have to look after them — unskilled as they are in the ways of the world," he complained. "It is no small thing to *dry-nurse* a couple of Indian boys, who, besides the ordinary frailties of humanity, are apt to develop certain Indian frailties. They have cost me more trouble for the last twelve month—favorably though I can speak of them in many respects—than our whole Scientific Department considered apart from them. The Indian Charity, I have reason to believe, was a burden to President Lord." The fund was clearly a burden to Smith as well, and he expressed "Doubts whether the Indian business ought to be continued."[29]

Once again, it was the SSPCK that kept Dartmouth on task and held it to its original pledge. Despite unfavorable reports about the state of Indian education at Dartmouth,[30] the SSPCK took the opposite view from presidents Lord and Smith: the rapid decline of the Indians meant they needed *more* education, not less. "We are led in this Country to understand that the native Indians are rapidly disappearing before the advance of the American nation," wrote John Tawse, the SSPCK investigator; "I should think that the only chance of preserving these tribes, not distinctly perhaps, but amalgamated with the Americans, would be by giving them a liberal Christian education, and thus enable them to compete with and keep their place among the people of another race." In other words, use the funds for their original purpose.[31] Dartmouth might be a reluctant host, but the insistence of the SSPCK and the persistence of a handful of Indian students kept Indian education alive at Dartmouth in the second half of the nineteenth century.

The trickle of Indian students from the West picked up again after the Civil War ended.

In January 1870 Colonel Eugene Baker led his U.S. cavalry in a dawn attack on a Blackfeet village on the Marias River in Montana. The inhabitants were huddled in their tepees, cold, and reeling from a recent smallpox epidemic. The soldiers killed 173 people, mostly old men, women, and children, and slaughtered 300 horses. It was the wrong village. The cavalry were after Mountain Chief's band; this was Heavy Runner' village.[32] Later that year, Robert Hawthorn, "a half-blood of the Blackfeet Tribe on the mother's side," entered Dartmouth. (His father was French.) Hawthorn was born in Kansas in 1842. According to his own account, he prepared himself for college, and he sold his cattle to come to Dartmouth, on assurances from Dartmouth professors that he would be supported by "the Indian fund." He entered the Chandler Scientific School but his continued education looked to be in peril in 1872 when President Smith suddenly informed him that funding would no longer be available. Hawthorn protested, saying he would never have come if he had

Robert Hawthorn. *Courtesy Dartmouth College, Rauner Library.*

thought there was any uncertainty about funding. So did Professor William Gage, who seems to have taken Hawthorn under his wing. Gage had encouraged him to come and had given him to understand that his education would be covered in full. Dartmouth's honor was at stake, and so was his own, Gage told Smith. He had boasted about Dartmouth's record on Indian education; "to turn about now and say it had failed even to take this *one* through would be for me to confess to a regular humbug," he declared. Their protests prevailed. Hawthorn graduated with his class in 1874.[33]

Choctaw Albert Carney had a rather more difficult time. Before the fall of 1868 he had had only private instruction, and he was not prepared to enter either the Academic or the Scientific departments of the College, so he was enrolled in the Agricultural College for a year. After that, it was decided he should go to Kimball Union Academy "under the patronage of his tribe," with the goal of preparing for college. He entered Dartmouth as a freshman in

Albert Carney. *Courtesy Dartmouth College, Rauner Library*
*(neg. 2426).*

the Academic Department in the class of 1875. He remained for two years, from 1871 to 1873, but apparently had persistent money problems and did not graduate. Nevertheless, he went on to pass the bar and became a judge. Just two years after he returned home, he was elected chief commissioner on the Choctaw Court of Claims, which in 1875–76 attempted to obtain compensation from the U.S. government for losses sustained during the Choctaws' removal from Mississippi in the 1830s.[34]

Cherokee Rollin Kirk Adair enrolled in the Agricultural College in 1874. Adair had begun his education in the elementary schools of the Cherokee Nation and apparently owed his continued education to his uncle, William Penn Adair, a prominent lawyer and senator in the Cherokee Nation who made good on a promise to care for Rollin and his siblings after their father was killed in the Civil War. Adair presented a thesis titled "Progress of Civilization among the Cherokees." President Smith had a good opinion of him and had "reason to believe that he has become a Christian since he came here." A former classmate who claimed to know Adair well recalled that he "was fitted for nothing but the N.H. College of Agriculture and the Mechanic Arts" and said he had heard that Adair "gradually reverted to the blanket" after he graduated in 1877. The classmate, who lived in Chelsea, Vermont, was evidently misinformed. Ironically, Adair took over his father's farm near Chelsea, Oklahoma. He became a merchant, became mayor of the town, and "proved himself a useful citizen to his community and his nation." From 1895 to 1899 he was superintendent of the Cherokee Male Seminary. His daughter-in-law said he "was considered a very well educated man and was always interested in civil and national affairs."[35]

President Smith, who had taken a dim view of Indian education just a few years earlier, now saw a need to renew the efforts for Indian education, or at least he told the SSPCK that he did. In the 1870s, in resistance to congressional pressure to establish a territorial government, the various tribes in Indian Territory attempted to form a consolidated tribal government. At a council held at Okmulgee, the capital of the Creek Nation in the Indian Territory, in December 1870, leaders from the Cherokee, Choctaw, Creek, Chickasaw, Seminole, Ottawa, Osage, Shawnee Quapaw, Seneca, Wyandotte, Peoria, Sac and Fox wrote and adopted a "Constitution of the Indian Territory," an intertribal charter that became known as the Okmulgee Constitution, and delegates met annually at Okmulgee for the next five years.[36] Joseph Folsom represented the Choctaws as a delegate and interpreter and Albert Barnes attended at least some of the meetings. "If the Indians are to have a Territorial Government," Smith wrote in 1876, "they will need educated men from among themselves. The Scotch Fund may find a higher use than ever." What was the maximum amount, Smith wanted to know, he could expect to draw from the fund?[37] The fund's original purpose was the education of Indians as missionaries, but changing times, the Indians, and now Dartmouth's president were shifting the emphasis toward education for self-government.

Another Cherokee, Walter Howard Luckadoe, spent a year at the Agricultural College in 1876–77 and then attended Kimball Union Academy until 1881. There he was known to be kind to others and of good Christian character on the whole, but not much of a scholar. He struggled with Latin and Greek and did poorly in algebra and geometry. Dartmouth's new president, Samuel C. Bartlett, saw signs of improvement and hoped he might join the freshman class in August 1881, but by the fall it was clear that "Luckadoe has disappointed us and must be dropped finally." Luckadoe left and was not heard from again. It was suggested that "he did not have a very clear sense of the difference between truth and falsehood" and that some of his actions bordered on insanity. John Tawse, secretary of the SSPCK in Edinburgh, regretted to hear that Luckadoe had "apparently returned to his original savage state" after all the care and expense that had been bestowed on him for the last two or three years.[38]

In 1882, R. S. Owen, secretary of the Board of Education in Tahlequah, the Cherokee capital, penned a letter of recommendation for Harvey Wirt Courtland Shelton and Ellis Cornelius Alberty. Shelton had graduated from the Cherokee Male Seminary that year. They were "sober, honest and industrious young men," Owen said, "belonging in every sense to the best class of our young people. They are Cherokee citizens by blood and have recently gone East, to New Hampshire, to be educated."[39] Both went initially to Kimball Union Academy. They did not make a good first impression: they were not professing Christians, and Shelton was not only guilty of "gross profanity" but also "a user of tobacco." The Academy's rules were quite explicit on both. Shelton claimed to have quit smoking and, within a matter of months, he and Albert showed evidence of changed lives and professed "to have found the Savior." The commissioners of the SSPCK approved funding for them both.[40]

After a year at Kimball Union Academy, Shelton entered Dartmouth with the class of 1887. He worked hard, did well, and earned respect, according to President Bartlett, but was compelled to leave during his junior year to take care of an aunt who had raised him and was now in ill health. Another story, from Tahlequah, gives a rather different version of his leaving. According to this account, Shelton wrote to his uncle, who had helped finance his education, to say that he could no longer subscribe to some of the religious doctrines he had been taught and beliefs he had formerly held. What should he do? "Come on home," replied the uncle. "You can go to hell in Tahlequah as easily as you can go to hell at Dartmouth." Shelton moved to Tahlequah and became a seminary instructor and clerk of courts for four years. He promoted scientific farming and had a cotton plantation during World War I. He died in Paris, Texas, in 1935.[41]

Alberty stayed at Kimball Union Academy a couple of years longer and by all reports was a good scholar. He "began to be discouraged for lack of means" and though he was ready for college in 1885, President Bartlett feared he would not be able to attend without more help and asked the SSPCK to allow Alberty $200 a year. Alberty's son recalled hearing his father tell of working in New Hampshire hay fields during the summer to earn extra money for college. But Alberty never made it to Dartmouth. He returned home because of ill health, either his own or that of a family member, and took up teaching at the Cherokee Male Seminary. "I think it a mistake but cannot remedy it," wrote Bartlett. Alberty later became superintendent of the Cherokee Orphan Asylum and an attorney. He was remembered as "a fine, tall, intelligent-looking gentleman of good manners and address" who earned "the confidence and respect of his people."[42]

While a handful of Indian students from the West went to Dartmouth, non-Indian Dartmouth graduates went in increasing numbers to the West. As politicians, businessmen, engineers, boosters, newspaper editors and territorial legislators, many Dartmouth alumni promoted transcontinental railroad development and the westward expansion of the nation, with a direct impact upon Native peoples even when they had no direct contact with them. Others had closer contact. John Ball (class of 1820) sat in on the U.S. Supreme Court in Washington to hear John Marshall's decision on the Cherokee case and then accompanied Nathaniel Wyeth's expedition to Oregon in 1832. He taught at the Hudson Bay Company school at Fort Vancouver for a winter before heading to San Francisco, sailing to Hawaii, and returning to New England aboard a whaler via Cape Horn.[43] Salmon P. Chase (class of 1826) played a key role in securing the Senate's passage of the Kansas-Nebraska Act in 1854. Sherman Hall and William Thurston Boutwell (both of the class of 1828), worked as missionaries with Indians in the upper Mississippi Valley. Albert Carrington (1834), from Royalton, Vermont, became a Mormon and was a member of the pioneer party to the Great Basin in 1847. He also participated in mapping and surveying the region with the Howard Stansbury expedition in 1849. He became prominent in Utah politics. Hyrum Smith, brother of Mormon prophet Joseph Smith, attended Moor's Charity School. Joseph William Drew (1844) studied law and medicine and taught in Massachusetts but moved to California in 1849 and then to Oregon, where he served as adjutant and quartermaster general in the Indian war of 1855–58.[44]

In 1863 President Abraham Lincoln created Arizona Territory by separating it from New Mexico and appointed John Noble Goodwin (1844) of Maine as territorial governor. It was a time of escalating violence between Apaches and Americans. In his message to the First Legislative Assembly (half of whom were miners) Goodwin portrayed the Apaches as savage enemies who must be removed as obstacles to progress:

But for them, mines would be worked, innumerable sheep and cattle would cover these plains, and some of the bravest and most energetic men that were ever the pioneers of a new country, and who now fill bloody and unmarked graves, would be living to see their brightest anticipations realized. It is useless to speculate on the origin of this feeling, or inquire which party was in the right or wrong. It is enough to know that it is relentless and unchangeable. They respect no flag of truce, ask and give no quarter, and make a treaty only that, under the guise of friendship, they may rob and steal more extensively and with greater impunity. As to them, only one policy can be adopted. A war must be prosecuted until they are compelled to submit and go upon a reservation.

The Arizona legislature called for volunteers and a war of extermination against the Apaches. Maricopa and O'odham Indians were enlisted as scouts to help hunt down Apaches, and bounties were paid on Apache scalps. Goodwin actively encouraged these volunteer companies and this war of extermination. In 1866 he wrote that the country demanded "fair, open and persistent war until the Apaches were "exterminated" or "bow[ed] their necks in submission." Then they would be placed on reservations "to labor or starve." He accurately predicted that defeating the Apaches would be a long and bloody process.[45]

President Ulysses Grant appointed George W. Emery (1858) governor of Utah territory in 1875. Missionary Edwin Hyde Alden (1859) served as an Indian agent. Born in Windsor, Vermont, in 1836, he was ordained by the American Missionary Society in 1864 and sent to New Orleans to take charge of the freedman school. After a spell as pastor back in Tunbridge, Vermont, he did home missionary work, organizing churches in Minnesota. In 1875, he was appointed U.S. Indian agent at the Fort Berthold Indian Reservation in Newtown, North Dakota Territory, where he was responsible for teaching farming techniques to the Arikaras, Hidatsas, and Mandans. He returned to Tunbridge after an absence of thirty-five years and served as pastor of the

Congregational Church from 1899 to 1903. He retired to his farm in Chester, Vermont, where he died in 1911.[46]

Dartmouth men in the West contributed to the rapid transformation of Indian country. By the last decades of the nineteenth century, it seemed to many that Indian people stood on the edge of an abyss. But those Indians who embraced the change and transformed themselves by education could lead their people away from the edge. Eleazar Wheelock had pointed to Samson Occom as a role model for the salvation of Indians in the eighteenth century. At the turn of the twentieth century, Dartmouth presidents pointed to Charles Eastman.

*Chapter Seven*

# CHARLES EASTMAN,
## 1858–1939

CHARLES ALEXANDER EASTMAN is Dartmouth's most famous Native son. A Wahpeton and Mdewakanton Dakota, the youngest of five children, he was named Hakadah, "the Pitiful Last," when his mother, Mary Eastman, daughter of soldier-artist Seth Eastman, died soon after he was born. His paternal grandmother raised him in traditional Sioux culture (and he earned the new name Ohiyesa, "unconquered" or "the winner," after a lacrosse game) but his father, Many Lightnings, had him change his name again and seek an American education. Now named Charles Eastman, he attended a series of schools, graduated from Dartmouth in 1887, and graduated from Boston University School of Medicine in 1890. He was a student, an athlete, a physician, a writer, a reformer, a lecturer, and a cultural intermediary between American and Native American ways of life. He served as a government physician on the Pine Ridge Reservation in South Dakota, as Indian inspector for the BIA, and as Indian secretary for the YMCA, and he helped found the Boy Scouts of America. He worked on special congressional legislation to settle Sioux land claims, he was a founding member and then president of the Society of American Indians, an organization committed to reforming federal Indian policy and championing the rights of all Indians, and he represented American Indians at the First Universal Races Congress in London. In his writings — *An Indian Boyhood, The Soul of the Indian, From the Deep Woods to Civilization*, and other books and essays — he tried to educate white society about tribal values and the first Americans' unique contributions to American civilization. In 1933, at the Chicago World's Fair, the Indian Council Fire granted him its first award for "the most distinguished achievement by an Indian."[1]

Yet when I assign *From the Deep Woods to Civilization* to students in my American Indian history classes, Eastman invariably gets mixed reviews.

Most acknowledge his achievements, but many, particularly the Native students—and this was the case at the University of Wyoming as well as at Dartmouth—are turned off, even angered, by the deferential tone and the almost fawning gratitude he displays toward his benefactors, and by the racialist discourse and apparent acceptance of many of the assimilation doctrines of the times. They often see him as an "apple" (red on the outside, white at the core) who curried favor with and craved approval from his white "superiors" and who served as a poster boy for the achievements of American schools in de-educating Indians. Attending college in an era when they are encouraged to study—and many later work for—the sovereignty of Native nations, the preservation of Native languages, and the revitalization of Native cultures, modern students often find it difficult to sympathize with someone who pursued an education predicated on the assumption that Native nations, languages, and cultures would disappear. As Gerald Vizenor has noted, tribal identities at the dawn of the twentieth century were surely different in many ways than at the dawn of the twenty-first. In Eastman's case, Vizenor wonders: "What did it mean to be the first generation to hear the stories of the past, bear the horrors of the moment, and write to the future?"[2]

Eastman's experience at Dartmouth reflects the complex and tension-filled relations between Indian people and the United States at that time. Surviving Dartmouth in the 1880s, like surviving in the United States, exacted a heavy toll on an Indian. Eastman's life spanned a period of far-reaching and often wrenching changes, not only for Native Americans but for American society as well. He was born in 1858, before the American Civil War and before the great clashes between the Sioux and the United States; he died in 1939, eight months before World War II broke out in Europe. He grew up during years of escalating conflict, when the United States slaughtered the buffalo herds on the plains, built railroads that spanned the continent, confined Plains Indians to reservations, and tried to systematically eradicate Sioux culture. He grew to manhood in a time of sustained assault on Native American manhood.

The ABCFM expanded its missions and established reservation boarding schools, such as the Santee Normal Training School on the Santee Reservation in Nebraska under the direction of Alfred L. Riggs in 1870. But off-reservation boarding schools proliferated after Captain Richard Henry Pratt opened Carlisle Indian Industrial School in Pennsylvania in 1879. The U.S. government embarked on a campaign to transform Indian youth. Children were shipped off to schools where they were subjected to military-style discipline and a rigid regimen and stripped of their Native clothing, hairstyles, and languages. The schools taught an Anglo-American curriculum that ignored or dismissed Native American history and culture, and inflicted punishments on students who were caught speaking their Native language. Students were taught reading, writing, and math. Boys received training in mechanical arts, girls in domestic service; they were being educated to occupy the lower echelons of American economy and society.

It was a hard time to be Indian, and perhaps the hardest time ever for a young Sioux man to try and make his way through Dartmouth. Many Indian students returned home to the reservation disconnected from their family, language, and culture, and with not much to show for all they had lost. Yet many Indian leaders, parents, and former students recognized that the white man's education could be a powerful weapon in the Indians' struggle to survive in the white man's world. Wolf Chief, a Hidatsa who went to school about the same time Charles Eastman did (although he was thirty years old) learned math so he could check traders' weights and later operate his own store on the Fort Berthold Reservation in North Dakota. Having learned to read and write, he bombarded the Office of Indian Affairs with complaints, fired off letters to newspapers, and even wrote to the president of the United States.[3] When American commissioners tried to negotiate a large land cession from the Crows in Montana in 1898, the chiefs brought forward "the boys we sent to school." They told the commissioners "they are young men now and can read and write; they are men now that we look on with confidence." One of the young men proceeded to read an itemized list of broken promises, missed payments, and delayed annuities. "This is the first time since I have dealt with Indians that they ever gave me anything on a piece of paper!" lamented one of the commissioners, who agreed to postpone further discussion of land sales.[4]

Like Wolf Chief and the Crow chiefs, Ohiyesa's father understood that education in the East could provide skills and tools for Indian survival rather than a recipe for Indian demise. At age fifteen, Ohiyesa believed his father had been hanged in the mass execution of Dakota warriors at Mankato following the "Great Sioux Uprising" in Minnesota in 1862. But in fact, President Lincoln had reduced the number of executions from more than 300 to 38, and Many Lightnings had escaped the hangman's rope. He served time in jail in Davenport, Iowa, converted to Christianity, and took his dead wife's surname, calling himself Jacob Eastman. He returned to his family, finding them in Manitoba, where they had fled after the war. He gave Ohiyesa his new name and urged him to learn the white man's ways. "We have now entered upon this life, and there is no going back," he told him. "Besides, one would be like a hobbled pony without learning to live like those among whom we must live."[5] After fifteen years of a traditional Dakota education, Ohiyesa was about to embark on seventeen years of Western education.

Jacob Eastman moved his family to Flandreau, South Dakota, where he had a homestead. The next year he entered Charles in Santee Normal Training School, where Charles's brother John was already a teacher. Charles learned to live indoors, to sleep in a bed, to speak and read English, to count and measure. "For a whole week we youthful warriors were held up and harassed with words of three letters. Like raspberry bushes in the path, they tore, bled, and sweated us — those little words rat, cat, and so forth — until not a semblance of our native dignity and self-respect was left." "I hardly think I was tired in my life until those first days in boarding school," he wrote later. "All day things seemed to come and pass with a wearisome regularity, like walking railway ties — the step was too short for me. At times I felt something of the fascination of the new life, and again there would rise in me a dogged resistance, and a voice seemed to be saying, 'It is cowardly to depart from the old things.'" When the teacher "placed before us a painted globe, and said that our world was like that — that upon such a thing our forefathers had roamed and hunted for untold ages, as it whirled and danced around the sun in space — I felt that my foothold was deserting me. All my savage training and philosophy was in the air, if these things were true."[6]

But he persevered. School superintendent Alfred Riggs became his friend and mentor. "Next to my own father," Eastman wrote in later life, "this man did more than perhaps any other to make it possible for me to grasp the principles of true civilization. He also strengthened and developed in me that native strong ambition to win out, by sticking to whatever I might undertake."[7] Riggs told him about Dartmouth, a college that had been founded for the education of Indians, and helped him to secure scholarships to finance his continuing education. After graduating in 1876, just months after the Sioux and Cheyenne annihilated George Custer's command at the Battle of the Little Bighorn, Eastman boarded his first train and traveled to Wisconsin, where he entered Beloit College. "I was now a stranger in a strange country," he recalled, "and deep in a strange life from which I could not retreat." He became fluent in English and spent at least three hours a day in physical exercise, a regimen he maintained throughout his college years.[8] Three years later, he transferred to Knox College in Illinois, where he learned the "conception of the home life and domestic ideals of the white man" and realized he needed to pursue a profession. He decided he could best help his people by becoming a doctor.

When Eastman arrived at Dartmouth, he was judged not yet ready to enter the freshman class and in January 1882 he began a year of preparation at Kimball Union Academy.[9] The SSPCK covered his expenses. But everything did not go smoothly. In his first six weeks at the academy he took Cicero and algebra, and mixed well with the other students, who included Harvey Shelton and Cornelius Alberty. But he was accused of plagiarism. He handed in a composition that was so good it attracted suspicion. It was turned over to Professor M. R. Gaines, who "saw at once that it was not his own production" and easily found the book "from which he had copied two pages, with the change of no more than half a dozen words." When Gaines questioned him, Eastman told him "several different things about it, none of which were consistent or satisfactory." Gaines continued to press and Eastman finally admitted the truth. "I was sorry to have to do it but I did not see any other way to help him to correct his fault," wrote Gaines. Eastman claimed he had been accustomed to that method of composition writing for years and did not realize he was doing anything wrong. He promised not to do it again and later handed in a composition of his own. "I regret the tendency on his part to resort to falsehood," said Gaines. He did not know if the school would be able to keep Eastman on the next term and saw no way that he could be prepared for Dartmouth before a year from the next commencement.[10]

By December, Eastman was still "not so ready as many" in his academic preparation, in part because he had to translate his thoughts from Dakota into English. But he was "trying in all respects to be a faithful exemplary Christian," and, said Gaines, "I can commend him most heartily in all things." A full year after the plagiarism incident, Gaines told President Bartlett at Dartmouth that Eastman seemed "much quickened" in his Christian life and that he had shown notable "mental and moral improvement."[11] By the summer of 1883 Eastman, now twenty-five, had received much exposure to American education and culture. He was ready for Dartmouth.

He arrived sharing many of the attitudes and aspirations of white American society. "I went to Dartmouth College, away up among the granite hills," he wrote in his autobiography; "the country around it is rugged and wild;

and thinking of the time when red men lived here in plenty and freedom, it seemed as if I had been destined to come view their graves and bones." Assuming, like most Americans, that the area's Abenaki inhabitants were extinct, he was determined to help his own people avoid the same fate. "Had our New England tribes but followed the example of that great Indian, Samson Occum, and kept up with the development of Dartmouth College, they would have brought forth leaders and men of culture. This was my ambition — that the Sioux should accept civilization before it was too late!"[12] Passages like that win Eastman few fans among Native people in New England, who were here then and are still here now.

Dartmouth's imposing buildings impressed him: "There was a true scholastic air about them," he said. He found that his years of college life in the West were "quiet compared with that of the tumultuous East." Thirty years later he reflected: "It was here that I had most of my savage gentleness and native refinement knocked out of me. I do not complain, for I know that I gained more than their equivalent."[13]

Football was still in its infancy at Dartmouth when Eastman arrived. (Dartmouth began playing football in 1881; in 1884 it lost to Yale by a score of 113–0!) But the national game was about to be transformed by Indians — in the form of the team from Carlisle Indian School with players like the legendary Jim Thorpe.[14] Popular and athletic, Eastman found himself elected as the freshman football captain on the evening of the first class meeting. "My supporters orated quite effectively on my qualifications as a frontier warrior, and some went so far as to predict that I would, when warmed up, scare all the Sophs off the premises!" He described himself as "a sort of prodigal son of old Dartmouth" and recalled that "nothing could have exceeded the heartiness of my welcome. The New England Indians, for whom it was founded, had departed well-nigh a century earlier, and now a warlike Sioux, like a wild fox, had found his way into this splendid seat of learning! Though poor, I was really better off than many of the students, since the old college took care of me under its ancient charter. I was treated with the greatest kindness by the president [Bartlett] and faculty."[15] Eastman became a prominent Dartmouth athlete. He captained the football team, was a champion distance runner, played baseball and tennis, and boxed. He joined a fraternity, Phi Delta Theta.

Eastman enrolled in the Latin scientific curriculum, which required taking courses in English, Latin, French, Greek, German, and linguistics. He also took classes in zoology, botany, chemistry, physics, natural history, political science, philosophy, and geometry, and for the first time in his life he became "really interested" in literature and history. Some of his studies were a challenge, especially math, President Bartlett reported during his freshman year, but he worked hard and made up for his early lack of preparation.[16] At Dartmouth he met the English poet Matthew Arnold, who evidently expected to see someone wearing buckskins and feathers and was taken aback by Eastman's polished manners and appearance. He also met Francis Parkman, Ralph Emerson, and Henry Wadsworth Longfellow.[17] At a time when Indian values and perspectives were targeted for obliteration in government boarding schools, at Dartmouth Eastman was "encouraged to ask questions and express my own ideas." He was an effective debater and would often present moral arguments citing an "Indian standpoint." In fact, he recalled, "This became so well understood, that some of my classmates who had failed to prepare their recitation would induce me to take up the time by advancing a native theory or first hand observation."[18]

Eastman graduated with honors, although an obituary written by a "friend" and classmate included a snipe: "To those who experienced Charlie's classroom work, it is quite interesting to read he graduated with honors. Truth to tell, we think the case might more veraciously be put by varying a Shakespeare passage to read, 'God made him an Indian; therefore let him pass for a scholar.' (For wasn't Dartmouth College founded to educate Indians?)"[19] At graduation, Eastman took part in what was then the class tradition of smoking a peace pipe. "It was under the Old Pine Tree that the Indians were supposed to have met for the last time to smoke the pipe of peace, and under its shadow every graduating class of my day smoked a parting pipe."[20]

The sspck financed Eastman's education at Kimball Union Academy and Dartmouth, paying for his tuition, board and rent, books, stationery, paper, stamps, clothing, shoes, rubber boots, oil, furniture, bedding, coal, firewood, washing and mending, and even fare to Nantucket and vacation expenses.[21] After he graduated, Eastman wrote to the sspck commissioners expressing his gratitude and his appreciation for "the rare opportunities given me for obtaining a most liberal and practical education." Friends in Boston were now supplying the means for him to pursue his medical studies, he said, "at the conclusion of which I expect to go back and settle among my people." He offered the commissioners his views on Indian education. Few Indians were prepared to go to college yet, but the more they were funded at prepara-

Charles Eastman, photographed while he was a student at Dartmouth.
*Courtesy Dartmouth College, Rauner Library.*

tory schools like Kimball Union Academy, "the more Indian youths would be likely to reach Dartmouth College." He was convinced that educating young Indians away from home was "the only way the Indian can be civilized and christianized." It was a time of tremendous change in Indian country and there was more opportunity "for an educated Indian to make himself useful." The government had opened some reservations and the Dawes or General

Allotment Act "brought the red man at the threshold of liberty and manhood, though many of them [are] far from being qualified to enter such a life." He concluded that "the Indian must be educated or else he will never fully understand the science of economy, the division of labor and the high order of society." He signed both his names: Charles Alexander Eastman and Ohiyesa.[22]

As Eastman made his way through Dartmouth and on to medical school, the assault on Indian lands, lives, cultures, and independence was reaching what many believed would be its final stages. Congress passed the Allotment Act in 1887, the year Eastman graduated. Reservations were intended to be crucibles of change, where government agents, teachers, and farmers instructed Indians in the arts of civilization and prepared them to take their place in American society. When Indians did not embrace the new ways, it seemed that reservations were failing in their purpose and functioning instead as bastions of traditional ways and communal landholding, and as obstacles to progress. Reformers grew impatient. Indians would have to be pushed into mainstream culture and forced to become hardworking Americans motivated by the acquisition of private property. Under the Dawes Allotment Act, named after Senator Henry Dawes of Massachusetts, who introduced the legislation, reservations were to be surveyed, divided into 160-acre sections, and the sections allotted to individual families. "Surplus lands" would be offered for sale to non-Indians. Allotment would terminate communal ownership and, its supporters believed, liberate Indians from the stifling hold of tribe and community, where kinship obligations and reciprocal generosity governed individual conduct. "There is no selfishness, which is at the bottom of civilization," said Dawes. Citizenship and allotment, said Commissioner Thomas A. Morgan, "necessarily looks toward the entire destruction of the tribal relation; the Indians are to be looked upon as individuals and not en masse; they are to stand on their own personal rights and be freed absolutely from the trammels of the tribe and the limitations of chieftaincy." Theodore Roosevelt praised allotment as "a vast pulverizing engine to break up the tribal mass."[23] Indian people often maintained old tribal connections and social bonds even as they adjusted to the new system—in some cases they continued to use the land as families and communities rather than as individual property owners.[24] Nevertheless, designed purportedly to lift Indians from backwardness and dependency, allotment stripped Indian tribes of two-thirds of their remaining lands and brought increased poverty and suffering.

The year before Eastman graduated, Geronimo, the famous Chiricahua Apache resistance leader and the last of the Indian "hold outs," surrendered. He and his handful of followers were sent by train to Fort Pickens, near Pensacola, Florida, as prisoners of war. Chiricahua scouts had assisted the army in tracking Geronimo and bringing an end to the war, but in a blatant breach of trust, the government rounded up the rest of the Chiricahuas—498 people, 399 of them women and children—bundled them onto trains, and shipped them off to prison in Fort Marion, Florida. Some of the Chiricahua scouts were still wearing their U.S. army uniforms. Conditions at Fort Marion were deplorable. Children were separated from their families and sent to Carlisle Indian School. By 1889, 37 of the 112 Chiricahua children sent to this school had died of tuberculosis. The citizens of Arizona Territory generally subscribed to the philosophy that the only good Apache was a dead one, but humanitarian groups in the East and army officers who had served with the scouts were outraged. The Indian Rights Association, based in Philadelphia, the Boston Indian Citizenship Committee, the Massachusetts Indian Association, and others lobbied for moving the prisoners. Returning them to Arizona was out of the question. Instead, the government relocated all the Chiricahuas to Mount Vernon Barracks, a disused arsenal near Mobile, Alabama. But the new prison was no better than the old one and the Chiricahuas continued to die. When Benjamin Harrison took office as president in 1889, the question of what to do with the Chiricahuas fell to his secretary of war, Redfield Proctor.

Redfield Proctor had graduated from Dartmouth in 1851 and attended law school. After serving in the Civil War he had practiced as an attorney but gradually devoted more time and energy to other business and to state politics. From 1878 to 1880 he served as governor of Vermont, and in 1880 he formed the Vermont Marble Company, which became the world's largest marble producer. By 1890 he employed 1,500 workers and, like some other industrial barons of the time who amassed great fortunes, turned some of his profits back into providing low-rent housing, free hospital care, accident insurance, and a library. Proctor and the Vermont delegation supported Harrison on every ballot at the Republican Party convention in Chicago in 1888; Harrison rewarded him with a cabinet post as secretary of war.[25]

Proctor appointed a commission to investigate alternative sites for the Chiricahuas. The Eastern Cherokee reservation in North Carolina seemed like a good possibility, but the governor of North Carolina responded to the prospect of having Apaches in his state by suggesting that Proctor's home state of Vermont would make a good home for them. A proposal to remove the Apaches to Indian Territory also ran into opposition. Proctor gave up trying to find them a new home: "I do not see what I can do for the Apache prisoners except to care for them the best I can where they are." It was up to Congress to move them. In 1891 Proctor visited Mount Vernon during a tour of military establishments in the South; he then headed west to the Apache reservation at San Carlos in Arizona. Bad as conditions were at Mount Vernon, they were far worse at San Carlos. Proctor thought the Chiricahuas were "very much better off" where they were; any Apache at San Carlos would "be glad to go to Mount Vernon."

In 1892 Grover Cleveland regained the presidency he had lost in 1888 and Harrison and Proctor left office with the Chiricahua controversy unresolved, and with the Chiricahuas still living, and dying, at Mount Vernon. In 1894 Congress authorized removing the 296 surviving Chiricahuas to Fort Sill, Oklahoma. After resigning as secretary of war, Redfield Proctor served four terms in the U.S. Senate and maintained an interest in Indians, but he died — of pneumonia in 1908 — with the Chiricahuas still in captivity.

In 1912, after twenty-six years, the longest captivity of a people in American history, Congress finally authorized the release of the Chiricahuas, giving them the choice of staying at Fort Sill or transferring to the Mescalero Apache reservation in New Mexico. One of the first Chiricahuas born out of captivity was Allan C. Houser (1914–1994), who became an internationally renowned artist and one of the major modernist sculptors of the twentieth century. In 1979 Houser came to Dartmouth as artist-in-residence. In 1992 President George Bush awarded him the National Medal of Arts; he was the first Native American to be so honored. (In 2007, David R. Raynolds [class of 1949] and Mae Reed Raynolds donated one of Houser's sculptures, *Peaceful Serenity*, to Dartmouth College. The sculpture stands on the grass in front of the Native American Studies Program building.)

One reason Proctor lost interest in the case of the Chiricahuas was because another event, even more scandalous, occurred elsewhere in Indian country while he was secretary of war, in which Charles Eastman also became caught up. Eastman, who developed an admiration for New England, and especially Boston, "as the home of culture and art, of morality and Christianity,"[26] began to give lectures and make connections. After he graduated from medical school in June 1890, through an introduction to commissioner of Indian affairs Thomas Morgan, Eastman secured an appointment as government physician on the Pine Ridge Reservation. He was the sole physician for some 6,000 people, but unlike his predecessors in the position, he took to his work with zeal and concern for his patients, and he was able to examine and question them in Sioux. He also met and became engaged to Elaine Goodale, a young reformer from New England who at the time was superintendent of Indian education for the reservations in Dakota Territory and who also spoke Sioux.[27] Impending tragedy hung over their courtship. More and more Sioux people were embracing the Ghost Dance religion, a revitalization movement that spread from tribe to tribe, promising a return of the buffalo and a restoration of the old ways. The American authorities became nervous that reports of Indians dancing portended a violent uprising and tensions mounted. "We seemed to be waiting—helplessly waiting—as if in some horrid nightmare, for the inevitable catastrophe," Elaine wrote.[28]

The catastrophe came in December. Indian police sent to arrest the Hunkpapa leader Sitting Bull assassinated him in his home. Two weeks later, the Seventh Cavalry intercepted and surrounded Big Foot's band of Miniconjou Sioux as, cold and hungry, they made their way to Pine Ridge. On the morning of December 29, after a botched attempt to disarm the Indians, the soldiers opened fire on the village. In the ensuing carnage, 200–300 people were shot down. Eastman treated wounded and mutilated survivors in a makeshift hospital at the Episcopalian mission chapel, where the pews were ripped out and the floor covered with hay and quilts on which to lay the victims. On New Year's Day, 1891, after a two-day blizzard, Eastman and others went out to the "battlefield" searching for survivors. He found a woman's body three miles from the site of the massacre "and from this point on we found them scattered along as they had been relentlessly hunted down and slaughtered while fleeing for their lives." Miraculously, they found five adults and two children who had survived the gunfire and the blizzard. Eastman himself found a blind old woman and a little girl about a year old. The girl was lying, warmly wrapped, near her dead mother. She was wearing a fur bonnet beaded with an American flag. Standing, stunned, amid the fragments of burned tepees and the frozen bodies was, wrote Eastman, "a severe ordeal for one who had so lately put all his faith in the Christian love and lofty ideals of the white man."[29]

Wounded Knee put a grisly end to Indian resistance. The same year, the U.S. Census Bureau declared that population in the West had increased to the point where the frontier could no longer be said to exist. Indians looked set to disappear along with the frontier.

Charles and Elaine went back East that spring to be married. Returning to Pine Ridge, Eastman became embroiled in a dispute with the Indian agent over payments to the Indians and resigned in 1893. He went into private practice in St. Paul, Minnesota. He also worked for the YMCA and between 1894 and 1897 established thirty-two YMCA chapters on Indian reservations. In 1897–99 he lobbied in Washington for the Santee Sioux to recover annuities canceled by Congress after the Minnesota war of 1862. He served as interpreter for an Oglala Sioux delegation before the Senate Committee on Indian Affairs in 1897.[30] In 1899 he worked for Carlisle Indian School, and the next year he was appointed agency physician at the Crow Creek Reservation in South Dakota. Eastman supported allotment, and in 1903 President Theodore Roosevelt assigned him the task of revising the allotment of tribal lands to individuals and assigning family names to the Sioux to protect their titles to land.

Back at Dartmouth, President Bartlett in the 1890s took up the tradition of trying to get the SSPCK to release its grip on the Indian funds and permit the College to use them for more general purposes. Reviewing Eleazar Wheelock's writings, Bartlett concluded that nowhere "is there to be found any fixed and precise definition of the aims and methods of this Institution, or any prescriptions or limitations as to the nature of its expenditures." Even before he died, the founder had modified "the Enterprise" so that educating Indians ceased to be its sole or even its primary purpose, and now the original goal had become impracticable. Citing Charles Eastman as the only recent example of an Indian who had completed his degree and gone on to a successful professional career, Bartlett proposed reopening Moor's Charity School and wondered: "Could we set in motion any mundane or celestial influences sufficient to induce the canny Scots in Edinburgh to let their annual income (if not principal) of the Charity fund go to the pay of a *teacher* of Indian youth in Moor's School directly instead of spending all on one or two pupils." He pitched his idea to the SSPCK, but the society refused to buy it. They reminded their Board of Commissioners in Boston, which supported Bartlett's proposal, "that the original purpose for which the Fund was collected was for the maintenance and education of native Indian Youths, with the view to their returning to their respective tribes as missionaries to teach Christian Knowledge among their own people." From the tenor of correspondence in recent years, the sspck saw little evidence of Indians having been educated to become missionaries. What was more, Bartlett's proposal suggested paying teachers' salaries at Moor's Charity School "irrespective of whether Indian Youths are being trained there or not." The directors of the fund could not support the school in any year unless Indian youths were in attendance that year and had mission work as their ultimate goal.[31] (In 1896, part of the Scotch Fund was used to hire a teacher at the Hanover High School, with the understanding that any Indian student could enroll there.)[32] The Board of Commissioners defended Dartmouth's record in using the funds, but not with much conviction. It was impossible to keep track of all of the Indian youth who had been aided by the fund, after they left, "but that they have not, on the average, rendered good service to their fellow Indians, we should be slow to admit." Eastman, who was not identified by name, furnished a model example: "He became a physician, married a prominent white lady, a well know[n] authoress, and has been doing excellent work among the Dakotas. His college education, which was secured through the Scotch Fund, helped powerfully in making him what he is."[33] President Bartlett too assured the society that its money had been well spent: Charles Eastman "was greatly improved and almost transformed by the influence of his College course," he said.[34] Eastman would serve as Dartmouth's sole model of success for many years to come.

He had to. Only one Indian student attended Dartmouth between Eastman's graduation and the end of the century; he did not stay long, and he said he "never did find use for much of anything I learned in college." Archibald Smamon Isaac or Isaacs, a member of the Snohomish tribe of Washington state, came to Dartmouth because he had heard it was an Indian college. He entered in 1896 with the class of 1900 but left after his freshman year. Returning to Washington, he worked for twenty-five years as a logger and doing odd jobs in the berry fields. He evidently developed a drinking problem and in later life he was in and out of jail and well known to the police and the welfare department, although apparently not disliked. When he died in August 1967 at age ninety, the *Seattle Times* described him as "one of Skid Road's most colorful characters."[35]

Eastman was convinced that Indian people must change if they were to have a chance of surviving, and many of his writings reflected the social Darwinism of the times. "The Indian no longer exists as a natural and free man," he wrote in *Indian Boyhood* (1902). "Those remnants which now dwell upon the reservations present only a sort of tableau—a fictitious copy of the past."[36] After working at the Crow Creek Reservation Eastman moved back to Minnesota for a time and then to Amherst, Massachusetts, where he stayed until 1919. In 1910, he assisted Ernest Thompson Seton in founding the Boy Scouts of America. In 1911, he was one of the charter members of the Society of American Indians and was selected by an international committee to represent American Indians at the First Universal Races Congress in London. In 1918 he was elected president of the Society of American Indians. From 1923 to 1925 he served as Indian inspector under Calvin Coolidge. Eastman wrote books and essays and was active on the lecture circuit, becoming increasingly vocal in demanding that the BIA be abolished and that Indians be granted citizenship. (Congress passed the Indian Citizenship Act in 1924.) He also advocated breathing more life into education and developing a more holistic education that involved fresh air exercise to develop muscles and morality as well as minds. "Sometimes education seems like eating shredded wheat biscuit without sugar and cream," he wrote. "There is no spirituality in it; there is no life in it."[37] He returned to England for a lecture tour in 1928, dining with the Earl of Dartmouth and former prime minister David Lloyd George, and cutting an impressive figure when he donned his Sioux regalia and war bonnet.[38]

He and Elaine had six children. Elaine encouraged and assisted him in his writings, and together they ran summer camps for girls and boys at Granite Lake in New Hampshire. Their second daughter, Irene, was preparing for a career in the opera but in 1918, at twenty-four, she died in Keene, New Hampshire, a victim of the great influenza epidemic that swept the western world at the end of World War I. Irene's death took an additional toll on a marriage that was already in trouble. In 1920, after thirty years of marriage, Charles and Elaine separated, citing irreconcilable differences.

As a student at Dartmouth, on the lecture circuit, and at college reunions, Eastman frequently dressed in full Sioux regalia and "played the part" of the Indian. In 1901, for the celebrations marking the hundredth anniversary of the graduation of Daniel Webster, he acted the role of Samson Occom in a series of tableaux staged by the Dartmouth Dramatic Club. Other "Dartmouth Indians"—white students in Indian dress and feathers—participated in a torchlight parade and danced around a bonfire. In 1904, Eastman was invited to return to Dartmouth in a commemoration marking the laying of the cornerstone of the new Dartmouth Hall and the visit of the sixth Earl of Dartmouth, the great-great-grandson of the original patron of the Col-

Charles Eastman at his fortieth class reunion. *Courtesy Dartmouth College, Rauner Library.*

lege. Hanover was decked out in gala attire, British and American flags were prominent at College Hall and the Hanover Inn, and there were dinners, football games, toasts and tableaux, songs and speeches. The earl was awarded an honorary degree. When President Tucker called on the earl to speak at a banquet, "the whole assembly rose and gave the distinguished Englishman two powerful 'Wah-Hoo-Wahs.'" The next evening at a bonfire, "a little group of fellows who had taken part in the tableaux as Indians were out in uniform and appointed themselves bodyguard to the earl."[39] Eastman played Occom once again, reenacting the Mohegan's first meeting with Wheelock in 1743 and his sermon at the London tabernacle of George Whitefield in 1766.[40] In 1927, at his fortieth reunion, Eastman posed, rode a horse, and had his portrait painted, all in full Plains Indian regalia. The Hood Museum of Art houses portraits donated by classmates of Eastman in full war bonnet.[41]

As Philip Deloria points out, including real Indian people in plays, tableaux, or Wild West shows added a sense of historical accuracy and authenticity; they were the "ultimate artifacts." By trying to project a more positive image of Indians that white Americans could understand, Eastman fell into the trap of "playing Indian." When he donned an Indian headdress, "he was connecting himself to his Dakota roots." But he was also "imitating non-

Indian imitations of Indians." He was, in short, indulging in Indian mimicry, combining in himself "a Dakota past and an American-constructed Indian Other."[42] For some people, such posturing makes Eastman an Uncle Tomahawk, pandering to white fantasies and perpetuating stereotypes. On one level, Eastman in war bonnet and buckskins portrayed the romantic Indian of a by-gone era and paraded vestiges of a culture he himself had left behind as he embraced the modern world. On another level, however, such displays represented a reassertion of Indian identity and culture in the face of American demands for assimilation and conformity. In the early twentieth century, more people began to display their Indian identities in public events and ceremonies. Often they adopted popular symbols of "Indianness" for these occasions. Sioux Indians who joined Wild West shows and played out prescribed roles found a way to celebrate their Native culture in the East and in Europe at a time when that culture was under siege back home.[43] Native American intellectuals took on some of the performative roles expected of Indians as a way of getting a public hearing for their cause. Eastman may have satisfied his classmates' expectations and fueled white stereotypes, but he also had his own agenda. Comfortable in starched collar and tie, he had no qualms about delivering a lecture wearing a war bonnet if it served his purposes and won points with his audience.[44]

Although Eastman absorbed Western learning and Western values and worked to bring about the assimilation of Indian people into mainstream society, he remained strongly attached to the traditional Sioux ways and values he had learned growing up and insisted that America had much to learn from Native people. As Bernd Peyer notes, "he viewed himself as a fairly successful 'transition' Indian who managed to master the white man's way and then took it upon himself to transmit ancient tribal values that still had social relevance for an increasingly morally deficient America."[45] He wrote primarily for non-Indian readers, many of them influential, and he told them much that they wanted to hear. He did not dwell on repression and injustice, and he employed the dominant discourse of racial hierarchy and progress. But he also advocated for Indian rights, criticized American hypocrisy, and took on the BIA. By running summer camps and writing books for young people, he introduced American youth to Indian ways of life at a time when government boarding schools were trying to convert Indian youth to the American way of life.[46] In his later years, he returned to the "deep woods," living in a cabin in Ontario and completing the circle of his life. "I am an Indian," he wrote at the end of his autobiography, "and while I have learned much from civilization, for which I am grateful, I have never lost my Indian sense of right and justice. I am for development and progress along social and spiritual lines, rather than those of commerce, nationalism, or material efficiency. Nevertheless, so long as I live, I am an American."[47]

He lived eighty years; he died in Detroit on January 8, 1939, after suffering a heart attack. He had witnessed many changes in his life and he had remade himself. But Charles Eastman, class of 1887, never entirely stopped being Ohiyesa.

*Chapter Eight*

# INDIAN SYMBOLS AND SOME
# INDIAN STUDENTS,
## 1900–1969

🎐 DARTMOUTH at the dawn of the twentieth century seemed to be further away than ever from fulfilling its founding mission. In 1901, after years of wrangling with successive Dartmouth presidents about how the Scotch Fund could or could not be used, the SSPCK sent its secretary as a special commissioner to Hanover to investigate the situation and to report on the state of educational and missionary work among the Indians in the United States and Canada. He found that the primary purpose of the Fund — "the return of educated youths to their own tribes as teachers and missionaries" — had not been achieved for years. "Those of strong character found profitable careers elsewhere, while the average Indian who returned home after living among white people usually lapsed into tribal ways and did more harm than good."[1] In 1915, the Supreme Court of New Hampshire ordered that the funds from Moor's Charity School be transferred to Dartmouth College. Moor's Charity School, which had long since ceased operation, formally ceased to exist after 145 years.[2] Soon after, the SSPCK finally gave up on Dartmouth. In 1922, "satisfied that the purposes for which the Fund was subscribed have entirely failed," the Society petitioned the Court of Session with an alternative scheme for the use of the funds previously earmarked for Indian education at Dartmouth. Drawing on negative reports stretching back over more than half a century, the SSPCK was clear about the causes of the failure:

(a) the impossibility of getting suitable beneficiaries of the fund and the difficulty of getting them to go back to their tribes after they have been educated; (b) the continually decreasing numbers of native Indians in North America and the distance of Dartmouth College at which the Government has placed the Indian Reservations; and (c) the activities and agencies of the various missionary societies of America and Canada among the native Indians which adequately meet the purposes for which the Fund was originally subscribed, so far as these purposes remain realisable at the present day.

The Society requested authority "to transfer the Fund for Indians in North America to their general funds and to use the income thereof for their general missionary purposes." In 1924, the petition was approved; the Court authorized the sspck "To apply the income of the capital sums forming the said Fund for Indians in North America and the accumulated interest thereon for the training and educating of native Christians in any selected Mission Field in the British Dominions beyond the seas for the work of missionaries among their own non-Christian people."[3]

By 1900, reformers and educators had developed increasingly pessimistic views of Indians' abilities and more limited objectives for themselves: Indians would be incorporated into American society, but they could never become fully "civilized" citizens.[4] Meanwhile, the 1900 national census placed Native American population at its nadir, recording a mere 237,000 Indians living in the United States. The count was low (census takers counted people as Indian if they thought they looked like Indians, and some Native people preferred to conceal their identity) but it seemed to confirm that Native Americans were on the brink of extinction. Given the prevailing attitudes and indications of impending Indian demise, it is perhaps not surprising that Dartmouth did little to honor its founding commitment for much of the twentieth century.

Few Indian students attended Dartmouth, but Dartmouth inscribed images of Indians that would affect Native students yet unborn and remain a point of controversy well into the twenty-first century. Cherokee scholar Rayna Green argues that for non-Indians to be able to play Indian, "real Indians" must be absent — either physically removed or removed from consciousness.[5] That certainly seems to have been the case at Dartmouth, where use of Indian images, symbols, and mascots flourished at a time when Indian students were notable for their absence. Longtime Dartmouth historian Jere Daniell wrote: "the college's main commitment to things native was through an increasing institutional use of racial symbols." For most of its history, Dartmouth's connection to Indians was through imitation and appropriation. Students played Indian, reenacted what they took to be old Indian traditions like smoking a farewell peace pipe, and used "the language of violence and the imagery of virile Indian warriors to reaffirm masculinity through intercollegiate athletics."[6]

"Playing Indian" in American society has a long history, stretching back to the Boston Tea Party and earlier. Non-Indians have appropriated Indian dress and acted out Indian roles for a variety of reasons, have created their own images of Indians, positive and negative, and have used their ideas about Indians to shape national identity. Indians were removed from their homelands and excluded from the nation, but they haunted the American memory and shared in the national story as historical curiosities. By 1900 Americans had created romantic images about the people they had defeated and dispossessed, and the stereotype of the savage warrior gave way to the stereotype of the disappearing Indian. James Earl Fraser's iconic sculpture "The End of the Trail," depicting a weary Indian warrior slumped over his dying pony, reflected American sentiments about the destiny of the first Americans. In the photographs of Edward Curtis, and in the imaginations of many Americans, "real" Indians faded into the sunset, disappeared from American consciousness and history, and were replaced by abstract and idealized Natives acting out prescribed roles. At a time when some people feared that influxes of foreign-born immigrants threatened to dilute the American character, images of Indian "primitivism" and Indian warriors could now be safely appropriated to represent distinctly American traits. Indians were proud, courageous, and free and had fought heroically against a superior foe. Once obstacles to American nation building, they could now be symbols of American national identity.[7] Schools and sports teams also expressed their "spirit" by latching onto stereotypical images of Indians as warriors, athletic, and outdoorsy. Modern-day Americans often look to, and appropriate aspects of, Indian cultures to claim connections with a way of life that appears more spiritual and more moral than the one they experience in the dominant capitalist culture.

At Dartmouth too, imagined Indians took the place of real ones. As Americans played Indian and played with images of Indians as expressions of a national identity, so Dartmouth men played Indian and made Indian images and associations a crucial part of their understanding of Dartmouth's identity. As in the nineteenth century "savage Indians served Americans as oppositional figures against whom one might imagine a civilized national Self," so stereotypical Indians, wild and free, served as oppositional figures against which Dartmouth men could imagine their own civilized and educated selves. As in eighteenth-century political protests and acts of civil disobedience—colonists dressed as Mohawks dumping tea into Boston Harbor, for instance—taking on an Indian identity absolved the "savages" of responsibility for wild behavior and breaking the rules.[8]

Beginning around 1854, graduating seniors on class day gathered around the stump of an old pine that reputedly marked the spot where Eleazar Wheelock taught his first class and/or where according to legend three Indians met to smoke the pipe of peace and bid each other farewell. A speaker would address the old pine, the class would sing their song, puff on clay pipes, and then lay them or smash them on the base of the pine. This was the ceremony in which Charles Eastman participated.

Poet Richard Hovey, class of 1885, wrote lines that became a popular song for generations of Dartmouth men:

> Oh, Eleazar Wheelock was a very pious man;
> He went into the wilderness to teach the Indian,
> With a Gradus ad Parnassum, A Bible and a drum,
> And five hundred gallons of New England rum.

Singing the song became a way for each new class to connect to the Dartmouth culture and Dartmouth past; for some students it no doubt represented the sum total of their knowledge of Dartmouth's founding and Indian history. The infamous "Indian yell" Wah-hoo-Wah! appeared as an expression of college fighting spirit. Robert Frost, who spent part of a year at Dartmouth as a member of the class of 1896, recalled twenty years later that he "wasn't much of a college man." "Much of what I enjoyed at Dartmouth was acting like an Indian in a college founded for Indians."[9] The sports section of the 1898 college yearbook depicted Indian warriors kicking footballs. Charles Dudley, class of 1902, devised a cane topped with a carved head of an Indian. The Indian head cane was adopted as the class cane in 1899 and the custom carried on for many years.[10] Long after the cane disappeared as a class symbol, Indian head canes continued to appear at commencement activities. Scrapbooks kept by Dartmouth students illustrate that by the turn of the century, participating in "Indian" rituals, songs, and play had become a way for successive generations of Dartmouth men to be initiated into the Dartmouth community and pass on Dartmouth "traditions."[11]

Students' scrapbooks also show that Indian images and Indian caricatures were being used to represent Dartmouth and its sports teams early in the new century. In 1908, for instance, a delegation of Dartmouth students attended

Hand-painted sign depicting a Dartmouth victory over Brown, 1905. *Courtesy Dartmouth College, Rauner Library.*

the Northfield Student Conference, a ten-day gathering of Christian students from colleges across the eastern United States and Canada. At the conference's celebration, when each delegation dressed in costume, the Dartmouth men donned Indian garb to represent their school. Ralph Walkingstick, class of 1918, is often credited with introducing the Dartmouth Indian yell, but the yell was on the scene a generation earlier.[12] Early twentieth-century football songs referred to the "Dartmouth Indians" who were intent on "massacring" and "scalping" their opponents, and posters, postcards, and newspaper cartoons depicted Dartmouth teams with Indian caricatures.[13] Prior to the 1920s, Dartmouth's intercollegiate athletic teams were known by a variety of names, including the Big Green, but not usually as "the Indians," that designation being reserved for the powerhouse Carlisle Indian School football team. But in 1922, before the Harvard game, Boston sportswriters began referring to the "Indians" from the north, and cartoons in Boston newspapers were soon depicting Dartmouth with an Indian figure. Before the end of the decade, the Indian symbol was appearing on football programs and team uniforms. By the 1930s, the Indian symbol was well established.[14]

In the depths of the Great Depression, the College commissioned renowned Mexican muralist José Clemente Orozco to paint a series of murals in the lower-level reading room in the basement of Baker library. Orozco was excited by the prospect of painting something that displayed the collision of indigenous and European civilizations on the American continent and the emergence of "an authentic New World civilization." He felt that this subject had a special significance for Dartmouth, which "has its origin in a continental rather than in a local outlook—the foundation of Dartmouth, I understand, predating the foundation of the United States."[15] Painted between 1932 and 1934, Orozco's *Epic of American Civilization* shifts the focus of America's history away from New England and provides a panoramic display of Mexican history from ancient Aztec society, to the devastating invasion of Spanish conquistadors and missionaries, to the deadening conformity of modern American society, the ruthless greed of capitalism, and the ravages of the military-industrial complex. It disturbed many people and outraged some alumni. Walter B. Humphrey, class of 1914, responded with a mural of his own. A cover artist for the *Saturday Evening Post* whose work is often mistaken for that of Norman Rockwell, Humphrey had designed the first "official" Indian head symbol for the College in 1932.[16] He now painted what he called "a real Dartmouth mural" on the walls of the Hovey Grill, a room in the basement of Thayer Dining Hall. The mural portrayed the song about Wheelock founding Dartmouth by bringing 500 barrels of rum to the New England woods. In the almost Disneyesque style popular at the time, stereotypical Indian men drinking the rum and scantily clad Native women, one reading a book she is holding upside down, surround a jovial Wheelock. Some people were offended by the public display of bare breasts and the disrespectful depiction of Dartmouth's founding father, but on a campus with few or no Native students, no one complained about the caricaturing of Indian people. But the Hovey murals, as they came to be known, would be there for Indian students to see in years to come. Born out of controversy, they would remain a source of controversy well into the twenty-first century.

By the middle of the century, Indian symbols were commonplace at Dartmouth and ingrained in the campus culture. Indian arrows littered the pages of the College yearbook, sports teams were referred to as "the Tribe," and the lacrosse team was called "the Indian stickmen."[17]

Only thirty Native American students attended Dartmouth between 1900 and 1969, many of them only for a year or two. Like others of their generations,

Panel from the "Hovey Murals" (1937–39), Walter Beach Humphrey (Dartmouth class of 1914). *Courtesy Hood Museum of Art, Dartmouth College. Commissioned by the Trustees of Dartmouth College, Hanover, New Hampshire.*

many found their lives disrupted by global conflict. Nevertheless, the almost forgotten stories of these men reveal much about the experiences of Indians at Dartmouth and in America during these years.

Two students from the Indian reservation at Old Town in Maine came to Dartmouth in the opening years of the century. Henry Hamilton entered the class of 1904 but did not graduate. He returned to Old Town, where he worked as a railroad mechanic. Horace Alysius Nelson, a Penobscot-Passamaquoddy, graduated from Old Town High School in 1900 at age twenty-two. The sole Indian in his class, he was only the second Penobscot to finish secondary school. (The first, seven years earlier, was Louis Sockalexis, who went on to a career in professional baseball.) Nelson entered Dartmouth on a "trial" basis, but as he was deemed unprepared for the academic demands of college, he spent a year at Hanover High School before matriculating in September 1901. After another year, perhaps because of illness, he returned home to Indian

Island, Maine, where he lived the rest of his life. He served a two-year term as Indian representative to the Maine state legislature in 1920–22 and as Penobscot tribal governor in the 1940s. Three of his seven children were dancers and performers.[18] Under the stage name Apid Elk, Winifred performed in circuses and appeared in the film *Drums along the Mohawk* (1939). Her younger sister became more famous: as Molly Spotted Elk, she pursued a career in dancing and film, appearing in the movie *Silent Enemy* (1930). Mildred, stage name Little Elk, also danced and did some film work.[19] Horace died in 1962. In memory of his brief time at Dartmouth, Winifred (then Winifred January) later willed to the Native American Studies Program a collection of basketry, beadwork, and art. Many of the baskets were made from sweet grass Horace had collected on the coast of Maine.[20]

Baseball player Jack Meyers attended classes at Dartmouth in 1905–6. Born in southern California in 1880, John Tortes Meyers was a member of the Cahuilla tribe. His father died when he was seven years old, leaving his mother to raise him. The family moved to Riverside, where Meyers attended high school but did not graduate. After high school he made a living as a catcher for semipro baseball teams in California and the Southwest. He was playing in a tournament in Albuquerque when he caught the eye of Ralph Glaze (class of 1906), a Dartmouth football and baseball star who made the majors as a pitcher with the Boston Americans in 1906–8. "I knew that Dartmouth's original charter had some provisions in it for helping the education of Indians," Glaze recalled. "So I asked John Tortes to consider going back to Dartmouth with me for a college education." Meyers thought about it for a minute and then said, "Wait till I get my glove." His catcher's mitt was his only luggage. Glaze persuaded Dartmouth alumni in his hometown of Denver to help send Meyers to Dartmouth; they supplied him with cash, train tickets, and even a fake high school diploma. Meyers's former semipro status rendered him ineligible to play on sports teams at Dartmouth, but he evidently tried out for the football team. A newspaper report described him as "a wonder physically towering above the rest of the student body" at 6 foot and 215 pounds and developing into a powerful lineman. However, "owing to his studies, which were unusually difficult to the Indian, he was not allowed to play regularly on the eleven." The newspaper assured its readers that "The big Indian is very popular with the students, and, like every student at the New Hampshire college, is immensely proud of old Dartmouth. He was recently elected to the Kappa Kappa fraternity." But, said Glaze, "Second semester was

John Tortes Meyers, photographed during his year at Dartmouth.
*Courtesy Dartmouth College, Rauner Library (neg. 3296).*

not so good. His lack of preparation became more apparent, there was sickness in his family back home, which worried him, and he hated the winter climate." Then the College found out about the phony diploma. President William Jewett Tucker offered to get him into Andover Academy to help prepare him for college, but "that was the end of John Tortes at Dartmouth." He left after just one year. Meyers himself said nothing about the diploma, just that he went home to California because his mother was ill and that by the time she recovered it was too late to return to Dartmouth.[21]

Whatever the reason for his departure, now twenty-five, he tried to make a living playing baseball. He played briefly for minor league teams and then joined the New York Giants in 1908. He was the Giants' regular catcher from 1910 to 1916, batting .300 over that period and .358 in 1912. Jack Meyers and the Giants won the National League pennant in 1911 but lost the World Series to the Philadelphia As and pitcher "Chief" Charley Bender from White Earth in Minnesota, a graduate of Carlisle Indian School in 1902 and a player repeatedly remembered as "one of the kindest and finest men who ever lived." The Giants won three consecutive pennants and Meyers led the batting in three seasons, but they lost the World Series to the Boston Red Sox in 1912 and to Philadelphia and Bender again in 1913. Dropped by the Giants in 1915, Meyers joined the Brooklyn Dodgers, winning the National League pennant in 1916. He retired at thirty-seven and enlisted in the Marines in 1917. After his discharge he joined the Buffalo Bisons for a season. Inevitably, and much to his chagrin, he was nicknamed "Chief" Meyers. When his baseball days were over, he returned home and became police chief for the Mission Indian Agency, and later worked for the Department of the Interior as an Indian supervisor.[22]

Toward the end of his life, Meyers said his biggest regret was that he never finished college. But he retained an affinity for Dartmouth. "You know, Dartmouth is just like the Giants: once a Giant, always a Giant," he said; "once a Dartmouth, always a Dartmouth. You never lose that affection for the old school, regardless if you just get in there and get a cup of coffee. They instill that spirit into you that lasts. Dartmouth men are very, very close, all over the world. They'll never turn you down." At eighty-six years of age, at the Dartmouth Club of New York, he presented the College with an autographed copy of the book *The Glory of Their Times*, which featured him as one of the stars of early baseball. He died in San Bernardino, California, on July 25, 1971, just four days shy of his ninety-first birthday.[23]

Alvis Kusic, a Tuscarora classmate of Meyers, also did not graduate. Neither did Victor Johnson, class of 1910, a Lummi from Washington State, who published a poem in *Dartmouth Magazine* in his freshman year. But Johnson did go on to earn a master's degree in education at the University of Washington. He taught in Hawaii as well as Washington and, he informed the Dartmouth Alumni Records Office in 1955, "retired from school work after thirty years, mostly in the Indian Service achieving the position of Supervisor of Indian Education for the Pacific Northwest."[24]

Several Native students attended Dartmouth around the time of World War I. David Hogan Markham, a Cherokee from Oklahoma who was related to Rollin Adair (class of 1877) and Harvey Shelton (1886), graduated in 1915. After graduate study in physics at the University of Chicago and a career in the Soil Conservation Service of the U.S. Department of Agriculture, in 1947 he was appointed director of conservation and reforestation for the Republic

of El Salvador for two years. Beginning in 1954 he worked with pipeline companies in Kansas, Missouri, Oklahoma, and Texas. He also directed a school
for boys in Phoenix, Arizona, and ran a boys summer camp in the Ozark
Mountains for ten years. He later donated several items to Dartmouth's Hood
Museum.[25]

Bertram Bluesky, a Seneca from Silver Creek, New York, who had attended
Carlisle Indian School when Jim Thorpe was there, arrived at Dartmouth in
the fall of 1914. "I would like to have it be the best college in the country from
now on, since I am attending it," he said. In the middle of his freshman fall,
he wrote a letter to the noted Native American physician Carlos Montezuma
describing his life at Dartmouth. It was a good college for any young student,
he said. Unlike some of the larger colleges, the student body was very unified,
with members of all classes coming together for debates and sports events.
"The whole of last week was devoted to preparing for the Princeton and Dartmouth Foot-ball game at Princeton," with much yelling and singing. Bluesky
would not be going to the game, although as a freshman he would do his part
in building a bonfire in the evening in the event the green team won. But like
Daniel Simon who had described Dartmouth as a hard school for poor students in the 1770s, Bluesky faced other challenges:

Doctor, I am penniless and I need outside aid. Three or four times this week I went without eating for whole days until late in the evening when apples and sandwiches came
around to be sold at a cheap price. Not only do I not have the proper sustenance but
I am also without bed clothing. I am using overcoats for blankets and an old sofa pil-
low for a head rest. I don't believe count Tolstoy had any more simple room than I have
here in Dartmouth College. I am trying to furnish my room with proper means but my
income from working is not enough even to buy me proper food. So please send me
some money.

Yours truly,
Bertram Bluesky.

After a year, Bluesky transferred to Fredonia State Teachers College in
Dunkirk, New York, and taught school in the neighborhood of the Cattaraugus Reservation.[26] Bluesky was also credited, along with Ralph Walkingstick,
with introducing the Dartmouth "Indian yell" in the fall of 1914. According to
some accounts, they did so at the Princeton game that Bluesky said he would
not be attending (Dartmouth lost 16–12).[27]

While Dartmouth students were devoting their energies and attention to the Princeton game, the world was falling apart in Europe. Three years later, the United States entered World War I. About 16,000 American Indians enlisted in the armed forces. Canada, as part of the British Empire, was already in the war, and some of its First Nations soldiers went early. Angus Splicer, a Mohawk from Kahnawake, seems to have attended Dartmouth only in 1912. He attended McGill University in 1915 but then enlisted in the Canadian Light Infantry. He was killed in action in June 1916, just about the date he would have graduated from Dartmouth.[28]

The war also altered Ralph Walkingstick's life. There was more to Simon Ralph Walkingstick (to give him his full name) than football games and Indian yells. He was a track athlete as well as a football player. In his freshman fall he replied to a letter of inquiry about Indian names with an informative letter not only about his own Cherokee name but also about the eighty-six-letter Cherokee syllabary invented by Sequoyah: "A bright Indian boy can learn to read and write in a few days," he said. "It is the only alphabet since the history of the world that has been invented by one man alone."[29]

In May 1917 Walkingstick left Dartmouth and joined the YMCA. He was appointed a secretary of the International Committee of the YMCA for work among British and Colonial troops, which carried the nominal rank of captain in the British army. He served overseas from December 1917 to July 1919, in India, Mesopotamia, and England.[30] In April 1918, delayed in Calcutta with a fever, he wrote to Professor Harold G. Rugg. He had seen and learned a great deal since he left Dartmouth, he said. "My class is graduating this year. I would like to be there with them, but I think this YMCA work is a greater thing just now." His position as part of the office staff was a thankless job and he was anxious to go to Mesopotamia, "where the soldiers are fighting and dieing [*sic*]." He saw several small engagements in Mesopotamia but no battles. In the summer he was hospitalized with influenza-pneumonia. The next April, the war over, he wrote Rugg again. He was about to leave for Bombay to take ship for America via Marseilles and London. "I have been in Mesopotamia about nine months, seen the Peace come, and now feel that it is time I went home and settled down for a while." He had seen all of the places of interest from Bible days but he was not impressed: "It is not a pretty country," he thought. "Quite the reverse. Everything has the color of dust, the women are all fat and cover their faces, the men wear evil looks, the children have sore eyes and dirty bodies, and, in fact, everything is as ugly as possible. It is

Ralph Walkingstick. *Courtesy Dartmouth College, Rauner Library*
*(neg. 2452).*

impossible to imagine that this was once a densely populated and beautiful
land. The supposed site of the Garden of Eden [above Hillal on the Euphra-
tes River] is as dreary and dusty and barren as the rest of the country." Dartmouth seemed far away. "No doubt all soldiers have left Hanover by now and
you are cheered to see everyone in civilian clothing once again." He hoped to
return to Hanover soon after he got back to America. He was discharged in
Baghdad on April 17, 1919.[31]

But he did not return to Dartmouth. He got a good job as state Indian
work secretary of the Oklahoma YMCA, serving the 135,000 Indians in the
state, and had a wife to support. He was just happy to be home in Muskogee:
"It is great to be alive in a real loveable climate after the months on that Mes-

opotamian desert," he said. "Old Abraham used his best judgment when he left there for the Promised Land." He continued to watch the progress of the football team and asked for news of the College, but he stayed in Oklahoma.[32] He worked as financial agent for Bacone College in Muskogee for a couple of years, as a sports writer for local Oklahoma newspapers, and for most of his career as a geologist in the oil business. He and his wife had five children (one, a son with the same name, was killed in action in the Philippines during World War II). The Dartmouth alumni record office had a difficult time tracking him down in later years. Respondents to its inquiries referred to hard times, "ups and downs," and possible drinking problems. But when "Old Stick" died in 1970, at age seventy-three, his obituary in the *Dartmouth Alumni Magazine* remembered happier times: "All will recall that glorious fall day when Ralph and Bertram Bluesky, in full chieftain costume, introduced the Indian Yell to the Dartmouth stands."[33]

Ironically, at just about the same time the SSPCK decided to wash its hands of Dartmouth, a Dartmouth Indian was preparing to return to his people as a minister. Born in a tepee on the Santee Sioux Reservation on the south bank of the Missouri River in Nebraska in 1892, Francis Philip Frazier was raised in a Christian home: his father and grandfather were both missionaries. He attended the Santee Indian School, Yankton College Academy, and Northfield Mount Hermon School in Massachusetts before entering Dartmouth with the class of 1920. He volunteered while he was a freshman and served in the Eighty-ninth Division of the 355th Infantry. He spent a year in France, including ninety days on the front line, and another six months in Germany.[34] After the war, he graduated from Oberlin College in Ohio in 1922 and attended the Chicago Theological Seminary. He was ordained as a Congregationalist minister and served his people first as pastor and later as superintendent of Dakota Association Churches, an association of Indian churches. (He also did a stint as a professional baritone singer in the late twenties, with a concert at Jordan Hall in Boston in 1927, and served as director of the Los Angeles Indian Center in the 1940s.) He and his wife, Suzie Meek Frazier, a Mesquakie or Fox Indian, had five children, one of whom drowned when he was just two years old.[35]

Frazier said his was "just an ordinary life," but he spent it working to improve the material and spiritual condition of his people. He developed rehabilitation projects with the tribal council on the Standing Rock Reservation straddling the border of North and South Dakota, where in the late 1950s

Philip Frazier with his wife and President Dickey at commencement in 1964, the occasion of his honorary degree. *Courtesy Dartmouth College, Rauner Library.*

and early 1960s most inhabitants lacked electricity or running water; income was paltry; one-quarter of the residents had been relocated to make way for the Oahe Dam; and most young people did not have a high school education. "I am an Indian American," Frazier said. "I lived in the isolated communities. I know their needs." The immediate need, he wrote to Dartmouth, was Christian education that would "help them to make the grades and adjustments in their thinking and way of life." Indian people had been deprived of incentive and rendered dependent on "some outside agent" for so long that they had lost their dignity, but "some of us Christian Indians want to help ourselves, secure our dignity and self respect and to secure income to build our own homes and feed our children and clothe them by our own efforts." He hoped the College might help.[36]

Francis was honored with the Twenty-fifth Annual Indian Achievement Award in 1958 for devoting his life to the service of his people and an honorary doctorate from Oberlin in 1960. Dartmouth awarded him an honorary doctor of divinity degree in 1964. In conferring the degree, President John Sloan Dickey linked the Frazier family tradition of missionary work and Dartmouth's own less than stellar tradition: "We here cannot sense the deprivation of dignity, mind and spirit you face in your people today without realizing how tragically unfulfilled is Wheelock's purpose to educate and Christianize the Indian. Your life witnesses the continuity of that purpose." Dickey felt that Dartmouth's first president would applaud the awarding of the degree.[37] Frazier died later that year.

Frell MacDonald Owl (class of 1927) also was awarded an honorary degree. He was born on the eastern Cherokee reservation in North Carolina in 1900, of Cherokee/Catawba and Scottish ancestry and a family that was determined to give the children a good education. After six grades in a boarding school for Cherokees, Frell, like others of his family, left for Hampton Institute in Virginia, a college originally established for black students that also admitted Indians. Many years later, he remembered his Aunt Sue (Susannah Owl), a devout Christian, sending him off with a sack full of sandwiches and parting lecture: "'You be a good boy and behave yourself and don't be like these good for nothings around here. Get a good education and get a job and save your money. Don't throw your money around like these good-for-nothings around here.' Then she pointed a finger at me and said, 'and don't you come back here married to no Catholic.' I really don't think she knew what a Catholic was but she felt she had to say that."[38]

Frell graduated as valedictorian in 1920 and was presented with a "Certificate of Educational Competency." The Dawes Act had linked citizenship to allotment, and subsequent legislation had authorized the BIA to issue fee patents and declare as citizens any Indians found "competent" to manage their own affairs. In 1917 the commissioner of Indian affairs, Cato Sells, expanded the list of Indians judged competent to be citizens to include students twenty-one years or older who received diplomas for completing a full course of study. The Certificate of Educational Competency described the recipient "as possessing such character, judgment, and educational qualifications as render him reasonably competent to transact his own business and to care for his own individual affairs." After two years at Phillips Andover Academy, Frell entered Dartmouth in 1923. A college dean questioned whether he was eligible to receive a $500 scholarship awarded to Indian students because the Certificate of Educational Competency meant he was now considered a U.S. citizen and was therefore not an Indian. Frell convinced him that he was still an Indian, whether or not he was a U.S. citizen.[39]

"Hoot" (as he was inevitably nicknamed at Dartmouth), became a member of Kappa Kappa Kappa, played varsity baseball, played the tuba in the

College Band and Community Symphony Orchestra, and joined various societies. Even so, he often felt homesick and missed being with Indian people. After graduation, he entered the BIA and "devoted his entire career to working among Indians." He taught at a federal Indian boarding school in Pierre, South Dakota, where he was adopted by a Sioux couple, worked for six months at Haskell Institute in Lawrence, Kansas, and then became principal of the government boarding school in Hayward, Wisconsin. But in the 1930s commissioner of Indian affairs John Collier tried to turn America away from the destructive assimilation policies of the past, and many government boarding schools were shut down. When Hayward closed its doors in 1933, Owl became a government negotiator with school boards and school districts in the state. In 1936–45 he was subagent at Lac du Flambeau Reservation in northern Wisconsin; in 1945–50 superintendent at Fort Thompson, South Dakota, supervising two Sioux reservations, and in 1950–54, superintendent at Red Lake Reservation in northern Minnesota. In 1954 he became superintendent of the Fort Hall Indian Reservation (Shoshone-Bannock), Idaho. He retired after thirty-three years of BIA service, and in 1961 he received the Department of the Interior Honor Award for meritorious service. In 1969, on its 200th anniversary, Dartmouth awarded him an honorary doctor of humane letters degree. President Dickey described him as having "worked to bridge the chasm between the Indian and the white man's world on which he had been required to depend as a stranger in his own land" and hoped that Dartmouth in its third century would remain committed like Owl to "integration through the power of education."[40]

Owl had "very definite ideas as to the present and future of his people — especially those still on the reservations." Indians had been too slow to change, he said; they must learn to adopt the white man's way — hold a job like whites, value time like whites, dress like whites. "The Indian problem is basically one of adjustment to a new way of life," he said. "There is no denying that the Indians face an acute cultural problem, the solution of which rests with them themselves." Like Frazier, he believed that education was the key to the "salvation of the Indian youth" and to progress. "Until more Indians are educated, the Indian group will remain static."[41]

Owl published several essays. In "Who and What Is An American Indian?" published in the scholarly journal *Ethnohistory* in 1962, he reviewed the various "categories" of Indians — full blood, mixed blood, enrolled, nonenrolled, tribal member, nonmember, and so on — explained the different criteria and

Frell Owl. *Courtesy Dartmouth College, Rauner Library.*

definitions employed by the federal government and the various tribes, and argued for a standard definition: "Although the United States serves as the legal guardian of American Indians, it has no clear-cut definition telling exactly what constitutes an American Indian." He also used the essay to attack full-bloods as obstacles to the kind of changes he thought necessary and had tried to promote in Indian country. Full-bloods, he said, generally lived on reservations, were wary of government personnel, scornful of mixed-bloods, often spoke their tribal language, and sometimes still wore their hair in braids. "The full-blood often lives in abject poverty, but he is an exceptionally proud person. Tribalism predominates in his thinking habits. Continued existence under Federal paternalism is his life's objective." The full bloods kept alive tribal culture and ceremonies and, because they often dominated tribal coun- cils, they dictated the pace of acculturation. "The full-blood is inclined to ignore the wisdom of non-Indians that might motivate change." In fact, said Owl, "he has the unique ability to resist change with Indian silence."[42]

Benedict Hardman, class of 1931, a Yankton Sioux who often used his tribal name, Tunkanawatena, in correspondence with Dartmouth, graduated four

Roland Sundown, in formal attire and in war bonnet. *Courtesy Dartmouth College, Rauner Library.*

years after Owl with a degree in English and philosophy. He earned a master's degree at the University of Minnesota in 1935, pursued a career as a newscaster and radio announcer, and then, returning to school, in 1985 became the first Indian to get a doctoral degree from the University of Minnesota. Hardman insisted on using the term "Indian." "No way will I ever use the euphemistic insulting term, Native American," he informed the Dartmouth Office of Public Programs. "I still proudly wear Indian head cuff links," he wrote in a letter to the *Dartmouth Alumni Magazine* in 1973. "I still have the Indian head sweater I wore as Dartmouth band leader in 1930–1931 when Roland Sundown '32, an Iroquois, and I were privileged to be in the forefront at Dartmouth athletic events. We were proud to be genuine Indians at an Indian school. I still and shall always refer to the Dartmouth Indians."[43]

Roland Burnett Sundown was a Seneca, reputed to be a descendant of captive Mary Jemison. He entered Dartmouth after attending Phillips Andover. In addition to performing as the "Dartmouth Indian" at football games, he also introduced the snow snake — a carved stave designed for skidding across the ice — to campus as a winter sport and donated a snow snake to the College museum. After Dartmouth, be became a teacher, first with the Indian Service in Alaska; then in New Jersey; then back in Canaan, New Hampshire, before working in Indian Service schools in Oklahoma and North Dakota. During World War II he served with the Army Counterintelligence Corps.[44] Then he went to graduate school where he studied the role of Indians in literature.

Others did not leave such an imprint at Dartmouth. Louis Poitras, from the Cheyenne River Agency in South Dakota, entered with the class of 1933

but stayed only one year.[45] Seneca John Snyder, 1936, came from Cattaraugus and attended Dartmouth in 1932–35 but left "under a double cloud." His
alumni file contains a terse note written by hand forty years later:

Dear Sir:

   I flunked out so I am not a graduate of Dartmouth College. Therefore, I am not an
alumnus.

   Please remove my name from your mailing list."[46]

Everett E. White (class of 1937) was a Mohawk from Akwesasne, a community on the banks of the St. Lawrence River, at the intersection of the borders
of New York, Ontario, and Quebec. Yet, like Sundown, he posed for photographs wearing full Plains Indian headdress when he was at Dartmouth. He
ran track and captained the freshman cross-country team but struggled as an
economics major and took a fifth year to graduate. He served in the army in
Germany and France and spent time in Greece administering economic aid
for the U.S. government. After the war he worked in the BIA.[47]

   Alexander Sapiel from Old Town, Maine, entered Dartmouth in 1934, cad-
died for the College president, and managed to graduate in 1938 before World
War II broke out, although he appears to have finished his degree at Duke.[48]

   The war disrupted lives at Dartmouth as it did everywhere else. As the
sleepy town of Hanover came to life on Sunday morning, December 7, 1941,
and students pulled out their books to study for final exams, events 6,000
miles away produced an abrupt awakening to realities of global conflict.
Exams no longer seemed important. Students searched their souls, called
home, and "drifted away from Hanover, one by one" to sign up, take their
chances, "and be transported beyond their control or their imagination" to
different parts of a world at war.[49] Within a year the navy commandeered the
Dartmouth campus. The names of those who did not return from World War
II are inscribed on a polished granite plaque on the back porch between the
Hopkins Center and the Hanover Inn.

   John Francis Imo, 1940, a Seneca, served in the Army Air Corps and did
not graduate.[50] Rudolph T. Lorraine, 1946, spent one year at Dartmouth but
left to join the army and did not return to campus.[51] Henry Gabriel Perley,
class of 1943, a Maliseet from Maine, also known as Henry Eagle, entered
Dartmouth in September 1939, the very month war broke out in Europe. He
was born in 1921, the son of Henry Red Eagle and Wanna R. Eagle Perley. He

William Cook with his wife and son on the Dartmouth
campus, October 1947. The cradle board was designed from
a model in the College museum. *Courtesy Dartmouth College,
Rauner Library.*

grew up in the Maine woods, but his parents were performers at Coney Island
in his early years. At Dartmouth, he took English honors and became vice-
president of Phi Sigma Epsilon and captain of the fencing team. As Henry put
it, he was in college "until the white man declared war and declared me in
it." He served for three years in the Army Air Corps as a radio operator and
received several citations.[52] After the war he resumed his studies and graduated cum laude in 1946, as did Albert Andrew Exendine, the other Indian in
his class.[53] Perley attended graduate school at Boston University, the University of Maine, and the University of Cincinnati. He taught English at Worcester Polytechnic Institute and Fairfield High School in Maine before going into
business with General Electric.[54]

Akwesasne Mohawk William John Cook (1949), also known as Chief Flying Cloud, flew a hellcat for forty months in the South Pacific and Philip-

pines theatre of the war before he came to Dartmouth. He was wounded in action in 1944 and won a purple heart, two Distinguished Flying Crosses, six air medals, and three campaign stars. He resumed his education after the war. At Dartmouth he was a football and lacrosse player and with his wife, Evelyn, ran an Indian craft shop on College Street. Cook also worked with local camps and gave lectures on Native American culture and folklore. Their first baby — Ronwi kanawaienton, or Louis Thomas Cook — was born while William was a student, and local newspapers gave plenty of publicity to "the first full-blooded Indian" born in Hanover. Recalled to active service as a captain in the Marine Corps in 1952, as a pilot instructor, Cook was killed when his twin engine Tigercat crashed on a night landing at Cherry Point, North Carolina.[55] Another Mohawk, Joseph Jacobs from Kahnawake, entered Dartmouth in 1946 but left after one year.[56] He was the last Indian admitted for almost twenty years.

Although few Indians attended Dartmouth in the first two-thirds of the twentieth century, Dartmouth continued its interest in Native people. Dartmouth men continued to go into Indian country, although not always with much sensitivity to Indians — the pioneering rock climber and later physician, Jack Durrance, class of 1936, was the first non-Indian to ascend Devil's Tower in Wyoming, a site held sacred by many tribes and more recently the source of considerable controversy as the National Park Service struggles to balance the religious rights of Native peoples with the recreational rights of climbers on federal land.[57]

In the early 1950s Roland E. Stevens, a graduate of the class of 1895 and still practicing as an attorney in White River Junction despite being in his eighties, served as counsel for the Iroquois. The Kahnawake Iroquois repeatedly claimed that Vermont owed them compensation for hunting lands they had lost in the northwestern corner of the state and now brought suit for $1.2 million. Dartmouth students took up their cause and launched a "Give Vermont Back to the Indians" campaign, selling buttons to help finance the lawsuit. It didn't do the Iroquois much good: in 1953 the Vermont legislature rejected their claim for the twelfth time.[58]

Whereas earlier generations had expended tremendous efforts to eradicate Native culture and transform Native people, Dartmouth scholars now began to study Native cultures and learn from Native people. John C. Ewers (class of 1931) became one of the country's foremost scholars in the ethnology of the Northern Plains Indians and the history of the West. In the latter half of the 1930s, he worked for the National Park Service, and then for the BIA in Browning, Montana, where he conducted fieldwork among the Blackfeet and supervised the development of a Plains Indian museum. After two years in the U.S. Navy during World War II, he was hired by the Smithsonian Institution, where he spent the rest of his career.[59] Wilcomb Washburn (class of 1948) also joined the Smithsonian, and beginning in 1968 was director of its American Studies Program. He published widely on American Indian history, although his conservative views often placed him at odds with Native people and a younger generation of scholars of Indian history, as well as with many Native students and faculty at Dartmouth, where he remained involved in the Native American programs.[60]

William N. Fenton, class of 1931, grew up in western New York, in the heart of the historic Seneca homeland. After graduate school at Yale, when anthropology was shifting away from old evolutionary theories and embracing the theoretical orientation of Franz Boas, which emphasized firsthand fieldwork and multidisciplinary approaches to understanding culture and culture change, Fenton devoted his career to the study of the Iroquois. He got his first job, in the depths of the Great Depression, as an employee of the Indian Service on the Tonawanda Reservation. He learned Seneca and was adopted into the Seneca Hawk Clan. He became senior ethnologist in the Bureau of American Ethnology at the Smithsonian Institution, director of the New York State Museum in Albany, and in 1968 joined the faculty of the Anthropology Department at the State University of New York, Albany, where he taught until his retirement in 1979. For another quarter of a century until his death in 2005, Fenton continued to research and write, and remained active in the Conference on Iroquois Research, which he cofounded in 1945. Although he sometimes took positions that were unpopular with Indian people — he opposed returning wampum belts from the state museum to Onondaga and denied that the Iroquois system of government served as a model for the U.S. Constitution, for example — Fenton enjoyed a reputation as "the Dean of Iroquois Studies."[61]

Dartmouth hired the renowned Arctic explorer and anthropologist Vilhjalmur Stefansson as consultant to the museum in 1947. Often known as the

"Prophet of the North," Stefansson had spent a dozen years in the Arctic, traveled an estimated 20,000 miles by dog sled, mapped some of the world's last uncharted landmasses, "discovered" the Copper Eskimo, and fundamentally influenced the way the non-Arctic world viewed and understood the Arctic. He also, during his time there, lived with an Inupiat woman named Fanny Pannigabluk and had a son with her.[62] Stefansson donated his 25,000-volume library and extensive collection of papers to Dartmouth. His work at the College in the 1950s and 1960s inspired the next generation of Arctic researchers (exemplified by the work of David Nutt and Elmer Harp, Bill Fitzhugh, and John Hobbie) and laid the groundwork for Dartmouth's continuing research in the Arctic, where climate change and globalization threaten Native lifeways and languages.

Vermonter Gordon M. Day began his career in forestry and after returning from service in World War II became chair of the forestry department at Rutgers. But in 1957, he took a position as research associate in the Anthropology Department at Dartmouth and devoted his energies full-time to Abenaki research. He carried out extensive community fieldwork, particularly at St. Francis, recording oral histories and material relating to Western Abenaki linguistics and ethnology. Between 1956 and 1985, he worked with more than three dozen Western Abenaki speakers. At a time when many anthropologists earned a poor reputation among Native people, Day was widely respected for his commitment and sensitivity to Abenaki issues and concerns. He deposited sixty reels of magnetic tape and 10,000 pages of manuscript on microfilm, plus notes, sketches, maps, and photographs, leaving Dartmouth with a vital resource not only for academic scholars but also for Abenaki people as they themselves attempt to preserve and revive the language. Day also prepared an Abenaki-English dictionary. He understood that the kind of work he did with Indian people was very different from the kind of work Eleazar Wheelock had had in mind: "It seems fitting," he said, "that the Dartmouth College Library should become the repository of a collection pertaining to the original inhabitants of Vermont, New Hampshire, and western Maine. Perhaps it is also a little incongruous when we reflect on the probable reaction of Dr. Wheelock to a suggestion that his little Indian pupils from the bark houses of St. Francis were themselves the bearers of a culture which merited study."[63]

By the 1960s, the College and campus had manufactured a variety of traditions, rituals, and ideas about Indianness that mythologized much of its own Indian history and linked successive generations of Dartmouth men in an imagined past, a shared culture, and a distinct identity.[64] However, the absence of Indian people, Rayna Green's prerequisite for inventing and imagining Indians, was about to become a thing of the past. In the early 1960s, Dartmouth's Tucker Foundation and a group of independent schools in New England launched Project ABC (A Better Chance) to help disadvantaged high school students strengthen their academic skills and achievement and encourage them to apply for college. Students spent a summer at Dartmouth, and those who wanted to complete their secondary education away from home were then placed in one of the community schools in the fall. One Native student enrolled in the summer program at Dartmouth in 1964, half a dozen in 1965. By 1969 a dozen schools and more than 130 students, about half of them Native, were participating, providing a pool from which Dartmouth could recruit in the future.[65] The Committee of Equal Opportunity also made a commitment to increase Native American admissions. Dartmouth had graduated only ten or eleven Native students in the previous hundred years, but in 1965 it admitted three: William Yellowtail, Gordon Maracle, and Gregory Dale Turgeon. The new arrivals were touted as evidence that Dartmouth had not forgotten its historic commitment to Indian education. Their admission, according to an alumnus of the class of 1921 writing in the *Dartmouth Alumni Magazine*, was

fresh affirmation of Dartmouth's abiding faith in its original mission . . . a reminder that the facile and amusing Indian symbolism garnishing the present-day College really stands for something and that the football cheers and cheerleaders, the College songs and souvenirs, and the place names are the mementos of an ideal which burned so hotly in one man's heart and head two centuries ago that he wrested a clearing from the wilderness to establish a new frontier of hope. Few colleges have a more meaningful motto.[66]

By 1969 there were seven or eight Native students on campus, significantly more than at any time in the previous century, and more were about to follow. As Native students became a presence, would they too regard the Indian mascot, the breaking of "peace pipes," and the depiction of drunken and half-naked Indian men and women in the Hovey murals as a meaningful motto and honoring a founding mission? Or would they see them as "nothing but fantasies," demeaning caricatures of themselves and their cultures?[67]

*Chapter Nine*

# THE RETURN OF THE NATIVES,
## 1970–2010

🏺 IN 1970 THE president of the United States and the president of Dartmouth College both announced a new era in Indian relations. In many regards a new era was already upon them. The 1960s and early 1970s brought dramatic changes to America, to Indian country, and to Dartmouth, and the presidents' respective announcements responded to demands and developments as well as charting new directions. The war in Vietnam, the civil rights movement, a growing counterculture, and widening generational attitudes divided American society. At the same time, Indian people mobilized to exert greater influence in running their own affairs and reverse the effects of past policies of dispossession, assimilation, and neglect. In 1961, delegates from more than sixty-five tribes attended the American Indian Chicago Conference and sent a Declaration of Indian Purpose to President John F. Kennedy. Later the same year, younger Indians expressed their impatience in trying to work with the U.S. government and formed the National Indian Youth Council in Gallup, New Mexico, demanding a new role in determining Indian policies. In 1968, the American Indian Movement was founded in Minneapolis; in the next five years it organized a march on Washington, occupied the BIA building, and staged a dramatic and televised standoff at Wounded Knee, South Dakota, drawing media attention to continuing injustices and demanding restoration of tribal sovereignty. In 1969, Indian students from the San Francisco Bay Area seized Alcatraz Island in the name of "Indians of All Tribes." Indians on the shores of the Great Lakes and on the Northwest Coast invoked nineteenth-century treaties to reassert their fishing rights. Many tribal chairmen and older, more conservative Indians disliked the militant tactics of the younger generation. But the new activism reflected a swelling desire for change in Indian country, and its reverberations were felt in Washington and at Dartmouth.

President Richard Nixon's special message to Congress on July 8, 1970, called for a new era of Indian self-determination. Veering away from failed past policies of paternalism and termination, the U.S. government would now enter into a partnership with Native communities, and Native people would have far more opportunity and responsibility for running their own affairs.[1] Congress followed up by passing the Indian Self-Determination and Education Assistance Act in 1975 and other laws designed to protect Indian rights and increase Indian participation.

President John Kemeny chose Dartmouth's bicentennial as the time to begin to make good on Dartmouth's promise and place new emphasis on Indian education. "Though the College he founded has prospered," said Kemeny, "only part of Eleazar's dream has come true." In two hundred years, only about a score of Native students had actually graduated. "Because I believe deeply in Eleazar's vision, I pledge my energies to the effort of translating the long-deferred promise of Dartmouth's charter into reality." For Kemeny and for Dartmouth, it was part of a larger commitment to equal opportunity and minority education. It was also a reflection of changing times. The historically low numbers of Indian students at Dartmouth were "a reflection of the deterioration of relations between whites and Indians," said Kemeny. "As the Indians were pushed farther West, it just didn't seem practical for them to attend." But after the social and political upheavals of the 1960s, the climate was very different. It was time for Dartmouth to do something.[2]

To achieve his goal of sixty Indians enrolled within four years, Kemeny announced in his inaugural address in March that Dartmouth would enroll fifteen Native students in the class of 1974. "The pronouncement was something of a shocker to the Admissions Office," recalled the former dean of admissions and financial aid, "because there were not 15 Native American candidates in the entire candidate pool."[3] Admissions had to scramble but they got the job done: Fifteen Native students from thirteen tribes and eight states matriculated in the fall, bringing the number of Indian students on campus to twenty-three, the largest enrollment in Dartmouth's history. Another group arrived the next year. Duane Bird Bear (1971), a Mandan-Hidatsa from Fort Berthold in North Dakota, Howard Bad Hand (1973, Rosebud Sioux), Travis Kinsley (1973, Tohono O'odham-Hopi), Dave Bonga (1974, White Earth Chippewa), Bruce Oakes (1974, Mohawk), and others helped shape the future Indian education at Dartmouth. In 1974 Eva Smith, a Shinnecock, became the first Native American woman to graduate from Dartmouth. As the dean of admissions and financial aid appreciated,

In attempting to bring to Hanover enough Native American students to create "critical mass," Dartmouth was, in a sense, recapitulating the history of the Bureau of Indian Affairs boarding schools. It is one thing to bring minority students to campus as individuals, with the understanding that as individuals they are expected to fit into the campus community as best they can. However, it is quite a different matter to enroll students with the understanding that they are not expected to lose their culture or be overwhelmed by the dominant white society.[4]

Dartmouth established the American Indian Program to provide cultural and academic support for its Native students. It hired as director thirty-year-old John Phillip Olguin, a Pueblo from Isleta, New Mexico, who had worked for the BIA, the Department of Health, Education and Welfare, and the Office of Economic Opportunity. Unlike other programs at academic institutions that were put together for Indians, this one was to be developed and run by Indians for Indians. "We're trying here to equip young Indians for positions as doctors, lawyers, sociologists, and teachers and we don't know the real recipe for doing that," Olguin explained. "But Dartmouth is giving us a chance to make mistakes. They're saying, in effect, 'Here's the expertise — what are you going to do about it?' It's a real challenge."[5]

In 1971 three Indians from Oklahoma entered Dartmouth Medical School — Ralph Dru, a Cheyenne, who had served in Korea and graduated from college on the G.I. Bill; Sarah Dye, a member of the Shawnee and Sac and Fox tribes, and Jeral Ahtone, a Choctaw-Kiowa. Dye and Ahtone graduated in 1975, a year when only twenty-two Native Americans graduated from medical schools all across the country. Ahtone — whose father had hitchhiked 110 miles every day for two years to earn a teaching certificate — completed his residency at Dartmouth in 1978 and later went to work for refugee populations in Pakistan, Indonesia, and Thailand. In 1984–85 he directed 250 clinics in Pakistan set up by the United Nations Office of the High Commissioner for Refugees. When he returned to the United States, he set up an anesthesia department in a hospital in a West Virginia coal mining town. He later became emergency room director at Kaufman Presbyterian Hospital in Texas.[6]

The presence of Native students was a symptom of a new Dartmouth; and Native students often bore the brunt of the backlash from members of the community who resented and resisted the changes. The difference in attitudes and agendas between young students who called themselves Native Americans and some of the older alumni like Frell Owl who were proud to think of themselves as Dartmouth Indians also reflected broader generational tensions across Indian country: younger voices challenged the status quo, demanded new ways of doing things, and adopted more militant tactics in dealing with a government that, like Dartmouth, had failed to honor its historic promises.

Michael Hanitchak (Choctaw-Chickasaw), director of the Native American Program from 1995 to 2010, entered Dartmouth with the class of 1973. In those early years, the Native students were just surviving. Hanitchak has seen many changes, mostly for the better, but sometimes "the school was a reluctant companion on the journey."[7] Nothing has highlighted that apparent reluctance more than the persistence of Indian imagery and stereotypes: college songs, chants, and war whoops at football games, cheerleaders in loincloths and paints, Indian head T-shirts, neckties, and jacket patches, murals in the Hovey Grill, Indian head canes and Indian pipes at graduation, and a whole range of "Dartmouth Indian" memorabilia.

Time and again since the 1970s, the Indian symbol has reared its head in one form or another, igniting heated debates about the traditions it ostensibly honored, the racism it demonstrated, and the freedoms of speech and thought that were being expressed or threatened. It has stirred emotions, generated countless letters to the student newspaper and the *Dartmouth Alumni Magazine*, and drawn occasional national media attention.[8] At first many people, including President Kemeny himself, he acknowledged, did not give it much thought, or just assumed that Indian students would be proud that their college had an Indian symbol. After all, some Indian students had taken part in these "traditions" in the past. But this was a new generation of Native students, politicized and sensitized by the events of the 1960s, and most of them hated it. In their eyes, Indian symbols did not honor a revered tradition but stood as stark reminders of a brutal history and were emblematic of the hypocrisy of an institution that had so far failed in its efforts to educate Indian youth. In 1971, Native Americans at Dartmouth issued a formal policy statement. Dartmouth had long been regarded as a school for the education of Indians, the statement read, but in fact for 200 years it had "nourished only a romantic notion of being an 'Indian' school through the creation and retention of a Dartmouth 'indian' [sic] mascot and assorted caricatures of Indian Americans." As "a microcosm of a larger society," Dartmouth "must reflect prevailing conditions," and there could be no place for caricatures of Indians "within an institution ostensibly committed to the education of Native Americans and others." The statement requested that all manifestations of the Indian symbol—from sports team mascots and Wah-hoo-wah cheers to the Hovey murals—be removed from campus. Additional recommendations included more active recruiting of Native American women and developing American Indian studies.[9]

In the spring of 1972, on the recommendation of a committee co-chaired by Native American Program director Stuart Tonemah (a Kiowa-Comanche from Oklahoma) and a young assistant professor of history named James Wright, the Faculty of Arts and Sciences unanimously approved the adoption of a Native American Studies Program. Howard Bad Hand and Duane Bird Bear approached Michael Dorris, a Modoc from Oregon, to teach in the program, and Dorris was hired, with a joint appointment in anthropology, to serve as chair. The new job was a challenge. "Nobody at Dartmouth knew what Native American Studies was supposed to be," Dorris recalled; "but the unpersuaded suspected that it somehow involved basket-weaving and mysticism, a sop to radical minority students."[10] The program was to consist of four core courses. Dorris made sure that his classes were academically rigorous and brought in visiting professors—Beatrice Medicine taught during the winter and spring terms in 1974. In 1975 a review committee strongly endorsed the program. In the committee's view, one of Dartmouth's unique strengths was that it did not have to answer to state legislatures, which had placed restraints on American Indian studies programs elsewhere in the country, while the College's small size meant it was "more likely than our larger and less intimate schools to become a 'living laboratory' for improved relations between Native Americans and their successors on this continent."[11]

In the fall of 1972, the Native American House opened at 18 North Park Street. It served as the residence and social/cultural space for Native students until a new Native American House, the former Occom Inn on North Main Street, was dedicated and opened in the fall of 1995. In 1973, the Native American Council was formed, an organization of representatives from students, administration, and faculty, including non-Natives as well as Natives, with oversight of all activities relating to Native Americans at Dartmouth. That same year, Dartmouth held its first powwow.

Meanwhile, the Alumni Council appointed an Indian Symbol Study Committee, chaired by Robert Kilmarx, class of 1950, a trustee and attorney from Providence, Rhode Island. Kilmarx admitted that the committee initially thought the whole thing was "silly," but they soon changed their minds. They found that the Indian symbols many alumni revered as hallowed traditions

Fritz Scholder, *Dartmouth Portrait #17* ("Big Green Indian"),
1973. Oil on canvas, acrylic background. Painted while Scholder
was artist-in-residence at Dartmouth, in the midst of some
heated debates about the Indian symbol. *Courtesy Hood Museum
of Art, Dartmouth College, Hanover, New Hampshire. Purchased through
the William B. Jaffe and Evelyn A. Jaffe Hall Fund.*

were, for the most part, relatively recent creations and had never been officially sanctioned by the College. It seemed that Dartmouth athletic teams had
not generally been known as "the Indians" until the 1920s, when newspaper
sports writers picked up the term, and the Indian symbol did not appear on
College athletic uniforms until 1928–29. The "Indian head" did not appear
on football jerseys until the 1965 season, and then only on the white, away-
game uniforms and not on the green, home-game uniforms until five years
later. Letters from alumni reflected "an overwhelming support of retention
of the symbol and lack of understanding of the Indians' point of view." In the
eyes of most Native Americans, the Indian symbol was "a grotesque misrep-
resentation" and "a racial slur" that illustrated the College's insensitivity to

Native American history, culture, and current issues and its lack of concern for the Native students on campus. The committee quoted President Kemeny: "Unless we can find the means to make these students feel a part of the Dartmouth family, we should not admit them in the first place." At Stanford, the student senate had established the Indian as the university's symbol in 1930 and voted to repeal the action in 1972. Since Dartmouth had never officially adopted the Indian symbol, it could hardly officially abolish it, but the committee recommended supporting efforts to end it. The Board of Trustees declared that using the symbol in any form was "inconsistent with the present institutional and academic objectives of the College in advancing Native American education." Many people, local businesses, teams, and organizations responded positively; it looked as if the Indian symbol might die by voluntary abandonment. The committee also recommended appointing a Native American Visiting Committee with review and advisory responsibilities for Dartmouth's Native American Program.[12] Frell MacDonald Owl was one of the early members.

Russell Ayers, class of 1929, was a second cousin of Ralph Walkingstick. He left Dartmouth after his freshman year and kept a low profile for the next decade, "being rather sheepish about my scholastic record." But his classmates made a point of including him in their activities, and he had fond memories of them — "the first palefaces I had ever associated with" — and the kindnesses they showed "an uncertain overgrown hill country cherokee [sic] boy."[13] He made a career in engineering and lived on Staten Island but got involved with Dartmouth again in the early 1970s. Sensing a new era in Indian affairs, Ayers saw opportunities for Dartmouth to take its Indian education to a new level. "For the first time ever the tide in congress seems to be drifting our way," he wrote to his classmate and class president Charley Dudley. "And whether our communities keep rotting or not is and always has been at the disposition of congress." He was under no illusions: under the old pretense of helping Indians to adapt, the government was "still neutralizing wild indians." (Ayers always spelled "indians" lowercase). "Actually, the pressure has never been anything but to break up their social structure, drive individual indians, particularly the young, out into the so-called mainstream. And finally, to dismember and to terminate the reservations. It is clear when you look at it from under the right flap." Everybody assumed it would be "a good thing to force indians out of their way of life" and that it was inevitable anyway, and the churches and colleges had been ringleaders in the work of cultural erosion. "Which is why I don't really think Dartmouth has the right slant in what they are trying to do. Good old Dartmouth, with the start it had, should by now have been the archives of things indian. Then it could proudly wear the indian symbol. That it did not makes me lukewarm about whether it ought to or not."[14]

Now, however, he saw a chance for Dartmouth to do something different. American business was now ready to do business with Indians, but it was "just not in the nature of bureaucracies to offer up the right kind of assistance to implement this." Impatient with past policies of compliance, "the more rambunctious young" were pushing their way into tribal councils, "to stop the rubber stamping, they contend"; but once on the councils "they find it takes more than simply being oppositional to do the sound thing." Ayers proposed a program of seminars at Dartmouth's Tuck Business School to help tribal council members deal with real and momentous issues. He knew that working with tribal councils meant getting into "a rather touchy area": the BIA would see this as proposing "an incipient business advisory for the various indian tribes of a sort most difficult to counter. And, by golly, we are." But it would reflect well on the College: "if Dartmouth is cocky enough to chance this, it can cement the old school's tradition as indian partizans as nothing else ever could, or will."[15]

In the wake of Wounded Knee and the FBI assault on the American Indian Movement, Ayers had trouble finding recruits. Responses to his letters and phone calls were so guarded that he went across country in person to drum up interest. Phones were tapped; infiltrators were everywhere, people told him. At first Ayers pooh-poohed the reports: Obviously, the FBI wanted to keep tabs on things, but it was hard to believe "that they would so ham-handedly seek to manipulate every council member especially and every conceivably influential indian as well." But he soon changed his mind: "Not anymore," he said. "It happened." On one occasion, Ayers himself was taken for "an FBI plant." He hoped things might return to normal—"whatever normal may turn out to be"—once the FBI surveillance abated. Self-determination was now "the thing," he explained to Dudley, but it had to mean more than simply letting Indians administer the programs that Washington concocted. There were still too many people deciding what was best for the Indians, but "no one who wants it to be the indians." Ayers still hoped that his Tuck program could help Indian people to better determine their own future, but he was not optimistic about it.[16]

Ayers's classmates turned to him to explain the furor over the Indian symbol as well as the complexities of Indian politics. In fact, he told Dudley, lots of people bugged him about it: "Not even just Dartmouth men. Some people who have never seen Hanover poke me in the belly and ask, 'why?'" So he knew getting rid of the Indian symbol was not a popular move. "And I will admit I do not quite know what it accomplishes. Protest seems to be a way of life among all the younger generation. And whether it makes any sense or not. Still, with indians, there has to be more to it than that." He worried that young Indians were imitating too closely the tactics of black militants, whose goals and agendas he felt were not appropriate for Indians, but he understood where they were coming from: "indians are still a very foreign element in this society," he wrote Dudley. "One of my standard cracks is that it took me forty years before I could really feel at ease amongst you folks." And it was worse for young Indians than it had been in his day, when many of the "old breed" of leaders were still around "who never made any concessions to the white man's ways."[17]

Few other alumni shared Ayers's perspective or sympathy. Developments on the Dartmouth campus threatened to transform the alma mater they loved and signaled disturbing shifts in the world they knew. To Arthur Appleton, class of 1936, in Chicago, Dartmouth had "changed so much that it is unrecognizable" to those who had attended ten, fifteen, or twenty years ago; he suggested changing its name to Kemeny College.[18] Ellis Briggs, class of 1921, a former U.S. career ambassador who had returned to live in Hanover, wrote a letter to the Manchester, New Hampshire, *Union Leader* under the banner headline "Goodbye to the Dartmouth Indian." It began: "The latest sacrifice on the altar of the New Revelation at Dartmouth College is the Dartmouth Indian himself, slain with his own tomahawk and scalped by his own sachems, in the shadow of his own wigwam." In keeping with the new orthodoxy, Ellis sniped, the books of James Fenimore Cooper would be burned at the next commencement and alumni donations in Indian pennies would henceforth be rejected.[19] Angry letters flooded into the president's office and the *Dartmouth Alumni Magazine*. Some alumni were outraged; some expressed dismay, some disgust. Some shook their heads in disbelief, baffled as to why Indians should take offense at depictions of proud Indian warriors. Others adopted a "get over it" tone.

Some older Native alumni had no time for the changes demanded by younger "Native Americans at Dartmouth." Signing himself "Mahkway-

Paykwa, Sagamore of the Maliseet," Henry Perley wrote from Thomaston, Maine, to say that he had seen nothing wrong with the Indian symbol when he was at Dartmouth. "If the militant redskins (and that's what we call them) want to make an issue, let them charge ahead," he said, "but they ain't my tribe." Dismissing the "frenzied mouthings of the adolescent wild ones," he emphasized that "the Native Americans at Dartmouth still do not speak for me."[20] Perley remained proud to be "a Dartmouth Indian" to the end of his life. That came tragically in April 1972 after he was physically assaulted by a stranger in Rockland, Maine, and died after brain surgery for the injuries inflicted. He was fifty-one. His check for reservations for his thirtieth reunion was in his pocket ready to mail. Perley had requested that his Native American artifacts be left to the College.[21] In honor of his memory, his classmates established a scholarship for Native American students at Dartmouth.

Charles Eastman's daughter, Eleanor Mensel, writing from Northampton, Massachusetts, expressed sadness at the demise of the symbol: "My father was very proud of his ethnic heritage and was also very proud to be a 'Dartmouth Indian,'" she wrote.[22] Benedict Hardman echoed her sentiments and steadfastly opposed doing away with the symbol.[23] And some of the Native students on campus found the issue was not clear-cut: "While I thought the symbol had to go, I was very proud of the Indian head on our football jerseys," recalls Jack Manning, a Fort Peck Sioux who played cornerback on the football team.[24]

"The reaction of a lot of alumni to being told that their Indian-head neckties were suddenly to be considered representations of racism rather than badges of undying loyalty to their alma mater was simply 'Now you've gone too far.'" As the clash of generations, of liberal and conservative values, of opposing views of what American society was and should be played itself out at Dartmouth, "the symbol," Calvin Trillin noted in the *New Yorker*, "became a symbol."[25] Bruce Duthu, a member of the Houma Tribe from Louisiana and now an attorney and professor of Native American Studies at Dartmouth, arrived on campus as a member of the class of 1980 to find that "the Indian symbol had become the touchstone for general debate about institutional capitulation to minority student interests." People who were unhappy with the admission of women, minority recruitment, establishing ethnic studies and women's programs, increasing sexual diversity on campus, and other departures from "tradition" fought to retain the Indian symbol as an emblem of the "good old Dartmouth" that was under assault. Some blamed Native students

for starting the trouble.[26] "Where will it end — this frenetic desire to elimi-
nate the customs, traditions and, yes, symbols, that once made Dartmouth
both unique and great?" asked one letter.[27] Someone urinated in the office of
the Native American Program. Someone deposited excrement at the door of
Michael Dorris's office. During his tenure as chair of Native American Studies,
Dorris had to deal with an almost annual resurgence of the Indian symbol and
engage in seemingly endless correspondence with alumni. Native students
kept asking why would people want to cling to something they knew was
offensive to other people unless they wanted to give offense? Dorris wrote:

> It was an ultimately boring, silly controversy, but it did hang on. Year after year the NAS
> students and I would have to explain why it was just as inappropriate for the Cauca-
> sian sons and daughters of Dartmouth to play stereotyped Indians (wild, savage, noble-
> hearted and stoic) as it would be if they took it into their heads to be rhythmic Blacks
> or wealthy Jews. The symbol became symbolic to all concerned, the issue on which the
> constituencies of a changing institution slugged out their differences. It was an annual
> nuisance that wore out me and every other Indian in town, but there was no way we
> could give up.[28]

The Board of Trustees reaffirmed their position on the symbol but the issue
frequently resurfaced, and polarized the campus and community. Students
and alumni debated possible alternative mascots; polls indicated a majority favored returning to the Indian symbol. In a letter to the student newspaper in 1978, James Wright, then an associate professor of history, accused
some pro-symbol students of racism: "If anyone believes the last conclusion
is too harsh, let me be clear," he wrote; "the arrogant assumption that anyone
can appropriate as 'theirs' a racial, cultural or religious group, and ignore this
group's reasoned protests, is racism. It is cultural rape."[29] The issue was cata-
pulted back into the spotlight in the winter of 1979, when two students wearing green war paint, feathers, and loincloths skated onto the ice at a hockey
game, an incident that attracted national as well as campus media attention.
Their action culminated a "winter of discontent" that also included sexist acts
against women and racist acts against African Americans. Students held a
rally on the college green and President Kemeny called a one-day morato-
rium on classes so the campus could discuss the issues. The administration
put the ice-skating students on probation. "I still can't understand why using
the Indian as a symbol hurts anybody's feelings," said one of them.[30]

That fall, in response to protests, the College decided to cover the Hovey murals during most of the year. The administration wanted to avoid censorship but ensure that the murals be displayed in an appropriate setting, not in a dining hall. Since moving the murals would have been expensive and potentially damaging, they were stored in place, covered with wooden panels that could be removed, at a cost of $500, for commencement and alumni reunions. It was a compromise that satisfied no one. One young Native woman found herself tending bar at a fiftieth reunion beneath depictions of virtually naked young Native women "holding Bibles upside down and lapping up rum at the feet of Eleazar Wheelock" — the Hovey murals had been uncovered for the occasion.[31] The question of what to do with the murals persisted: Were they art or just "pub art"? Was it not censorship to keep them covered? Why cover them and not the Orozco murals that some people found equally disturbing? Shouldn't they be portrayed in an educational setting and discussed with appropriate artistic and historical context? Michael Dorris gave a lecture beneath the Hovey murals on the occasion of the Columbian Quincentennial, but they continued to alienate rather than educate. Plans for demolishing Thayer Dining Hall in the first decade of the new century pushed the controversy to the forefront again: should the murals be removed at great expense or should they just be demolished along with the building? Determined to avoid any form of censorship, the College opted to remove them to a different space, but then financial crisis in 2009–10 caused the administration to rethink its plans for Thayer Hall.

Conservatives fought back against what they saw as the stifling liberal ethos of the new College and an administration that was riding roughshod over Dartmouth's traditions. Orton Hicks, class of 1921, kept up a regular correspondence with Michael Dorris for years. Hicks had returned to Hanover after a career in the motion picture industry, had served as vice-president of the College from 1958 to 1966, and had remained active in alumni affairs. He (inadvertently, he said) wrote Dorris on "Indian head" stationery and intended "to keep fighting the rest of my life to bring back the Indian symbol." He wished that the Native Americans at Dartmouth would show "some sensitivity to the feelings of thousands of alumni," and he felt the College was wrong "to let a group of about 40 Native Americans tell 40,000 alumni what they call themselves." He once thought the controversy might die out with the passing of the pre–World War II generation but came to believe "that the Indian symbol will never die until the Native Americans ask for its return."[32]

*Little Man . . .*
*Be a Big Man*

"Be a Big Man." Some supporters of the Indian
mascot insisted that it honored Native Americans.
*Courtesy Dartmouth College, Rauner Library.*

Alumni mounted and supported campaigns to reverse the liberal trend
and restore the Indian symbol, or at least a "dignified" version of it.[33] In 1980,
a group of conservative students established the *Dartmouth Review*, an independent and frequently inflammatory newspaper, with hefty financial backing and some high-level connections, including the right-wing columnist
William F. Buckley, Jr. The *Review* took on the administration for coddling to
the interests of whining minorities and took up the restoration of the Indian
symbol as a campaign.[34] *Review* staff handed out Indian T-shirts each year to
incoming freshmen and made available for sale to parents and alumni Indian
head canes, Indian patches, Indian symbol boxer shorts, and "heavy, green
Indian doormats."

At an October 1983 football game, members of the freshman class rushed
up the east stands at Memorial Field at halftime, unfurled a huge Indian
banner, and yelled "Wah-hoo-wah." The act produced the usual flurry of
responses, counterresponses, and debates. President David T. McLaughlin

issued a statement reaffirming the Board of Trustees' original position on the symbol and called for a reaffirmation of Dartmouth's principles of community. The student newspaper stopped accepting materials on the Indian symbol because of an "oversaturation" of letters and columns in which the arguments had become "repetitive and duplicative."[35] The next fall, the captains of the football team urged students to unite behind the Indian symbol.[36] Not surprisingly, there was another football field incident involving a banner. McLaughlin declared the use of the symbol at athletic events "indefensibly wrong."[37] A similar incident occurred in the 1986 season.

Conservative predictions that the 1980s would reverse the trends of the 1960s at Dartmouth proved inaccurate. The College experienced even more changes after James O. Freedman became president in 1987. The first president since 1822 with no prior connection to the school, he brought an outsider's perspective. He pushed Dartmouth to become a first-tier academic institution and a hospitable place for intellectuals and minorities, and he took on the *Dartmouth Review*, denouncing it for its racism and sexism.

At his first commencement ceremony in June 1988, Freedman handed her diploma to Stacey Coverdale, a Shinnecock from Long Island. Twelve hours later, Stacey was killed when the car driven by her father was hit head on by a speeding Saab driven by a Dartmouth junior. Stacey died of a torn aorta. Several months after her death, she and other Native students appeared in the documentary film *A Way of Learning*, directed by Abenaki filmmaker Alanis Obomsawin. The film focused on the value of a liberal arts education for Native Americans but also emphasized that American Indian cultural values were preserved and even enhanced at Dartmouth where, for instance, students could satisfy the "foreign language" requirement with their Native language. The film, to many people, was surprisingly upbeat. The Indian symbol was mentioned only once — by Stacey Coverdale: "I've had a lot of confrontations on having to espouse my views on the Indian symbol and being of color," she said. "But the people I've met here are talented and beautiful and wonderful." The film was dedicated to Coverdale.[38]

The Indian symbol controversy died down but showed a Rasputin-like refusal to die out, and other issues of cultural appropriation surfaced. Native students took on the "tradition" in which members of the graduating class would puff on clay pipes and then smash them at the stump of an old pine tree where Eleazar Wheelock had reputedly held Dartmouth's first classes. Responding to Native student complaints that in their cultures pipes are sacred objects and pipe smoking a sacred ritual, and with considerable support from the student body, in 1992 the graduating class's Senior Executive Committee voted unanimously to abolish the practice.[39]

Speaking at an event to mark the 500th anniversary of Columbus's voyage to America, Nicole Adams, 1995, a member of the Colville Tribe of Washington, acknowledged that progress had been made but cautioned that Dartmouth and the country as a whole still had a lot to learn about Native Americans and their cultures. "We are reminded of this every time when we hear chants of 'wah-hoo-wah.' We are reminded of this every time we see gross caricatures of our people in every corner of the campus."[40]

Native students sometimes experienced racism and stereotyping from Native as well as non-Native students. Marianne Chamberlain, from Wolf Point, Montana, described herself as "the lightest-skinned person in my family." When she walked into the Native American house as a freshman and "found a bunch of Native American–looking people sitting around a drum, singing and drinking beer and hard alcohol," she stared in disbelief. Wasn't this the very image Indian people had been fighting against forever? "Here I was at an Ivy league college looking at this stereotype come to life." The head singer looked at her and asked: "Hey, white girl, do you know what kind of song this is? You don't belong here, go back to the city." Marianne replied that it was a slide step song and that on her reservation they were taught never to sing and drum while intoxicated because singing is sacred. She turned and left, alienated from the students and the house she had expected to be her community.[41]

Dartmouth is not a racist institution, generally. But, like anywhere else, it is a place where racist attitudes and behaviors linger, bubble up in unexpected ways, and resurface with depressing regularity. In that, it is probably no different from other institutions in America. However, the relative isolation of the College makes it a self-contained world that accentuates the disruptive impact of such things. Hanover is a small town; with no larger city or community to absorb the shock waves, it sometimes seems that racist incidents and offensive behaviors reverberate endlessly around the campus. In the fall of 2006, a series of such incidents occurred in rapid succession. During orientation week, the *Dartmouth Review* distributed T-shirts exhibiting the Indian symbol to first-year students. On Columbus Day, a group of fraternity pledges, some of whom had evidently been drinking, violated a sacred drumming ceremony on the green, running through the drumming circle, clapping and mock dancing. During homecoming weekend, before the football game against Holy Cross, T-shirts appeared depicting an Indian and a crusader (the Holy Cross mascot) engaging in oral sex. Then, more than thirty years after the College had publicly disavowed using Indian symbols, the Development Office published an alumni calendar that included a picture of an Indian head cane carried at graduation. Next, Dartmouth crew teams held a costume party with the theme "Cowboys, Barnyard Animals, and Indigenous People." With the administration constrained by its commitment to freedom of speech, the Native American Council took out a two-page letter in the student newspaper to draw attention to what was going on and to urge action. The same day, President Wright sent a letter to the students, urging them to unite against racism, ignorance, and prejudice, and explaining that the Indian symbol persisted because it "was easier than confronting our history." The next day, Dartmouth's athletic director apologized for having invited the "Fighting Sioux" of the University of North Dakota to compete in a December hockey tournament scheduled years in advance. There was the usual round of meetings, discussion groups, educational sessions, and letters to the editor.[42]

After Thanksgiving, the *Dartmouth Review* featured a cover illustration of an Indian brandishing a scalp, and the headline "The Natives are Getting Restless!" The lead article, "NADS on the Warpath," accused Native students of being oversensitive and ready to stir up trouble about imagined slights or anything else they could come up with.[43] The following day, 500 people responded in a campus-wide "Solidarity Against Hatred" rally on the green, and President Wright made clear that this kind of intolerance had no place in the Dartmouth or its traditions that he knew. The next month, the "Fighting Sioux" arrived on campus to defeat the Dartmouth ice hockey team.

As writer Louise Erdrich (class of 1976) explained, even in normal years, Native students at Dartmouth often become "exhausted cultural emissaries, and each deals with stereotypes peculiar not only to Native Americans, but to his or her tribe."[44] To many Native students it seemed that Dartmouth, having made great efforts to recruit them, clung to "traditions that fostered a student culture that alienated them."[45] Calvin Trillin had written in his 1977 *New Yorker* article that Native students "hated having their experience at Dartmouth dominated by [the Indian symbol]. They hated having to explain constantly why it offended them. They hated being considered humorless and hypersensitive because they objected to it."[46] Thirty years on, not much had changed. As one non-Native alumnus had acknowledged sadly in 1980, "debate over the Indian symbol is a permanent part of the Dartmouth experience."[47]

That debate is part of a long-standing and often heated controversy in America about Indian sports mascots in particular and Indian cultural appropriation and representation in general. Native Americans have sued the Washington Redskins and lobbied other teams, schools, and colleges to change their symbols. In 2005 the American Psychological Association called for the retirement of all Indian mascots, symbols, and images by sports teams, schools, colleges, and organizations, citing a growing body of research that demonstrated the harmful effects of such racial stereotyping, especially on the self-esteem of young Native Americans.[48] The NCAA banned the use of Indian nicknames and mascots by college sports teams playing in its post-season tournaments. The University of Illinois stopped using its famous "Chief Illiniwek" as a mascot and logo. But some professional, college, and high school teams retain theirs in the face of criticism, and some Indian people say they have no problem with it.[49] These contests resonate with particular irony at a college ostensibly founded to educate Indians, but they are not unique to Dartmouth. In the face of huge odds, Indians have survived in America, but the "White Man's Indian" — the imagery of Indian people constructed and appropriated by non-Indians — has also survived, embedded for many people in their vision of themselves, their college, and their country. When real Indians meet imaginary Indians, conflict and anger almost always occur. After years of wrestling, and much hand wringing, Dartmouth has not successfully resolved or removed the issue. Neither has America.

For some Dartmouth alumni, taking a stand against reassertions of Indian rights was not confined to the Dartmouth campus. Slade Gorton, class of 1949, earned a reputation as a modern-day Indian fighter. Gorton, whose family corporation was a wholesale fish distributing firm, opposed Indian fishing rights on the Northwest Coast in the 1970s. Several tribes staged "fish-ins" to draw public attention to their rights embodied in nineteenth-century treaties to fish in their "usual and accustomed places" and then took their case to court. In 1973 the United States, representing fourteen tribes, sued the state of Washington, represented by its attorney general, Slade Gorton.

Judge George Boldt in U.S. District Court upheld the Indians' treaty rights and interpreted their right to fish "in common" with non-Indian citizens to mean taking an equal share; in other words, 50 percent of the harvestable fish. Many non-Indians in the area were outraged, Boldt was burned in effigy, and anti-Indian racism soared. Gorton referred to Indians as "super citizens" who benefited from special rights, and he campaigned to overturn the decision. He traveled to Washington, D.C., to present the state's argument that the Indians should only be entitled to equal access to the fishing grounds, not guaranteed an equal share of the catch, but the Supreme Court in 1978 upheld Boldt's ruling in a six-to-three opinion.[50]

After Gorton became a U.S. senator (Republican) in 1981, he built a record promoting what many people saw as anti-Indian legislation — some called him the "Custer of the Senate." In 1995, he became chair of the Senate Appropriations Committee's Subcommittee on Interior and Related Agencies (including the BIA) and tried to cut $200 million from the tribes' $1.7 billion annual appropriation. He presented legislation that would have deprived the Lummi Indian Nation of Washington of federal funding if they did not give up a lawsuit over water rights against non-Indian landowners on their reservation. "The battle, bluntly, is not over water," he said. "It's over power." The bill failed. In 1996, he introduced legislation to tax Indian gaming operations at 34 percent, a move that did not pass the committee.[51]

A *New York Times* editorial in 1997 described him as having "a 25-year gripe about the Indians."[52] In 1998, he introduced to Congress his "American Indian Equal Justice Act," which would have required tribes to surrender their sovereign immunity in order to receive federal funds and required all tribes receiving federal funds to undergo means-testing. Democratic Senator Daniel Inouye, a champion of Native rights in the continental United States if not in his own Hawaii, described the bill as a measure "to assure that commercial activities conducted on Indian lands are rendered incapable of competing in [the] free market place." Ada Deer, assistant secretary of the interior for Indian affairs from 1993 to 1997, called it "termination by appropriation." The House rejected the bill, but it reflected a broader conservative suspicion of tribal power and hostility to tribal rights.[53]

One journalist described Gorton as "The Last Indian Fighter" and "Public Enemy No. 1" for American Indians, driven by a "perverse obsession with punishing some of the poorest people on the continent."[54] In 1998, tribes formed an organization they called the First American Education Project to raise funds for a media campaign against Gorton. They tried to avoid a back-lash of anti-Indian sentiment by focusing on his record on environmental issues. In 2000, American Indian activists campaigned to prevent Gorton's reelection to his senate seat. He was defeated by 2,229 votes.[55]

Meanwhile, Dartmouth's Native American programs continued to grow. Twenty years after Kemeny's renewed commitment, more than 125 American Indian, Alaska Native, and Native Hawaiian students were enrolled at Dartmouth, representing 55 different tribes or groups. Dartmouth had more Native students than all the other Ivy League schools combined, and the graduation rate among its Native students was 80 percent, compared with the national average of 10 percent.[56] While some alumni stopped contributing in protest against the College's stand on the Indian symbol, others reaffirmed or increased their financial support. In 1991, Dartmouth's Native American programs received their largest donation: a $1.6 million endowment from Gordon W. Russell, class of 1955. By the first years of the twenty-first century, thirty years after it started with one half-time faculty member, Native American Studies had grown into a permanent program offering a major and a minor, and with five tenure-track faculty, supplemented by adjuncts and regular visitors, teaching more than 400 students a year in courses on history, culture, law and policy, tribal governance, sovereignty and indige-nous rights, archaeology, anthropology, literature, gender issues, film, and representation. Many students carry out independent research, some write honors theses, and some carry out internships in Native communities and organizations.

Students regularly apply what they have learned and the skills they have acquired in confronting challenges and pursuing opportunities to benefit Native communities. For many Native students, college is a prelude to tribal service, either back home or on a larger national scale. Native alumni go on to become artists, authors, doctors, lawyers, politicians, professors, teach-ers, tribal administrators, and community workers. Those who return home sometimes experience a difficult readjustment, a reentry period in some ways as challenging as the adjustment they faced when they first came to Dart-mouth. But time and again, Native students have used their education to ben-efit and strengthen Native nations and communities.

William Yellowtail grew up on his family's ranch on the Crow Reservation in Wyola, Montana. He graduated from Dartmouth in 1971 with a degree in geography and environmental studies. In 1984 he was elected to the first of three terms as a Montana state senator, representing Big Horn, Rosebud, and Powder River counties. Yellowtail has also been the executive director of the Montana Inter-Tribal Policy Board and director of human resources development and education for the Crow Tribe and has served in various tribal, state, and national organizations and committees and the Montana Environmental Quality Council. In 1993, President Bill Clinton named him regional administrator for the EPA's Region 8 office, headquartered in Denver. Then forty-five, Yellowtail was the first Native American and first non-Coloradoan to hold the post, which involved directing the operations of more than 600 employees and oversight of federal environmental programs dealing with air, water, and land in Montana, Colorado, North Dakota, South Dakota, Utah, and Wyoming, and for twenty-seven tribes. In 1996 Yellowtail made an unsuccessful bid for a seat in the U.S. House of Representatives. In 2006, Montana State University appointed him to the Katz Endowed Chair in Native American Studies, formerly occupied by the renowned Southern Cheyenne educator and scholar Henrietta Mann. Preferring to look forward rather than dwell on the past, Yellowtail said he would develop curriculum and leadership activities that focused on the future of Native peoples in the West and centered on "personal Indian sovereignty," which he described as the "mindset and point of view of building your own world, charting your own destiny, being in charge of your own self, your family and your future."[57]

Lori Arviso Alvord, class of 1979, came to Dartmouth when she was sixteen. Born Lori Cupp, she had grown up in Crownpoint, New Mexico, a "tiny, dusty, reservation bordertown," and was the first person from her town ever to go to an Ivy League college; in fact, she says, she was "the first ever to see one." She "entered a world so different from my home that I could hardly believe both places existed on the same continent!" Her memories of her arrival in Hanover are mostly of the color green. "Green cloaked the hillsides, crawled up the ivied walls, and was reflected in the river where the Dartmouth crew students sculled." The landscape was "lush, beautiful, and threatening." She felt lucky to be there, but she was lonely, far from home, and in culture shock.[58] She made it through Dartmouth, went on to medical school at Stanford University, and became a doctor. In fact, she became the first Navajo woman surgeon. She worked at the Gallup Indian Medical Center, an Indian Health Service hospital serving the Navajo Reservation, and returned to Dartmouth as an assistant professor of surgery and psychiatry and associate dean at the Medical School from 1997 until 2010.

Louise Erdrich, a member of the Turtle Mountain Band of Chippewa, grew up in Wahpeton, North Dakota, where her German-American father and her French-Ojibwe mother both taught at the BIA school. She came to Dartmouth in 1972 as a member of the first coeducational class, and met Michael Dorris, whom she later married and with whom she often collaborated in writing. She graduated from Dartmouth in 1976 and then earned a master's degree in creative writing at Johns Hopkins. In 1984 her first novel, *Love Medicine*, was awarded the National Book Critics Circle Award. A steady stream of novels followed, firmly establishing her as an author of international acclaim.[59] Her novels are typically complex, interconnected stories about Ojibwe people in North Dakota and mixed-blood families living on and around the reservation. In 2009 *A Plague of Doves* was a finalist for the Pulitzer Prize in fiction. In 2007 she declined an honorary doctorate from the University of North Dakota in protest against the university's Fighting Sioux mascot. In 2009 she accepted an honorary doctorate from Dartmouth and was the featured commencement speaker.

Alvin Warren graduated from Dartmouth in 1991 with a degree in history with high honors and certification in Native American Studies. He wrote his honors thesis on Pueblo Indian land grants. When he returned home to Santa Clara, New Mexico, the tribal governor asked him to create a land claims program. He established and directed the Santa Clara Pueblo Land Claims/ Rights Protection Program and was able to assist the tribe in regaining more than 16,000 acres of traditional lands. In 2004–5, Warren was the national director of the Trust for Public Land's "Tribal Lands Program." In addition to assisting Native peoples in mapping, protecting and reacquiring traditional land, he served in his tribal government as interpreter, treasurer, and council member and was elected to two consecutive terms as lieutenant governor of Santa Clara. He served on the New Mexico Indian Affairs Commission. In 2007, Governor Bill Richardson appointed him chairman of the Commission and, a year later, cabinet secretary of the New Mexico Indian Affairs Department, a position that entails dealing with state government as well as with the twenty-two tribes in New Mexico. His grandmother's sister, 102 years old at the time, put it very plainly, telling him in Tewa: "Now all of us Indian people in the whole state are your responsibility." For Warren, there was a direct, if

Navajo Graduates, 2004. Jonathea D. Tso kicks a leg while celebrating graduation with classmates Sheina Yellowhair, Poonam Aspaas, Sophia Manheimer, and Marla Yazzie. *Photo by Linda M. Welch. Courtesy of the photographer and the graduates.*

unexpected, connection between his undergraduate research at Dartmouth and his career of service and leadership for his people in New Mexico.[60] When he returned to Dartmouth in the fall of 2008 for the first time since his graduation, he brought a donation from the Pueblo tribes to serve as seed money for internships for Dartmouth Native students.

Jonathea D. Tso graduated from Dartmouth in 2004 with a double major in Native American Studies and Environmental Studies. She then spent two and a half years taking care of her grandmother and her sheep in Cove, Arizona, and pursued a degree in Navajo language and Diné studies at Diné College. In 2007–8, Jonathea was chosen Miss Navajo Nation. Winning the Miss Navajo pageant required, among other talents, demonstrating fluency in the Navajo language and the ability to butcher a sheep. The position involved serving as a Navajo cultural ambassador, and Jonathea used her year to promote appreciation of Navajo culture, particularly among young people.

Much has changed in America and at Dartmouth in the forty years since two presidents announced a new era. Many Indian communities remain plagued by poverty and poor health, and continue to suffer from the legacies of colonialism and failed government policies, but all over the country, Indian nations have rebuilt their governments, revitalized their cultures and communities, fought to preserve their rights and their languages, and proved effective in developing their economies and exerting political influence. At the end of the twentieth century, two-thirds of Native Americans lived in cities. Consequently, many Native students coming to Dartmouth are not "straight off the rez," and some grew up in social and educational environments similar to those of the majority of students. For other Native students, "college is the first place they have ever lived where being a member of one's particular clan or tribe, or coming from one's particular reservation or region of the country, means little or nothing to anyone else."[61] Adjusting to an East Coast Ivy League college, balancing tribal values and Western education, and dealing with cultural misunderstanding and intolerance still pose significant personal challenges. Yet instead of being permanently separated from their home, family, and upbringing, Native students more often draw strength from them. In the 1950s and 1960s, Frell Owl maintained that Indians faced "an acute cultural problem." Jodi Archambault, a member of the Standing Rock Sioux tribe and a 1991 Dartmouth graduate, saw things differently:

I always felt short-changed in terms of academics as a result of attending reservation schools. Now I realize how privileged and fortunate I am to have such strong ties to my people and culture. People often express sympathy for Indians who live on reservations, particularly Pine Ridge, but I think we are rich beyond any American's dream . . . we have our Lakota culture. This culture is and always has been the solution, not the problem.[62]

In 2009 President Obama named Jodi Archambault Gillette an associate director of the White House Office of Intergovernmental Affairs, which serves as a conduit between the White House and state and local governments. She is the first Native American to hold the post and has responsibility for overseeing Indian and tribal affairs in the office. Later that year, the U.S. Senate confirmed Obama's nominee, Hilary Tompkins, who served from 2005 to 2008 as chief counsel to Governor Bill Richardson for the state of New Mexico, as solicitor for the Department of the Interior. Tompkins, Dartmouth class of 1990 and a Navajo, is the first Native American and the second woman to hold that office.

Many of the Natives who "returned" to Dartmouth in the last forty years have since returned to Indian Country, broadly defined, and are helping to shape the future of their nations and this nation.

# CONCLUSION

## Eleazar Wheelock Meets Luther Standing Bear

🦌 IN 1997, in an edition marking the twenty-fifth anniversary of coeducation at Dartmouth, the *Dartmouth Alumnae* [sic] *Magazine* featured a cover picture of a Native American woman — Sarah Harris, class of 2000, a descendant of Samson Occom. Recalling Sarah Occom's request to Eleazar Wheelock to educate her son, the magazine editor noted: "You could say a woman started it all."[1] The school that Eleazar Wheelock created with the money Samson Occom raised has grown to include many different people and perspectives. The growth has often been slow and sometimes painful, but Dartmouth has become, at last, a school for "the education and instruction of youth of the Indian tribes in this land . . . and also of English youth and any others." Ironically, in the process, Dartmouth has become a very different place from the one Wheelock envisioned.

When Wheelock founded Dartmouth, it never occurred to him that he or his school had anything to learn from Indian people. Indian ways of knowing and learning were simply primitive superstitions that must be eradicated if Indian students were to make any progress. In Wheelock's vision for Dartmouth, the few Indian students who attended were to be educated in English ways and Christianity so they could serve as missionaries who would convert other Indians to English ways and Christianity.

Not much changed as English colonial education for Indians gave way to American education for Indians. In 1819, Congress passed the Civilization Fund Act, providing for an annual appropriation of $10,000 to introduce "the habits and arts of civilization" among the Indians by employing "capable persons of good moral character, to instruct them in the mode of agriculture suited to their situation; and to teach their children in reading, writing, and arithmetic." The act represented a commitment by the U.S. government to permanent involvement in Indian education, but it was an education to

MARCH                                                    1997

# DARTMOUTH
## ALUMNAE MAGAZINE

# A Woman's Place

Sarah Harris '00 carries on
a two-century tradition of
women putting their stamp
on the College.

*Dartmouth "Alumnae" Magazine* cover. Cover artist, Rob Day; art director, Dave Nelson. The publication's title was changed for this special issue recognizing women at Dartmouth. *Courtesy Dartmouth College.*

change Indians; the prevailing belief held that Indians could only survive if they ceased being Indians. With the establishment of government-sponsored boarding schools later in the century, the campaign to transform Indian children by eradicating their culture became a crusade. In 1891 Congress made school attendance mandatory for Indian children. Two years later it authorized the BIA to withhold rations and annuities from parents who refused to send their children to school. By 1900 congressional funding for Indian education reached almost $3 million, and 21,568 Indian students were enrolled in school. After the military subjugation of the continent, the United States waged a new war on Indian pupils to remake them into individual citizens, not tribal members. The schools tried to strip students of their Native languages, Native clothing, Native heritage, and Native identity and provide them instead with minimal education and training to function at the lower levels of American society. Like British educational efforts in Ireland and the Highlands of Scotland, such campaigns "were designed to absorb supposedly deficient peoples into larger, dominant nations, leading not to cross-cultural fertilization but to the erasure of minority cultures and identities." Indian education was "education for extinction," cultural genocide waged with good intentions by people who sought to save Indians from themselves.[2]

Yet amid the hardship and heartbreak of the boarding schools, Indian students resisted the educational assault and refused to succumb to the assimilation philosophies and practices of their teachers. They engaged in numerous small acts of subversion and rebellion, built bonds of friendship and loyalty with other Indian students, and found humor and humanity in the midst of alienation and regimentation. Within the confines of the white man's schools, they created a subculture of survival and sustained their own Indian communities.[3] Some used their education to pursue Indian agendas; many combined their Indian and Western educations in ways their teachers would never have sanctioned, or even imagined. Luther Standing Bear, the first Lakota student to attend Carlisle Indian School in Pennsylvania when it opened in 1879, looked back on the education he received and regretted the missed opportunities for creating a truly American school based on the fusion of Indian and Western systems of knowledge. Instead, "we went to school to copy, to imitate; not to exchange languages and ideas, and not to develop the best traits that had come out of uncountable experiences of hundreds of thousands of years living upon this continent." White people certainly had much to teach

Indians, but Indians had much to teach them, wrote Standing Bear; "what a school could have been established upon that idea!"[4]

Dartmouth could very easily have continued in the tradition of Eleazar Wheelock and the boarding schools, less blatantly and less brutally but just as effectively de-educating Indian students as it prepared them for success in the non-Indian world. The late Lakota scholar and activist Vine Deloria, Jr., delivered some scathing indictments of Western education. He criticized mainstream colleges for training professionals but not producing people. Certainly, Dartmouth graduates populate the offices of corporate America. Native students can, if they wish, attend Dartmouth, graduate with the credentials and skills they need to succeed in mainstream America, and have little to do with the Native community on campus, their Native community at home, or their Native heritage. For some students, Dartmouth is a path to a high-paying career rather than an opportunity to broaden the mind and feed the soul. But Dartmouth does, and must do, more than make its graduates marketable. "Education is more than the process of imparting and receiving information," wrote Deloria; "it is the very purpose of human society and . . . human societies cannot really flower until they understand the parameters of possibilities that the human personality contains."[5] Similar words and identical sentiments can be found in the speeches of past Dartmouth presidents James Freedman and James Wright, who steered the College into the twenty-first century with the firm belief that it should prepare students to live well, not just to make a good living.

Dartmouth is not, at least not yet, the kind of truly American school Luther Standing Bear longed for, but it is a far cry from the place Eleazar Wheelock imagined. It is now an institution that recognizes value in diversity, and a place where far more students embrace their Native identity than set it aside. Living in a Native American community, albeit a rather transient and academic one, sharing experiences with Native students from all over North America, and having the opportunity to take classes that concentrate on Native issues can enhance Native students' appreciation of their culture and identity, as well as increase consciousness of Native rights and sovereignty. Dartmouth can provide an environment where "Indianness" thrives, in the very place where Wheelock intended it should wither.

At Dartmouth, as elsewhere, Native American Studies is still emerging as an academic discipline and is breaking new ground. Native and non-Native scholars explore issues of space, gender, artistic expression, representation,

Chief Killer (Noh-hu-nah-wih), Cheyenne, 1849–1922. *Untitled* (School at Fort
Marion), 1875–78. Graphite, ink, and crayon on paper. Cheyenne artist Chief Killer
provides his perspective on the American educational process as he experienced
it while a prisoner of war in Fort Marion, Florida. The Indian prisoner-students,
wearing army uniforms and with their hair cut short, lack individuality as they sit
in orderly rows while teachers write on the blackboard and use flash cards. This
was the kind of education that Luther Standing Bear found deadening and limiting.
*Courtesy Hood Museum of Art, Dartmouth College, Hanover, New Hampshire. Purchased through
the Robert J. Strasenburgh II 1942 Fund.*

colonialism, indigenous sovereignty, and nationhood as essential lines of
inquiry in attempting to better understand the Native American—and, therefore, the American—past and present. Students learn about Native American ways of living, organizing societies, and understanding the world; they
also learn about relationships with colonial power and the unique rights and
political aspirations of Indian peoples in the United States and Canada. Students explore the intersection of Indian and European histories and systems
of knowledge—so Native faculty at Dartmouth assign Locke, Rousseau, and
Foucault alongside tribal origin stories, the epic of the founding of the Iroquois League, and the writings of Vine Deloria, Jr.

Dartmouth's acquisition of the Mark Lansburgh collection of Plains Indian

The Occom Pond Singers, Dartmouth's powwow drum group, perform an honor song for President Jim Yong Kim at the inauguration of the College's seventeenth president, September 22, 2009. *Courtesy photographer Tom McNeill and the drummers.*

ledger drawings in 2007 illustrates how "Indian education" has changed since the College was founded. Over thirty years, Mark Lansburgh, class of 1949, brought together one of the largest and most diverse collections of nineteenth-century Native American drawings in private hands. Historically, Plains Indians warrior-artists depicted visual narratives of war and hunting on buffalo robes and tipis to publicly memorialize their heroic deeds. From the 1850s through the 1870s, however, American expansion transformed life on the Great Plains. Smallpox, cholera, and other alien diseases decimated Native populations, treaties lopped off huge chunks of Native American homelands, and commercial hunting, aided and abetted by a government campaign of systematic slaughter, virtually exterminated the buffalo herds that had constituted the foundation of Plains Indian economy and culture. Relocated to reservations, Native people were subjected to government programs of "civilization" that replaced hunting with farming, outlawed their dances and rituals, and took their children away to boarding schools. As a result of exposure to American settlers, soldiers, and government agents, Plains warrior-artists adopted new perspectives, themes, materials, and styles to portray their personal experiences, and developed a new and unique genre using bound ledger books and lined paper. The drawings provide Native alternatives to the many romanticized and ahistorical representations of Plains cultures. The Hood Museum of Art now holds more than 130 ledger drawings, making Dartmouth a resource for the study of Plains Indian art. Ledger drawings generate intellectual and cultural discussions that range far beyond the Great Plains in their implications and relevance. Dartmouth is no longer an institution that thinks it has nothing to learn from Indians or from its Native students.

In the first 200 years of Dartmouth College, about sixty Native students attended (see appendix 2). Since the College recommitted itself to honoring its founding pledge, more than 700 Native students from more than 160 tribes, from Abenaki to Zuni, have attended. In the first years of the twenty-first century, Dartmouth matriculated between thirty and forty Native students every year. In the fall of 2009, the number passed fifty; for the first time in Dartmouth's history, Native American students composed 5 percent of the entering class. Yet Native American students are not just statistics to show that Dartmouth is finally living up to its historic mission. They connect Dartmouth to Native worlds and worldviews that are lost to most of modern America, to tribal communities and concerns that seem far removed from a privileged Ivy League college, and to a constantly changing "Indian country" that exists in eastern cities and Alaska as well as on western reservations. Indian students are an essential resource in creating the kind of educational environment that Luther Standing Bear hoped for, and they have been a major influence in the evolution and growth of Native American Studies at Dartmouth.

Nevertheless, despite a more congenial and relevant curriculum, a generally improved social and political climate, and more educational and career opportunities than ever before, Dartmouth can still be a hard place to be Indian. What sustains Dartmouth's Native students through difficult times is . . . Dartmouth's Native students. Year after year, following Dartmouth's commencement ceremonies, Native graduates give personal testimonies acknowledging the support of friends and peers, and declare that they "would not have made it without NAD." Like their grandparents and great-grandparents who grouped together and built their own communities to combat the homesickness, austerity, and racism they confronted in boarding schools, so Native American students have built a community at Dartmouth. The people Wheelock intended to change at Dartmouth have helped to change Dartmouth and ensured that, at least in some respects, Dartmouth is, after all, an Indian school. In the young Native American men and women it attracts, educates, and graduates, perhaps Dartmouth finally does have a role and a place in the heart of Indian country, albeit one Eleazar Wheelock would neither recognize nor understand.

# Appendixes

The following lists of Indian students who attended Moor's Charity School and Dartmouth before the College recommitted itself to Indian education in 1970 are based on several previous compilations, supplemented and modified by research in the College archives, particularly the financial records for Moor's Charity School and the SSPCK. According to David McClure and Elijah Parish, 150 Indians attended Moor's Charity School during Eleazar Wheelock's lifetime.[1] If that figure is accurate, many have been lost in the records or escaped notice and remain anonymous. Compiling a full and accurate count of the Native students, discovering exactly when they arrived and departed, and even, in some cases, knowing which school they were in at a particular time is difficult, and at this point perhaps almost impossible. In some cases, there may be no more than a brief record of an expense for an Indian student — or a student who appears to be Indian — in the financial records of Moor's Charity School. These lists are the most complete yet, but given the uncertainties in the records, they should not be regarded as definitive or final, or even, in some cases, completely accurate.

1. David McClure and Elijah Parish, *Memoirs of the Rev. Eleazar Wheelock, D. D., Founder and President of Dartmouth College and Moor's Charity School; With a summary history of the College and School, to which are added copious extracts from Dr. Wheelock's Correspondence* (Newburyport, Mass.: Edward Little and Co., 1811), 64.

| Name | Tribal Affiliation | Year of Arrival or First Mention | Year of Departure or Last Mention | Comments |
|---|---|---|---|---|
| Samson Occom | Mohegan | 1743 | 1747 | |
| John Pumshire | Delaware | 1754 | 1756 | Went home ill |
| Jacob Woolley | Delaware | 1754 | 1759 | "[R]un away"; entered the College of New Jersey (Princeton) in 1759 |
| Samson Woyboy | Pequot | 1757 | | Left after 19 weeks because of "bodily infirmities of long standing" |
| Joseph Woolley | Delaware | 1757 | 1765 | Cousin of Jacob Woolley; went to teach at Onoquaga |
| Hezekiah Calvin | Delaware | 1757 | 1766 | Went to teach in Mohawk country; died of consumption (tuberculosis) |
| Joseph Johnson | Mohegan | 1758 | 1766 | Went to teach in Oneida country; married Occom's daughter; licensed to preach, at Dartmouth, 1774 |
| David Fowler | Montauk | 1759 | 1761 | Taught in Oneida, Mohawk, and Montauk country; married Hannah Garrett |
| Aaron Occom | Mohegan | 1760 | 1766 | Son of Samson; entered and left several times; died 1771 |

| Name | Tribal Affiliation | Year of Arrival or First Mention | Year of Departure or Last Mention | Comments |
|------|--------------------|----------------------------------|-----------------------------------|----------|
| Isaiah Uncas | Mohegan | 1760 | 1764 | "[P]resumptive chief of the Mohegans"; died 1773 |
| Amy Johnson | Mohegan | 1761 | 1764? | Sister of Joseph Johnson; "had left" by 1766 |
| Joseph Brant | Mohawk | 1761 | 1763 | Became prominent war chief and British ally in the Revolution |
| Negyes | Mohawk | 1761 | 1761 | Left after several months |
| Center | Mohawk | 1761 | 1761 | Died soon after leaving |
| Miriam Storrs | Delaware | 1761 | 1764 | |
| Moses | Mohawk | 1761 | 1766 | Assistant school teacher |
| Johannes | Mohawk | 1761 | 1765 | Assistant school teacher; interpreter |
| Sarah Wyog | Mohegan | 1762 | 1768 | "[M]uch dancing and Lude conduct;" "rusticated" (expelled) in 1764 but probably readmitted |
| Enoch Closs | Delaware | 1762 | 1765 | "Ran away" |
| Samuel Tallman | Delaware | 1762 | 1767 | |
| Abraham Major | Mohawk | 1762 | 1765 | Teacher to Mohawks |
| Abraham Minor | Mohawk | 1762 | 1765 | Teacher to Mohawks |
| Peter | Mohawk | 1762 | 1769 | Teacher to Mohawks |
| Patience Johnson | Mohegan | 1762 | 1764 | "[D]ismissed as incorrigible" |
| Samuel Ashpo | Mohegan | 1762 | 1763 | Entered at 44; left for teacher-missionary work |

| Name | Tribal Affiliation | Year of Arrival or First Mention | Year of Departure or Last Mention | Comments |
|---|---|---|---|---|
| Daniel Mossuck | Tunxis | 1762 | 1762 | Stayed only a few months; soldier in Revolution |
| Jacob Fowler | Montauk | 1762 | 1766 | Brother of David Fowler; pupil of Occom; tutor at the Charity School 1774–76 |
| Emmanuel Simon(s) | Narragansett | 1763 | 1763 | Asked to be readmitted in 1767 |
| Hannah Poquiantup | Niantic | 1763 | 1763 | Stayed only a few months; married John Matthews in 1789 |
| Hannah Garrett | Pequot resident with Narragansetts | 1763 | 1766 | Married David Fowler |
| Mary Secutor | Narragansett | 1763 | 1768 | Returned to school 1767 |
| William Major | Mohawk | 1764 | 1766 | Said to be "natural son" of Sir William Johnson |
| William Minor | Mohawk | 1764 | 1767 | |
| Elias | Mohawk | 1764 | 1769 | |
| Susannah | Mohawk | 1765 | 1767 | |
| Katharine | Mohawk | 1765 | 1767 | "Katherine & Mary went away Jan. 9, 1767" |
| Mary | Mohawk | 1765 | 1767 | Also known as Molly |
| David or Dawet | Oneida | 1765 | 1766 | Returned home |
| Mondius or Mundus | Oneida | 1765 | 1768 | Taken home due to illness; became school teacher at Oneida |
| Jacob | Oneida | 1765 | 1769 | Went home spring 1767; returned in the fall |

| Name | Tribal Affiliation | Year of Arrival or First Mention | Year of Departure or Last Mention | Comments |
|---|---|---|---|---|
| Sarah Simon(s) | Narragansett | 1765 | 1769 | |
| Charles Daniel | Narragansett | 1765 | 1767 | Father withdrew him |
| John Green | Mohawk | 1766 | 1767 | "Went home suppose Feb. 16, 1767" (Wheelock) |
| William | Oneida | 1766 | 1768 | Returned home with his sister Hannah, who had been "several Months in this school" in 1768 |
| Son of Tekawanda? | Seneca | 1766? | | The Seneca war chief, Tekawanda, promised in 1765 to send his adopted son to school the next year |
| Margaret | Mohawk | 1766 | 1767 | Went home Jan. 9, 1767 |
| Paulus | Mohawk | 1766 | 1767 | "[W]ent home in a few months;" "Went home suppose Jan 9, 1767" (Wheelock) |
| Seth | Mohawk | 1766 | 1767 | "Went home suppose Feb. 17, 1767" (Wheelock) |
| John Shattock | Narragansett | 1766 | 1767 | Died of consumption, 1770 |
| Toby or Tobias Shattock | Narragansett | 1766 | 1767 | Died of smallpox in Edinburgh, 1768 |
| Toby Shattock's wife and child | Narragansett | 1766 | 1767 | Mother worked at the school |
| Abigail | Narragansett | 1767 | 1767 | Also known as "Nabby" |
| Martha Rogers | Narragansett | 1767 | | |
| John Secuter | Narragansett | 1767 | | Brother of Mary |

| Name | Tribal Affiliation | Year of Arrival or First Mention | Year of Departure or Last Mention | Comments |
|------|-------------------|----------------------------------|-----------------------------------|----------|
| Hannah Nonsuch | Niantic or Narragansett | 1767 | 1768 | |
| Hannah (Hannah Hail) | Oneida | 1767 | 1769 | Taken out of school |
| Cornelius | Oneida | 1767 | 1769 | Taken out of school |
| Peter Minor or Little Peter | Oneida | 1767 | 1769 | Taken out of school |
| William Minor | Oneida | 1767 | 1768 | Died at school |
| James Simon(s) | Narragansett | 1767 | 1769 | Enlisted in Revolution 1775 |
| Apollos | Mohawk | 1767 | 1768 | Died at school |
| Nathan Clap | Mashpee or Nausett from Yarmouth, Cape Cod | 1767 | 1768 | "At school a short time and turned out badly"; "expelled July 9, 1768"; sent to the Oneidas |
| Jacob | Oneida | 1767 | | |
| John Matthews | Narragansett | 1767 | 1772 | Went to teach the Tuscaroras; married Hannah Poquiantup 1789 |
| Peter Major | Oneida | 1768 | 1769 | |
| William Sobuck | "Indian" | 1768 | | Large "x" placed next to his name |
| Joseph | Oneida | 1768 | | |
| James Niles | Narragansett | 1768 | | |

*1770 — Moor's Charity School moves from Lebanon, Connecticut, to Hanover, New Hampshire*

| Name | Tribal Affiliation | Year of Arrival or First Mention | Year of Departure or Last Mention | Comments |
|------|-------------------|----------------------------------|-----------------------------------|----------|
| Abraham Simon(s) | Narragansett | 1768 | 1776 | Moved with Wheelock to Hanover; in 1772, received "common wages of a schoolmaster after he begins to instruct a number of Indians" |

| Name | Tribal Affiliation | Year of Arrival or First Mention | Year of Departure or Last Mention | Comments |
|---|---|---|---|---|
| Daniel Simon(s) | Narragansett | 1768–69 | 1777 | Moved with Wheelock to Hanover, entered Dartmouth |
| Caleb Watts | | 1770 | 1775 | "[A] mulatto, though classed as an Indian" |
| Ebenezer Mitchell | | 1771 | | |
| John Konkapot | Stockbridge | 1771 | 1775 | Enlisted in army as John Stockbridge |
| Peter Pohquonnappeet | Stockbridge | 1771 | 1775 | Entered Dartmouth College |
| Samuel Squintup | Stockbridge | 1771 | 1774 | Enlisted in Revolution |
| Joseph Mecheekampauh | Stockbridge | 1771 | 1775 | |
| Paul Umpeethawe | "Indian" | 1772 | 1775 | |
| "Peter Indian" | | 1772 | | |
| "Indian Captive" | Mattagnessawack | 1772 | 1773 | Found near Penobscot by Ripley but does not seem to have come |
| "Indian Captive" | Natick | 1772 | 1773 | From St. Francis |
| John Phillips | Kahnawake | 1772 | 1780 | Son of a captive |
| Thomas Stacey | Kahnawake | 1772 | 1783 | "[S]on to Mr. Stacey, who was captivated from Ipswich" |
| Benjamin Towsey | Stockbridge | 1772 | 1775 | |
| Eneus/Eneas | "Indian" | 1772 | 1775 | From Canada; died 1776 |
| Lewis Vincent | Huron, Lorette | 1772 | 1781 | Brother of Sebastian; served as scout in the Revolution |
| Sebastian Vincent | Huron, Lorette | 1772 | 1775 | Also known as Basteen, brother of Lewis |

| Name | Tribal Affiliation | Year of Arrival or First Mention | Year of Departure or Last Mention | Comments |
|---|---|---|---|---|
| Andrew Indian | | 1773 | | |
| David Naunauneckenuck | Stockbridge | 1773 | | Enlisted in Revolution. |
| David Indian | | 1773 | | May refer to David Phillips or David Naunauneckenuck |
| Talbot or Tabot Phillips | Kahnawake | 1773 | 1780 | Son of a captive |
| John Popnahaunauk | Stockbridge | 1773 | 1776 | |
| James Mittamore | | 1773 | 1774 | "James Indian" enlisted 1775 |
| Stephen Jacob | | 1773 | 1775 | |
| John Sauk | Kahnawake | 1773 | 1780 | |
| Isaac Chauncy | | 1773 | 1776? | "Isaac Indian" |
| Mary Cachnawaga | Kahnawake | 1773 | 1774 | Mention of "Mary and her sisters" in 1774 |
| John Trohnehanewha | | 1773 | | |
| Abraham Tawhawpeat | Stockbridge? | 1773 | 1776? | "Abraham Indian" |
| Isaac Waunaupeat | | | 1776? | "Isaac Indian" |
| "Aaron, son of Harris" | Stockbridge | | | |
| Bill Nolauksin | | | | |
| Isaac Tribou | | 1774 | 1776 | From Canada |
| Benedict Gill | St. Francis | 1774 | 1777 | Withdrew |
| Anthony Gill | St. Francis | 1774 | 1777 | Withdrew |
| Francis Joseph Gill | St. Francis | 1774 | 1780 | Referred to as "Joseph Gill" |

| Name | Tribal Affiliation | Year of Arrival or First Mention | Year of Departure or Last Mention | Comments |
|------|--------------------|--------------------------------|----------------------------------|----------|
| Francis Gill II | St. Francis | 1774 | 1779 | Referred to as "Joseph Gill Junior" |
| Montuit Gill | St. Francis | 1775 | 1777 | Withdrew |
| Wesha/Wisha | | 1776 | 1776 | From Canada |
| John Baldwin/ Bolden | | 1778 | 1788 | "One of Wheelock's Indians in Captain Freeman's Company" |
| Jean Batiste | | 1779 | 1781 | |
| Joseph Brant, Jr. | Mohawk | 1800 | 1803 | } Sons of Joseph Brant |
| Jacob Brant | Mohawk | 1800 | 1803 | |
| Joseph Taukerman | St. Francis | 1803 | 1805 | |
| John Taubausanda | St. Francis | 1803 | 1804 | |
| Louis Annance | St. Francis | 1803 | 1809 | |
| Paul J. Gill | St. Francis | 1803 | 1810 | Went to Dartmouth but did not graduate |
| John Stanislaus | St. Francis | 1804 | 1807 | |
| Stanislaus Joseph (Gill?) | St. Francis | 1805 | 1808 | |
| William Gill | St. Francis | 1806 | 1809 | |
| Eleazar Williams | Kahnawake | 1807 | 1807 | |
| Vincent | Huron-Lorette | 1807 | | Son of Sebastian Vincent |
| Francis or Obean Noel Annance | St. Francis | 1809 | 1813 | Class of 1814; did not graduate |
| Ignatius | Algonquin | 1809 | 1813 | |
| Louis Langford | Kahnawake | 1810 | 1816 | Went to Canada 1815 |
| Simon Annance | St. Francis | 1815 | 1816 | Came and left a couple of times |
| Unknown, John? | From Saratoga | 1815 | | |

| Name | Tribal Affiliation | Year of Arrival or First Mention | Year of Departure or Last Mention | Comments |
|------|-------------------|-------|-------|----------|
| James Stevenson | Seneca | 1815 | 1817 | |
| Jacob Jameson | Seneca | 1815 | 1817 | |
| John Weal? | Stockbridge or St. Regis | 1815 | | |
| John Whalebone | Seneca | 1815 | 1816 | |
| John Alexander | | 1817 | | "An Indian Youth at the school" |
| Rev. Paul Pierre Osinikhirhine | St. Francis | 1822 | 1827 | |
| Peter Hooker Augustine | Oneida | 1826 | 1829 | |
| Peter Annance | St. Francis | 1826 | 1831 | To Kimball Union, 1830 |
| Joseph Alex Masta | St. Francis | 1827 | 1836 | Brother of John Batiste Masta |
| Joseph Williams | St. Francis | 1828 | 1830 | Sent home |
| James Joseph Annance | | 1829 | 1831 | |
| Cartnache Annance | St. Francis | 1830 | | son of Louis Annance |
| John Stanislaus, Sr. | St. Francis | 1832 | 1835 | Father of John Stanislaus, Jr. |
| John Stanislaus, Jr. | St. Francis | 1832 | 1846 or 1847 | Son of John Stanislaus, Sr., came at age 4 |
| Maris Bryant Pierce | Seneca | 1834 | 1836 | |
| Lewis Benedict | St. Francis | 1835 | 1847 | Started Moor's, 1844 |
| Jonathan Edwards Dwight | Choctaw | 1838 | 1839 | Left to teach "his countrymen" |
| John Batiste Masta | St. Francis | 1841 | 1846 | Went on to Dartmouth Medical School |

| Name | Tribal Affiliation | Year of Arrival or First Mention | Year of Departure or Last Mention | Comments |
|------|-------------------|-------------------------|--------------------------|----------|
| Archelaus Annance | St. Francis | 1841 | 1844 | Ran away |
| Jeremiah Slingerland | Stockbridge | 1841 | 1843 | Went on to seminary in Maine and missionary work. |
| Joseph P. Folsom | Choctaw | 1844 | 1850 | Entered Dartmouth College in 1851 |
| Elijah Tahamont | St. Francis | 1843 | 1848 | |
| Elijah Solon/ Tolon/Lolon | St. Francis | 1843 | | May be Tahamont |
| Simon B. James | Choctaw | 1845 | 1855 | Entered Dartmouth College in 1855 |
| Wallace King | Seneca | 1848 | 1849 | "A poor student" |
| John Tecumseh Henry | Ojibwa | 1849 | 1851 | Dismissed as "fickle and unstable" |
| James Ward | Cherokee | 1851 | 1852 | Killed in Civil War |
| Charles Stewart | Choctaw | 1852 | 1856 | |
| John Lawless | St. Francis | 1854 | 1856 | Dismissed because he "did not answer expectations"; seems to be last student at Moor's Charity School |

| Name | Tribal Affiliation | Year of Arrival or First Mention | Year of Departure or Last Mention | Comments |
|---|---|---|---|---|
| Daniel Simon | Narragansett | 1770 | 1777 | Only Indian students to graduate before 1800 |
| Peter Pohquonnappeet | Stockbridge | 1771 | 1780 | |
| Lewis Vincent | Huron | 1775 | 1781 | |
| Frances Joseph Gill/Annance | St. Francis | 1778 | 1783 | Did not graduate |
| Paul J. Gill | St. Francis | 1806 | 1808 | Did not graduate |
| Noel Annance | St. Francis | 1803 | 1813 | Did not graduate |
| Peter Hooker Augustine | Oneida | 1829 | 1830 (?) | Did not graduate |
| James Joseph Annance | St. Francis | 1831 | 1835 | |
| Louis Benedict | St. Francis | 1834 | | |
| Maris Bryant Pierce | Seneca | 1835 | 1840 | |
| John Batiste Masta | St. Francis | 1845 | 1850 | Half-brother of Peter Paul Osunkerhine; attended Dartmouth Medical School |
| Simon B. James | Choctaw | 1855 | 1856 | Attended Kimball Union Academy and the Agricultural College and left Dartmouth after freshman year; killed in Civil War |
| Joseph Pitchlynn Folsom | Choctaw | 1850 | 1854 | |
| Charles J. Stewart | Choctaw | 1852 | 1855 | Did not graduate; "not highly competent" |

| Name | Tribal Affiliation | Year of Arrival or First Mention | Year of Departure or Last Mention | Comments |
|------|-------------------|------|------|----------|
| James Ward | Cherokee | 1851/ 1852 | 1853 | Did not graduate; killed in Civil War |
| Jeremiah E. Foreman | Cherokee | 1857 | 1859 | Did not graduate |
| DeWitt(e) Clinton Duncan | Cherokee | 1857 | 1861 | |
| Albert Barnes | Cherokee | 1857 | 1861 | Chandler School |
| Edward W. Pierce | Seneca | 1863 | 1864 | Son of Maris B. Pierce; attended Thetford Academy, Chandler School; did not graduate from Dartmouth |
| Chester Lay | Seneca | 1863 | 1864 | Did one term of private instruction to prepare for Dartmouth but returned home instead; funded by SSPCK |
| Daniel Twoguns | Seneca | 1863 | 1864 | Did one term of private instruction to prepare for Dartmouth but did not attend; funded by SSPCK |
| Charles Alfred Carson | | 1868 | 1872 | Alumni file and classmates refer to his "Indian ancestry" and "my Indian classmate" |
| Robert Hawthorn | Blackfoot | 1870 | 1874 | |
| Albert Carney | Choctaw | 1871 | 1873 | Previously attended the Agricultural College and Kimball Union Academy; did not graduate from Dartmouth |

| Name | Tribal Affiliation | Year of Arrival or First Mention | Year of Departure or Last Mention | Comments |
|---|---|---|---|---|
| Rollin K. Adair | Cherokee | 1876 | 1877 | Attended Agriculture College |
| Walter Howard Luckadoe | Cherokee | 1876 | 1881 | Attended Agriculture College, left for Kimball Union Academy; entered Dartmouth in 1880 but was dropped from SSPCK funding in 1881 |
| Harvey Wirt Courtland Shelton | Cherokee | 1883 | 1886 | Attended Kimball Union Academy and Agriculture College but did not graduate from Dartmouth |
| Cornelius (Ellis) Alberty | Cherokee | 1883 | 1885 | Attended Kimball Union Academy; did not graduate from Dartmouth |
| Charles Alexander Eastman | Dakota Sioux | 1883 | 1887 | |
| _____? Miles | Unspecified, from Indian Territory | 1885 | 1888 | Wanted to study medicine |
| Alonzo Mitchell | Cherokee | 1886 | | Attended Agriculture College |
| Charles A. Hoffman | Santa Agency | 1890 | 1893 | All four attended Kimball Union Academy with funding provided by Dartmouth but did not attend Dartmouth |
| Charles Whistler | | 1890 | 1893 | |
| Zachariah T. Carnell | Choctaw | 1891 | 1893 | |
| George H. Hughes | Choctaw | 1892 | 1893 | |
| Archibald Smamon Isaac(s) | Snohomish | 1896 | 1897 | Did not graduate |

| Name | Tribal Affiliation | Year of Arrival or First Mention | Year of Departure or Last Mention | Comments |
|---|---|---|---|---|
| Henry L. Hamilton | Penobscot-Passamaquoddy | 1900 | 1901 | Did not graduate |
| Horace A. Nelson | Penobscot | 1901 | 1903 | Did not graduate |
| John Tortes Meyers | Cahuila | 1905 | 1906 | Did not graduate |
| Victor H. Johnson | Lummi | 1906 | 1909 | Did not graduate |
| Alvis Kusic | Tuscarora | 1908 | 1909 | Did not graduate; received A.B. from Whitworth in 1917 |
| John H. Pierce | Iroquois | | 1910 | |
| David Hogan Markham | Cherokee | 1911 | 1915 | |
| Angus Splicer | Mohawk | 1912 | 1914 | Transferred to McGill in 1915; killed in World War I in 1916 |
| Henry Wateo | "Indian student" | 1912 | 1915 | |
| John S. Martinez | Monte Vista, Calif. | 1913 | 1917 | Did not graduate |
| Bertram Bluesky | Seneca | 1914 | 1915 | Did not graduate |
| Simon Ralph Walkingstick | Cherokee | 1914 | 1917 | Did not graduate; left during World War I |
| Francis P.H. Frazier | Sioux | 1916 | 1917 | Did not graduate; received A.B. from Oberlin in 1922 |
| Frell McDonald Owl | Cherokee | 1923 | 1927 | |
| Russell O. Ayers | Cherokee | 1925 | 1927 | Did not graduate |
| Benedict Edward Hardman | Yankton Sioux | 1927 | 1931 | |
| Roland Burnett Sundown | Iroquois | 1928 | 1932 | |

| Name | Tribal Affiliation | Year of Arrival or First Mention | Year of Departure or Last Mention | Comments |
|---|---|---|---|---|
| Louis A. Poitras | Cheyenne River Sioux | 1929 | 1930 | Did not graduate |
| Alexander A. Sapiel | Penobscot | 1934 | 1936 | Did not graduate |
| John E. Snyder | Seneca | 1932 | 1935 | Did not graduate |
| Everett E. White | Mohawk | 1933 | 1938 | Class of 1937; remained an extra year |
| John Francis Imo | Seneca | 1936 | 1940 | Did not graduate |
| Rudolph T. Lorraine | Mohawk | 1942 | 1943 | Did not graduate |
| Henry Gabriel Perley (aka Henry P. Eagle) | Penobscot | 1939 | 1943/ 1946 | Studies interrupted by World War II |
| Albert A. Exendine, Jr. | | 1939 | 1943/ 1946 | Studies interrupted by World War II |
| William John Cook | Mohawk | 1946 | 1949 | |
| Joseph H. Jacobs | Abenaki from Kahnawake | 1946 | 1947 | Did not graduate |
| William P. Yellowtail | Crow | 1965 | 1971 | |
| Brian Maracle | Mohawk | 1965 | 1969 | |
| Gregory Dale Turgeon | | 1965 | | Did not graduate |
| Harry James Buckanaga | Sioux | 1966 | 1970 | |
| Duane Bird Bear | Mandan-Hidatsa | 1967 | 1971 | |
| Richard Buckanaga | Sioux | 1968 | 1972 | Did not graduate |
| John W. "Jack" Manning | Fort Peck Sioux | 1968 | 1972 | |

| Name | Tribal Affiliation | Year of Arrival or First Mention | Year of Departure or Last Mention | Comments |
|---|---|---|---|---|
| Howard Bad Hand | Lakota | 1969 | 1973 | |
| Travis Kinsley | Hopi-Tohono O'odham | 1969 | 1973 | |
| Michael Hanitchak | Choctaw-Chickasaw | 1969 | 1974 | |

# NOTES

Unless otherwise noted, manuscript citations in the notes refer to holdings in Dartmouth's Rauner Library.

## Introduction

1. "A Proposal for Introducing Religion Learning, Agriculture, and Manufacture among the Pagans of America," Ms. 763427.2.

2. *Narrative of the Captivity of Mrs. Johnson*, various eds., quoted in Colin G. Calloway, ed., *Dawnland Encounters: Indians and Europeans in Northern New England* (Hanover, N.H.: University Press of New England, 1991), 200.

3. Luther Standing Bear, *Land of the Spotted Eagle* (1933; reprint, Lincoln: University of Nebraska Press, 1978), xxvii.

4. Nathan Lord to John Tawse, May 9, 1853, SSPCK Records, folder 1-5.

5. Laura J. Murray, ed., *To Do Good to My Indian Brethren: The Writings of Joseph Johnson, 1751–1776* (Amherst: University of Massachusetts Press, 1998), 247.

6. Russell Ayers to Charley [Dudley], Aug. 24, 1974, Russell Ayers, Alumni file, 1929.

7. Bill Bray (now Lonefight), "Refuse to Kneel," in Andrew Garrod and Colleen Larimore, eds., *First Person, First Peoples: Native American College Graduates Tell Their Life Stories* (Ithaca, N.Y.: Cornell University Press, 1997), 53.

8. Philip J. Deloria, *Indians in Unexpected Places* (Lawrence: University Press of Kansas, 2004).

9. Joanna Brooks, ed., *The Collected Writings of Samson Occom, Mohegan: Leadership and Literacy in Eighteenth-century Native America* (New York: Oxford University Press, 2006), 5; Bernd C. Peyer, *The Tutor'd Mind: Indian Missionary-writers in Antebellum America* (Amherst: University of Massachusetts Press, 1997), 101.

10. Brooks, *Collected Writings of Samson Occom*, 58, 104.

11. James Axtell, "The Power of Print in the Eastern Woodlands," in Axtell, *After Columbus: Essays in the Ethnohistory of Colonial North America* (New York: Oxford University Press, 1988), 86–99; Hilary E. Wyss, *Writing Indians: Literacy, Christianity, and Native Community in Early America* (Amherst: University of Massachusetts Press, 2000).

## Chapter 1

1. Jere R. Daniell, "Eleazar Wheelock and the Dartmouth College Charter," *Historical New Hampshire* 24 (Winter 1969), 3–44.

2. Francis Jennings, *The Invasion of America: Indians, Colonialism, and the Cant of Conquest* (New York: Norton, 1976), 53–56, 242–43, 362.

3. David McClure and Elijah Parish, *Memoirs of the Rev. Eleazar Wheelock, D.D., Founder and President of Dartmouth College and Moor's Charity School; With a summary history of the College and School, to which are added copious extracts from Dr. Wheelock's Correspondence* (Newburyport, Mass.: Edward Little and Co., 1811), quotation at 11.

4. Dick Hoefnagel, with the collaboration of Virginia L. Close, *Eleazar Wheelock and the Adventurous Founding of Dartmouth College* (Hanover, N.H.: Hanover Historical Society/Durand Press, 2002).

5. Wheelock to Whitefield, Mar. 1, 1756, Ms. 756201.

6. McClure and Parish, *Memoirs of the Rev. Eleazar Wheelock*, 259, 263.

7. Wheelock to Nathaniel Whitaker, Dec. 21, 1766, in Leon Burr Richardson, ed., *An Indian Preacher in England: Being Letters and Diaries Relating to the Mission of the Reverend Samson Occom and the Reverend Nathaniel Whitaker to Collect Funds in England for the benefit of Eleazar Wheelock's Indian Charity School, from which grew Dartmouth College* (Hanover, N.H.: Dartmouth College Publications, 1933), 193.

8. Eleazar Wheelock, *A Plain and Faithful Narrative of the Original Design, Rise, Progress and Present State of the Indian Charity-School at Lebanon in Connecticut* (Boston: Richard and Samuel Draper, 1763), 14. This is the first in a series of nine publications promoting Wheelock's efforts (1763–75), the first seven written by Wheelock and the last two by Rev. Nathaniel Whitaker; all except the first are titled *A Continuation of the Narrative of the Indian Charity School.*

9. Wheelock to Whitefield, Mar. 1, 1756, Ms. 756201; Wheelock, *Plain and Faithful Narrative* (1763), 16–17.

10. Wheelock, *Plain and Faithful Narrative* (1763), 11.

11. James McCallum, *Eleazar Wheelock, Founder of Dartmouth College* (Hanover, N.H.: Dartmouth College Publications, 1939), 75; Wheelock to Earl of Dartmouth, Sept. 4, 1776, Ms. 766504.4; also in Richardson, *Indian Preacher in England*, 163.

12. Margaret Connell Szasz, *Indian Education in the American Colonies, 1607–1783* (Albuquerque: University of New Mexico Press, 1988).

13. *Mamusse wunneetupanatamwe Up-Biblum God naneeswe Nukkone Testament kah wonk Wusku Testament: Ne quoshkinnumuk nashpe wuttinneumoh Christ noh asoowesit John Eliot* (Cambridge, Mass.: Printeuoop nashpe Samuel Green kah Marmaduke Johnson, 1661–63), Rauner Library, Dartmouth College.

14. Alden T. Vaughan, *New England Frontier: Puritans and Indians 1620–1675*, rev. ed. (New York: Norton, 1979), 281–84.

15. Daniel Gookin, *Historical Collections of the Indians in New England*, Collections of the Massachusetts Historical Society 1 (1792; reprint, Towtaid, N.J., 1970), 87.

16. David J. Silverman, *Faith and Boundaries: Colonists, Christianity, and Community among the Wampanoag Indians of Martha's Vineyard, 1600–1871* (Cambridge: Cambridge University Press, 2005).

17. Patrick Frazier, *The Mohicans of Stockbridge* (Lincoln: University of Nebraska Press, 1992); Rachel Wheeler, *To Live upon Hope: Mohicans and Missionaries in the Eighteenth-century Northeast* (Ithaca, N.Y.: Cornell University Press, 2008).

18. Hoefnagel, *Eleazar Wheelock and the Adventurous Founding*, 10.

19. Michael Leroy Oberg, *Uncas, First of the Mohegans* (Ithaca, N.Y.: Cornell University Press, 2003).

20. Occom wrote the first draft of his narrative in Boston as he was waiting to sail to England on his fund-raising tour; he wrote the longer version in response to questions raised about his identity as a recently converted Mohegan. Samson Occom, *A Short Narrative of My Life* (1768), manuscript and typescript in Rauner Library; Joanna Brooks, ed., *The Collected Writings of Samson Occom, Mohegan* (New York: Oxford University Press, 2006), 32, 42–43, 51–54.

21. Brooks, *Collected Writings of Samson Occom*, 13–14.

22. W. DeLoss Love, *Samson Occom and the Christian Indians of New England* (1899; reprint, Syracuse, N.Y.: Syracuse University Press, 2000), quotation at 37; Bernd Peyer, "The Betrayal of Samson Occom," *Dartmouth Alumni Magazine* 91 (Nov. 1998), 32; Lisa Brooks, *The Common Pot: The Recovery of Native Space in the Northeast* (Minneapolis: University of Minnesota Press, 2008), 84–86.

23. Franklin B. Dexter, ed., *Diary of David McClure, 1748–1820* (New York: Knickerbocker Press, 1899), 192.

24. Wheelock to unknown, 1756, Ms. 756900.1, quoted in Hoefnagel, *Eleazar Wheelock and the Adventurous Founding*, 17.

25. Brainerd to Wheelock, Mar. 23, 1757, in James Dow McCallum, ed., *The Letters of Eleazar Wheelock's Indians* (Hanover, N.H.: Dartmouth College Publications, 1932), 29–31; Wheelock to Whitefield, quoted in Hoefnagel, *Eleazar Wheelock and the Adventurous Founding*, 19.

26. Wheelock, *Plain and Faithful Narrative* (1763), 30; Brooks, *Common Pot*, 231. John Pumpshire interpreted at the treaties held at Easton, Pennsylvania, in 1756 and 1757: Susan Kalter, ed., *Benjamin Franklin, Pennsylvania, and the First Nations: The Treaties of 173–62* (Urbana: University of Illinois Press, 2006), 187, 199, 256, 258, 260, 263, 266, 269, 272, 277, 280, 282, 286.

27. Wheelock, *Plain and Faithful Narrative* (1763), 30–31; McCallum, *Eleazar Wheelock*, 83; Wheelock to Wm. Hyslop, Dec. 1, 1760, National Archives of Scotland, Edinburgh, GD95/12/2.

28. Frederick Chase, *A History of Dartmouth College and the Town of Hanover, New Hampshire*, ed. John K. Lord, 2 vols. (Vol. 1: Cambridge, Mass.: John Wilson and Sons, 1891), 17; Wheelock to Hyslop, Dec. 1, 1760, National Archives of Scotland, GD95/12/2.

29. Chase, *History of Dartmouth College*, 1:15.

30. McCallum, *Eleazar Wheelock*, 109–10; McClure and Parish, *Memoirs of the Rev. Eleazar Wheelock*, 64; Hoefnagel, *Eleazar Wheelock and the Adventurous Founding*, 20, 23–24; Moor's deed of Indenture, July 17, 1755 Ms. 755417.2.

31. Hoefnagel, *Eleazar Wheelock and the Adventurous Founding*, 24–25; Wheelock to Johnson, Dec. 11, 1761, June 27, 1762, in James Sullivan et al., eds., *The Papers of Sir William Johnson*, 15 vols. (Albany: State University of New York, 1921–65), 10:345, 469; Wheelock to Brainerd, Nov. 6, 1761, Ms. 761606.1; McClure and Parish, *Memoirs of the Rev. Eleazar Wheelock*, 19 (accomplishments adapted to their sex). On Indian women at Moor's Charity School, see Szasz, *Indian Education in the American Colonies*, chap. 9; on

hierarchy, see Stacy L. S. Hogsett, "'The Tawnee Family': The Life Course of Value Adaptation for Eleazar Wheelock's Indian Scholars," Ph.D. diss., University of New Hampshire, 1998.

32. Laura J. Murray, ed., *To Do Good to My Indian Brethren: The Writings of Joseph Johnson, 1751–1776* (Amherst: University of Massachusetts Press, 1998), 54.

33. On Johnson, see Fintan O'Toole, *White Savage: William Johnson and the Invention of America* (New York: Farrar, Straus, and Giroux, 2005).

34. Sullivan et al., *Papers of Sir William Johnson* 9:480; 10:271, 272–74, 279–80, 309, 313–14, 344–45, 468–70; E. B. O'Callaghan, ed., *The Documentary History of the State of New-York*, 4 vols. (Albany: Public Printers, 1850–51), 4:197 (Johnson's mite).

35. James Axtell, "Dr. Wheelock's Little Red School," in Axtell, *The European and the Indian: Essays in the Ethnohistory of Colonial North America* (New York: Oxford University Press, 1981), 94; Wheelock, *Plain and Faithful Narrative* (1763), 40–42; Wheelock to Johnson, June 27, 1762, July 5, 1763, Apr. 17, 1764, Aug. 25, 1764, in Sullivan et al., *Papers of Sir William Johnson* 10:470, 729; 11:134, 339 ("as remote as may be"); Wheelock to Johnson, Aug 20, 1762, and Jan 20, 1763, Ms. 762470 and Ms. 763120.2.

36. Dexter, *Diary of David McClure*, 6–7.

37. McCallum, *Letters of Eleazar Wheelock's Indian Students*, 76–77.

38. "List of private persons & their donations for Wheelock's charity school," June 1763, ledger B, Moor's Indian Charity School Records, box 4, 26.

39. Wheelock to Oliver, Dec. 17, 1762, Ms. 762667.2; Wheelock to Wentworth, Oct. 29, 1764, Ms.764579.3, quoted in Hoefnagel, *Eleazar Wheelock and the Adventurous Founding*, 29; Chase, *History of Dartmouth College*, 1:37–38.

40. *An Account of the Society in Scotland for Propagating Christian Knowledge, from Its Commencement in 1709* (Edinburgh: A. Murray and J. Cochrane, 1774), 4; *An Account of the Funds, Expenditure, and General Management of the Affairs of the Society in Scotland for Propagating Christian Knowledge* (Edinburgh: J. Paterson, 1796), 8–9, 27–29, 50–51, 56–64; "The Highlands and Islands Education Trust: Historical Report," typescript, Rauner Library. For a full discussion of the work of the SSPCK, in both the Highlands and America, see Margaret Connell Szasz, *Scottish Highlanders and Native Americans: Indigenous Education in the Eighteenth-century Atlantic World* (Norman: University of Oklahoma Press, 2007), and Donald E. Meek, "Scottish Highlanders, North American Indians and the SSPCK: Some Cultural Perspectives," *Records of the Scottish Church History Society* 23 (1989), 378–96.

41. *Account of the Society in Scotland for Propagating Christian Knowledge*, 13–17; Meek, "Scottish Highlanders, North American Indians and the SSPCK," 378–96; Frederick V. Mills, "The Society in Scotland for Propagating Christian Knowledge in British North America, 1730–1775," *Church History* 63 (1994), 15–30.

42. *Account of the Funds, Expenditure, and General Management*, 27–29.

43. Hilary E. Wyss, "Writing Back to Wheelock: One Young Woman's Response to Colonial Christianity," in Kristina Bross and Hilary E. Wyss, eds., *Early Native Literacies in New England: A Documentary and Critical Anthology* (Amherst: University of Massachusetts Press, 2008), quotation at 99.

44. Confessions of Hannah Nonesuch and Mary Secutor, Mar. 11, 1768, Ms 768211.1-2; the girls' confessions are also in McCallum, *Letters of Eleazar Wheelock's Indians*, 232–33, 236–38 (McCallum identifies Hannah as Mohegan); Tammy Schneider, "'This Once Savage Heart of Mine': Joseph Johnson, Wheelock's 'Indians,' and the Construction of a Christian Indian Identity, 1764–1776," in *Reinterpreting New England Indians and the Colonial Experience*, ed. Colin G. Calloway and Neal Salisbury (Boston: Colonial Society of Massachusetts, 2003), 232–63

45. Letter of recommendation, July 29, 1768, Ms. 768429.1.

46. Jacob Woolley's Confession, and Woolley to Wheelock, Apr.9, 1763, in McCallum, *Letters of Eleazar Wheelock's Indians*, 254, 265; Fowler to Wheelock, May 2, 1765 (gold ring), ibid., 88; Nathan Clap to Wheelock, June 28, 1768; Kirkland to Wheelock, Dec. 29,1768, ibid., 68–69, 140.

47. Wheelock, *Plain and Faithful Narrative* (1763), 44 ("great fondness"); Wheelock to Oliver, 17 Dec. 1762, Ms. 762667.2 ("correct & punish"); Axtell, "Dr. Wheelock's Little Red School," 100.

48. McClure and Parish, *Memoirs of the Rev. Eleazar Wheelock*, 32–33.

49. Wheelock to Johnson, May 16, 1763, in O'Callaghan, *Documentary History of the State of New-York*, 4: 211.

50. Daniel to Wheelock, Nov. 30, 1767, Ms. 767630.3, also quoted in Hoefnagel, *Eleazar Wheelock and the Adventurous Founding*, 23.

51. William S. Simmons and Cheryl L. Simmons, eds., *Old Light on Separate Ways: The Narragansett Diary of Joseph Fish, 1765–1776* (Hanover, N.H.: University Press of New England, 1982).

52. Sarah Simon to Wheelock, Oct. 12, 1767, Ms. 767562.4; McCallum, *Letters of Eleazar Wheelock's Indians*, 220–21.

53. McClure and Parish, *Memoirs of the Rev. Eleazar Wheelock*, 19; Wheelock, *Plain and Faithful Narrative* (1763), 20–21.

54. Wheelock to Sarah Symons, June 27, 1768, Ms. 768377.2.

55. Sarah Simon to Wheelock, Apr. 4, 1769, Ms. 769254.1; McCallum, *Letters of Eleazar Wheelock's Indians*, 227. For the similar experiences of Indian parents and students at American boarding schools in the twentieth century, see Brenda J. Child, *Boarding School Seasons: American Indian Families, 1900–1940* (Lincoln: University of Nebraska Press, 1998).

56. The five children Sarah sent to Wheelock were Emmanuel, Sarah, James, Abraham, and Daniel. McCallum, *Letters of Eleazar Wheelock's Indians*, 219.


## Chapter 2

1. David McClure and Elijah Parish, *Memoirs of the Rev. Eleazar Wheelock, D.D., Founder and President of Dartmouth College and Moor's Charity School; with a summary history of the College and School, to which are added copious extracts from Dr. Wheelock's Correspondence* (Newburyport, Mass.: Edward Little and Co., 1811), 212.

2. Ms. 763427.2; Wheelock to Amherst, Apr. 2, 1763, and Amherst to Wheelock, May 23, 1763, in E. B. O'Callaghan, ed., *The Documentary History of the State of New-York*, 4 vols. (Albany: Public Printers, 1850–51), 4:210, 212. The proposal is also quoted in Dick Hoefnagel, with the collaboration of Virginia L. Close, *Eleazar Wheelock and the Adventurous Founding of Dartmouth College* (Hanover, N.H.: Hanover Historical Society/Durand Press, 2002), 34, and in Frederick Chase, *A History of Dartmouth College and the Town of Hanover, New Hampshire*, ed. John K. Lord, 2 vols. (Vol. 1, Cambridge, Mass.: John Wilson and Son, 1891), 1:32–33.

3. McClure and Parish, *Memoirs of the Rev. Eleazar Wheelock*, 223–24; Smith to Wheelock, Mar. 30, 1764, Ms. 764230, and in Leon Burr Richardson, ed., *An Indian Preacher in England: Being Letters and Diaries Relating to the Mission of the Reverend Samson Occom and the Reverend Nathaniel Whitaker to Collect Funds in England for the Benefit of Eleazar Wheelock's Indian Charity School, from which grew Dartmouth College* (Hanover, N.H.: Dartmouth College Publications, 1933), 20.

4. Joanna Brooks, ed., *The Collected Writings of Samson Occom, Mohegan* (New York: Oxford University Press, 2006), 266–67.

5. Brooks, *Collected Writings of Samson Occom*, 270.

6. Alden T. Vaughan, *Transatlantic Encounters: American Indians in Britain, 1500–1776* (Cambridge: Cambridge University Press, 2006).

7. Brooks, *Collected Writings of Samson Occom*, 86.

8. Rev. Peter Jillard to Wheelock, Mar. 2, 1767, in Richardson, *Indian Preacher in England*, 227.

9. Margaret Connell Szasz, "Samson Occom: Mohegan as Spiritual Intermediary," in Szasz, ed., *Between Indian and White Worlds: The Cultural Broker* (Norman: University of Oklahoma Press, 1994), 69. The terms of the English trust and a list of the English subscribers are provided in Eleazar Wheelock, *Continuation of the Narrative of the Indian Charity School* (London, 1769), 75–84, and 85–128.

10. Samson Occom to Wheelock, Feb. 12, 1767, Ms. 767162.2; Mary Occom to Wheelock, July 15, 1767, Ms. 767415; Wheelock, *Continuation of the Narrative* (London, 1769), 129.

11. Chase, *History of Dartmouth College*, 1: chap. 2.

12. Whitaker to Wheelock, Mar. 7, 1767, Ms. 767207, and quoted in Hoefnagel, *Eleazar Wheelock and the Adventurous Founding*, 36.

13. Colin G. Calloway, *The Scratch of a Pen: 1763 and the Transformation of North America* (New York: Oxford University Press, 2006), 53–55; Julian P. Boyd, ed., *The Susquehannah Company Papers*, 11 vols. (Ithaca, N.Y.: Cornell University Press for the Wyoming Historical and Genealogical Society, 1962), vol. 2, especially 158–59, 175 (Johnson to Wheelock quotation), 313, 317; Wheelock to Johnson, Apr. 30, 1762, in James Sullivan et al., eds., *The Papers of Sir William Johnson*, 15 vols. (Albany: State University of New York, 1921–65), 10:441 ("better sort of people"); Hawley to Wheelock, Sept. 19, 1761, Ms. 761519.

14. Sullivan et al., *Papers of Sir William Johnson*, 6:472, 492, 530, 543; 12:657, 748–50, 919–20.

15. Atkinson quoted in Hoefnagel, *Eleazar Wheelock and the Adventurous Founding*, 37; Colin G. Calloway, *The Western Abenakis of Vermont, 1600–1800: War, Migration, and the Survival of an Indian People* (Norman: University of Oklahoma Press, 1990), 11.

16. Colin G. Calloway, ed., *Dawnland Encounters: Indians and Europeans in Northern New England* (Hanover, N.H.: University Press of New England, 1991), 123–24.

17. Calloway, *Western Abenakis of Vermont*, 183–86; Cohos quotation in Wheelock's commission for Cleaveland and Wright, July 20, 1768, Ms. 768667.1, quoted in Hoefnagel, *Eleazar Wheelock and the Adventurous Founding*, 37.

18. Johnson to Wheelock, Aug. 8, 1765, Ms. 765458.1 and 765458.2.

19. Eleazar Wheelock, *Continuation of the Narrative of the Indian Charity School* (London, 1771), 27.

20. Ms. 769213.3, 769213.6, 769253.1, 770900.4–6; Chase, *History of Dartmouth College*, 1:126.

21. The full text of the charter can be found at www.dartmouth.edu/~govdocs/case/charter.htm.

22. Jere R. Daniell, "Eleazar Wheelock and the Dartmouth College Charter," *Historical New Hampshire* 24 (winter 1969), 3–44; James Axtell, "Dr. Wheelock's Little Red School," in Axtell, *The European and the Indian: Essays in the Ethnohistory of Colonial North America* (New York: Oxford University Press, 1981), 108.

23. *Petition of the Society in Scotland for Propagating Christian Knowledge to Settle Scheme for Application of Trust-Fund* (Edinburgh: T. and A. Constable, 1922), 3.

24. Quoted in Chase, *History of Dartmouth College*, 1:155.

25. Wheelock to Johnson, May 31, 1768, in Sullivan et al., *Papers of Sir William Johnson*, 6:236; McCallum, *Letters of Eleazar Wheelock's Indian Students*, 232; Wheelock, *Continuation of the Narrative* (London, 1769), 70; Wheelock to Secretary Keen, Apr. 5, 1769, Ms. 769255.

26. Wheelock to Robert Keen, May 31, 1768, in Richardson, *An Indian Preacher in England*, 339.

27. Sullivan et al., *Papers of Sir William Johnson*, 6:455–58 ("bigots" and "Cubs"), 472–73, 491–93, 528–30, 542–44; 7:749; 12:349–50, 598–99, 748–50.

28. Hoefnagel, *Eleazar Wheelock and the Adventurous Founding*, 96–99; Wheelock to the English Trust, Oct. 8, 1767, Ms. 767558.1; Wheelock to Whitaker, Nov. 28, 1767, Ms. 767628.1, and in Richardson, *An Indian Preacher in England*, 321. Ralph Wheelock's journal of his mission to Iroquois country in 1768 is in Wheelock, *Continuation of the Narrative of the Indian Charity School* (London, 1769), 44–54.

29. Hoefnagel, *Eleazar Wheelock and the Adventurous Founding*, 46–48.

30. Franklin B. Dexter, ed., *The Diary of David McClure, 1784–1820* (New York: Knickerbocker Press, 1999), v, 23, 143.

31. Bryant F. Tolles, Jr., "The Evolution of a Campus: Dartmouth College Architecture before 1860," *Historical New Hampshire* 42 (1987), 329–82; Chase, *History of Dartmouth College*, 1:236; Leon Burr Richardson, *History of Dartmouth College*, 2 vols. (Hanover, N.H.: Dartmouth College Publications, 1932), 1:118.

32. "A Catalogue of the members of Dartmouth College & Mores School," Mar. 1,

1771, Ms. 771190, lists five Indians "on charity": Abraham and Daniel Simon, Samuel Squintup, Caleb Watt, and Ebenezer Mitchell. "A catalogue of the students in Dartmouth College and School," 1772, McClure Ms. 772900.3, lists Simons and Watts, Peter Pohquonnappeet, and two other Stockbridge Indians as "miscellaneous scholars," preparing for college. John Konkapot of Stockbridge is also listed at this time. Brooks, *Collected Writings of Samson Occom*, 99n70.

33. Chase, *A History of Dartmouth College*, 1:230–32; Dexter, *Diary of David McClure*, 24.

34. David Towsey to Wheelock, Dec. 17, 1771, Ms. 771667; Wheelock to David Towson [*sic*], Jan. 12, 1772, Ms. 77212.2.

35. Bernd Peyer, "The Betrayal of Samson Occom," *Dartmouth Alumni Magazine* 91 (Nov. 1998), 36. Compare Wheelock's statements eight years earlier: Eleazar Wheelock, *A Plain and Faithful Narrative of the Original Design, Rise, Progress and Present State of the Indian Charity School at Lebanon, Connecticut* (Boston: Richard and Samuel Draper, 1763), 16–17.

36. Harold Blodgett, *Samson Occom, The Biography of an Indian Preacher* (Hanover, N.H.: Dartmouth Publications, 1935), 116–17.

37. Wheelock to Occom, Jan. 22, 1771, Ms. 771122; Occom to Wheelock, July 24, 1774, Ms. 771424; also in Brooks, *Collected Writings of Samson Occom*, 98–100.

38. Wheelock to Occom, Feb. 24, 1772, Ms. 772174.1; Richardson, *History of Dartmouth College*, 1:122–23 ("primarily designed for them").

39. Occom to Wheelock, June 1, 1773, Ms. 773351; Wheelock to Occom, July 21, 1773, Ms. 773421; Peyer, "Betrayal of Samson Occom," 36.

40. Chase, *A History of Dartmouth College*, 1:244–48.

41. James Dow McCallum, ed., *The Letters of Eleazar Wheelock's Indians* (Hanover, N.H.: Dartmouth College Publications, 1932), 221.

42. Daniel Simond [*sic*] et al. to Wheelock, Feb. 16, 1773, Ms. 773166; McCallum, *Letters of Eleazar Wheelock's Indians*, 222.

43. The meetings with the Oneidas and Onondagas are in Ms. 772174.2 and Ms. 772331, and in McCallum, *Letters of Eleazar Wheelock's Indians*, 276–88.

44. Chase, *History of Dartmouth College*, 1:309.

45. Dexter, *Diary of David McClure*, 26–27, 142.

46. Dexter, *Diary of David McClure*, 62–64.

47. Dexter, *Diary of David McClure*, 80–81. Red Jacket's speech is in Peter Nabokov, ed., *Native American Testimony: A Chronicle of Indian-White Relations from Prophecy to the Present, 1492–2000* (New York: Penguin, 1991), 57–58.

48. Dexter, *Diary of David McClure*, 83. McClure was not the only Presbyterian missionary in this period to receive a polite but firm refusal from the Delaware council, many of whom leaned toward the Moravians: C. A. Weslager, *The Delaware Indians: A History* (New Brunswick, N.J.: Rutgers University Press, 1972), 293–94.

49. Dexter, *Diary of David McClure*, 109, 122–23, 142. From Fort Pitt, McClure sent Wheelock an account of his two-week stay in a Delaware village on the Muskingum; Mac Cluer to Wheelock, Oct. 26, 1772, Ms. 772576.

50. Dexter, *Diary of David McClure*, 143; Tolles, "Evolution of a Campus," 338–39; Richardson, *History of Dartmouth College*, 1:131.

51. Dexter, *Diary of David McClure*, 176.

52. John Demos, *The Unredeemed Captive: A Family Story from Early America* (New York: Knopf, 1994); Evan Haefeli and Kevin Sweeney, *Captors and Captives: The 1704 French and Indian Raid on Deerfield* (Amherst: University of Massachusetts Press, 2003).

53. Dexter, *Diary of David McClure*, 88. Crèvecoeur said that Indian society exerted an "imperceptible charm" on white people and that there was something "singularly captivating" in their social bond. Hector St. John de Crèvecoeur, *Letters from an American Farmer*, ed. Warren Barton Blake (London: J. M. Dent, 1962), 214–16; Leonard W. Labaree, ed., *The Papers of Benjamin Franklin*, 35 vols. (New Haven, Conn.: Yale University Press, 1959–99), 4:481–833.

54. Emma Lewis Coleman, *New England Captives Carried to Canada between 1677 and 1760 during the French and Indian Wars*, 2 vols. (Portland, Me.: Southworth Press, 1925; reprint, Bowie, Md.: Heritage Books, 1989); Axtell, *The European and the Indian: Essays in the Ethnohistory of Colonial North America*, 161–206, 351n66: Alden T. Vaughan and Daniel K. Richter, "Crossing the Cultural Divide: Indians and New Englanders, 1605–1765," *Proceedings of the American Antiquarian Society* 90 (1980), 23–99.

55. Eleazar Wheelock, *Continuation of the Narrative of the Indian Charity School* (Hartford, Conn., 1775), 11; Gordon M. Day, "Dartmouth and Saint Francis," *Dartmouth Alumni Magazine* 52 (Nov. 1959), 28–30; Axtell, "Dr. Wheelock's Little Red School," 106–7.

56. Chase, *History of Dartmouth College*, 1:307.

57. Report on Ripley's mission to Canada, Sept. 21, 1772, Ms. 772521.2; Eleazar Wheelock, *Continuation of the Narrative of the Indian Charity School* (May 1771 to Sept 1772) (Portsmouth, N.H., 1773), 9, 11, 38–40 (Ripley mission and "thirst for learning"); Eleazar Wheelock, *Continuation of the Narrative of the Indian Charity School* (Sept. 1772 to Sept. 1773) (Hartford, Conn., 1773), 7–9 ("Indian Temper"); Wheelock to Thornton, Sept. 23, 1772, Ms. 772523; Wheelock to Trumbull, Mar. 16, 1775, Ms. 775216. 2; McCallum, *Eleazar Wheelock*, 191–92 ("likely Indian boys"); McCallum, *Letters of Eleazar Wheelock's Indians*, 26; Chase, *History of Dartmouth College*, 1:311. The four Kahnawakes requested permission to visit Sir William Johnson, whence they returned home; on Feb. 27, 1773, Wheelock also wrote a letter of good conduct for Basteen Sawvanhas and Lewis Sawantawman (Sebastian and Lewis Vincent), "Indians of the Tribe at Lorett," who had been in his school for some months and were about to visit Sir William Johnson, Ms. 773177. Neil Goodwin, "We Go As Captives" (unpublished ms., cited with author's permission), contains information on the Stacey and Phillips families.

58. Thomas Kendall, "Diary and account book, 1772–1774," Ms. 772900.3, quotations at 6, 9, 11 of typescript.

59. Maccluer to Mrs. Walcutt, Mar. 23, 1771, Ms. 771223.4, and Thomas Walcutt Papers, Massachusetts Historical Society, reel 2; McClure to Mrs. Walcutt and Mrs. Walcutt to McClure, May 21, 1771, Ms. 771321 and 771321.1.

60. Wheelock to Elizabeth Walcutt, Sept. 3, 1771, Ms. 771503.2.

61. Elizabeth Walcutt to Macclure, Feb. 10, 1772, McClure Ms. 772160.2 and Walcutt Papers, reel 2: Elizabeth Walcutt to Thomas, May 26, 1771, Sept. 28, 1771, Feb. 11, 1772, May 7, 1772, June 10, 1772, Sept. 28, 1772, Dec. 31, 1772, Jan. 30, 1773, Mar. 18, 1773, May 19, 1773, June 14, 1773, Sept. 23, 1773, Mar. 13, 1774; Benjamin Walcutt to Thomas, Jan. 21, 1772; Thomas to mother, Jan. 13, 1772, Jan. 24, 1772, Apr. 13, 1772, Jan. [?], 1773, Apr. 20, 1773; Thomas to brother, Apr. 12, 1772.

62. Thomas Walcutt to mother, Jan. [?], 1773, Sept 1, 1773; Thomas Walcutt to "Far Distant Friend," Jan. 13, 1772; Mother to Thomas, Sept. 9, 1773, Walcutt Papers, reel 2.

63. Frisbie's account of his 1774 mission is in Eleazar Wheelock, *Continuation of the Narrative of the Indian Charity School* (Hartford, Conn., 1775), 44–54.

64. Frisbie to Elizabeth Walcutt, May 30, 1774, Walcutt Papers, reel 2.

65. Elizabeth to Thomas, June 10, 1774, Walcutt Papers, reel 2.

66. Thomas to mother, St. Francis Village, Sept. 10, 1774, Walcutt Papers, reel 2.

67. Daniel Simon to Thomas Walcutt, Mar. [?], 1775, Walcutt Papers, reel 2.

68. Elizabeth to Thomas, Mar. 7, 1775, Walcutt Papers, reel 2. Elizabeth served as care-taker of the Indian boys from 1774 to 1776; McCallum, *Letters of Eleazar Wheelock's Indian Students*, 119n; Wheelock, *Continuation of the Narrative of the Indian Charity School* (Hartford, Conn., 1775), 12–13.

69. Wheelock to Walcutt "at Canada," Mar. 7, 1775, Walcutt Papers, reel 2; Wheelock, *Continuation of the Narrative of the Indian Charity School* (Hartford, 1775), 14–15.

70. Wheelock, *Continuation of the Narrative* (Hartford, 1773): 26; MacClure to Rev. J. Caldwell, Dec. 1, 1774, McClure Ms. 774651.1.

71. Day, "Dartmouth and Saint Francis," 28–30.

72. Jane Marcou, *Life of Jeremy Belknap . . . with selections from his correspondence and other writings . . . arranged by his grand-daughter* (New York: Harper and Bros., 1847), 66, 68, 72.

73. Laura J. Murray, ed., *To Do Good to My Indian Brethren: The Writings of Joseph Johnson, 1751–1776* (Amherst: University of Massachusetts Press, 1998), 240–41.

74. "Summary of Expenses, 1767–1817," Moor's Indian Charity School Records, box 1.

75. Wheelock to John Thornton, Apr. 1, 1774, Wheelock to SSPCK directors, Apr. 1, 1774, Ms. 774251.1-2; SSPCK to Wheelock, Oct. 3, 1774, Ms. 774553.2.

## Chapter 3

1. David McClure and Elijah Parish, *Memoirs of the Rev. Eleazar Wheelock, D.D., Founder and President of Dartmouth College and Moor's Charity School; With a summary history of the College and School, to which are added copious extracts from Dr. Wheelock's Correspondence* (Newburyport, Mass.: Edward Little and Co., 1811), 75.

2. Timothy Dwight, *Travels in New-England and New-York*, 4 vols. (1821; reprint, Cambridge, Mass.: Harvard University Press, 1969), 2:74–75, 78.

3. Wheelock to Gov. Trumbull, Mar. 16, 1775, Ms. 775216.2; Wheelock to David Macluer, Mar. 20, 1775, Ms. 775220.1; Wheelock to Trumbull, Mar. 27, 1775, Ms. 775222.2; Wheelock to the Provincial Congress, June 28, 1775, Ms. 775378.1; James Dow McCallum, *Eleazar Wheelock, Founder of Dartmouth College* (Hanover, N.H.: Dartmouth College Publications, 1939), 198–99; Frederick Chase, *A History of Dartmouth College and the Town of Hanover, New Hampshire*, ed. John K. Lord, 2 vols. (Vol. 1, Cambridge, Mass.: John Wilson and Son, 1891–1913), 1:355.

4. On Brant and Kirkland, see Alan Taylor, *The Divided Ground: Indians, Settlers, and the Northern Borderland of the American Revolution* (New York: Knopf, 2006); Christine Sternberg Patrick, "The Life and Times of Samuel Kirkland, 1741–1808: Missionary to the Oneida Indians, American Patriot, and Founder of Hamilton College" (Ph.D. diss., State University of New York, Buffalo, 1993); James Kirby Martin and Joseph H. Glatthaar, *Forgotten Allies: The Oneida Indians and the American Revolution* (New York: Hill and Wang, 2006).

5. Daybook, 1771–72, Moor's Indian Charity School Records, box 5, 27, 33; Records of the Dartmouth College Treasurer, DA-2, 1745, ledger A (1770–75), 6 (Wheelock's notation).

6. Wheelock to Trumbull, Mar. 27, 1775, Ms. 775222.2; Wheelock to Trumbull, Mar. 16, 1775, Ms. 775216.2; Wheelock to Macluer, Mar. 20, 1775, Ms. 775220.1; Karim M. Tiro, "James Dean in Iroquoia," *New York History* 80 (1999), 391–422.

7. Wheelock to Provincial Congress, June 28, 1775, Ms. 775378.1; Wheelock to Silas Deane, Aug. 6, 1775, Ms. 775456.2; Peter Force, ed., *American Archives: Documents of the American Revolution 1774–1776*, 9 vols. (1837–53), ser. 5, 2:125, 1362.

8. Dean to Wheelock, Dec. 25, 1775, Ms. 775675.2.

9. Wheelock to Macluer, Mar. 20, 1775, Ms. 775220.1; Wheelock to Trumbull, Mar. 16 and 22, 1775, Ms. 775216.2 and 775222.2; Wheelock to Deane, Aug. 6, 1775, Ms. 775456.2; Col. Hurd to Gen. Schuyler, July 13, 1776, in Force, *American Archives*, ser. 5, 1:263.

10. Leon Burr Richardson, *History of Dartmouth College*, 2 vols. (Hanover, N.H.: Dartmouth Publications, 1932), 1:156; Resolutions of the U.S. Continental Congress, Sept. 19, 1776, Ms. 776519, and in Force, *American Archives*, ser. 5, 2:1362; Wheelock to Commissioners of Indian Affairs, Oct. 13, 1777, and May 27, 1778, Ms. 777563.1 and Ms. 778327; Wheelock to Congress, Nov. 1, 1778, and Apr. 2, 1779, Ms. 778601 and Ms. 779252.1.

11. Chase, *History of Dartmouth College* 1:387; Wheelock to Joseph Louis Gill, Nov. 1, 1777, Ms. 777601, and reprinted in Colin G. Calloway, ed., *Dawnland Encounters: Indians and Europeans in Northern New England* (Hanover, N.H.: University Press of New England, 1991), 243–45.

12. Copy of Last Will and Testament of Eleazar Wheelock, Apr. 2, 1779, Ms. 7779252; Wheelock to Congress, Apr. 2, 1779, Ms. 779252.1.

13. Richardson, *History of Dartmouth College*, 1:156–67; Memorial of John Wheelock, Papers of the Continental Congress, 1774–1789, National Archives microfilm, M247 (204 reels), reel 52, item 10:423–24; reel 172, item 1:42.

14. Occom to John Thornton, 1776, Ms. 776900.2, and in Joanna Brooks, ed., *The Collected Writings of Samson Occom, Mohegan* (New York: Oxford University Press, 2006),

113; Harold Blodgett, *Samson Occom: The Biography of an Indian Preacher* (Hanover, N.H.: Dartmouth College Publications, 1935), 164–65.

15. Colin G. Calloway, *The American Revolution in Indian Country: Crisis and Diversity in Native American Communities* (Cambridge: Cambridge University Press, 1995).

16. James Dow McCallum, ed., *Letters of Eleazar Wheelock's Indians* (Hanover, N.H.: Dartmouth College Publications, 1932), 296–97; "List of Indians in the Indian Charity School," Rauner Library, Dartmouth College, and typescript, Historical Room, Stockbridge Town Library, Stockbridge, Massachusetts, "Stockbridge Indians" box; *Minority Military Service: Massachusetts, 1775–1783* (Washington, D.C.: National Society, Daughters of the American Revolution, 1989).

17. Eric P. Kelly, "The Dartmouth Indians," *Dartmouth Alumni Magazine* 22 (Dec. 1929), 123; Chase, *History of Dartmouth College*, 1:374n1; James L. Farley, "A Compendium of the Military Activities of the Inhabitants of the Town of Hanover and the College District during the Revolutionary War" (senior thesis, Dartmouth History Dept., 1942), 39–40.

18. Daybook, 1772–73, Moor's Indian Charity School Records, box 5, 350. Peter may have been Peter Pohquonnappeet, but the latter is usually referred to by his full name in the College records.

19. Calloway, *American Revolution in Indian Country*, chap. 2; Calloway, *The Western Abenakis of Vermont, 1600–1800* (Norman: University of Oklahoma Press, 1990), chap. 11.

20. The following paragraphs are based on Colin G. Calloway, "Sentinels of the Revolution: Bedel's New Hampshire Rangers and the Abenaki Indians on the Upper Connecticut," *Historical New Hampshire* 54 (1990), 271–95.

21. Bedel to Wheelock, Feb. 17, 1776, Ms. 776167.

22. Calloway, *Revolution in Indian Country*, 83–84.

23. Farley, "Compendium of the Military Activities," 39–40.

24. Wheelock to Johnson, Feb. 27, 1773, in James Sullivan et al., *The Papers of Sir William Johnson*, 15 vols. (Albany: State University of New York, 1921–65), 12:1012 (fragmented version of the same letter, 8:726).

25. Dick Hoefnagel with the collaboration of Virginia L. Close, *Eleazar Wheelock and the Adventurous Founding of Dartmouth College* (Hanover, N.H.: Hanover Historical Society/Durand Press, 2002), 76–77; "Evidence in John Payne's Trial," April 1775, Ms. 775290. College accounts list "Lewis Indian" and "Lewis Loret" as well as Lewis Vincent. They were likely the same person; Daybook, 1774–75, Moor's Indian Charity School Records, box 5, 1, 45, 187, 209.

26. Students to Wheelock, Mar. 14, 1777, Ms. 777204. Lewis Vincent's expenses are detailed in Records of the Dartmouth College Treasurer, DA-2, 1746, ledger B (1775–82), 46.

27. Chase, *History of Dartmouth College*, 1:390, 548; part of a copy of a letter from Maj. Gen. Gates, June 26, 1778, Ms. 778376; Wheelock to the Board of Commissioners for Indian Affairs, May 27, 1778, Ms. 778327; Farley, "Compendium of the Military Activities," 39–40.

28. Wheelock's testimonial, July 3, 1775, Ms. 775403.4; McCallum, *Letters of Eleazar Wheelock's Indians*, 234; J. S. to Capt. Mathews, Apr. 13, 1781, Papers and Correspondence of Governor-General Sir Frederick Haldimand, 1758–84, British Museum, Additional Manuscripts 21,840: 12 (reel 92 in microfilm ed.).

29. John Sauck to [?], July 10, 1775, Ms. 775410 (letter in Mohawk), and in McCallum, *Letters of Eleazar Wheelock's Indians*, 234–35. Daybook, 1774–75, Moor's Indian Charity School Records, box 5, lists expenses for John Sauk, e.g. 71, 137–38. Records of the Dartmouth College Treasurer, DA-2, 1746, ledger B (1774–91), list of expenses incurred in 1780, 10.

30. Chase, *History of Dartmouth College*, 1:409–14; Students to Wheelock, Mar. 4, 1777, Ms. 777204; Wheelock to Stacey, Nov. 6, 1777, Ms. 777606.2; Neil Goodwin, "We Go As Captives," unpublished manuscript, cited with permission.

31. Eleazar Wheelock, *A Continuation of the Narrative of the Indian Charity School* (Portsmouth, N.H., 1773), 38.

32. Calloway, *Western Abenakis of Vermont*, 34–39.

33. John Duffy, *Epidemics in Colonial America* (Baton Rouge: Louisiana State University Press, 1953), 20–21, 51, 57, 104.

34. Elizabeth A. Fenn, *Pox Americana: The Great Smallpox Epidemic of 1775–82* (New York: Hill and Wang, 2001).

35. Ripley to John Wheelock, Mar. 7, 1776, Ms. 776207, quoted in Hoefnagel, *Eleazar Wheelock and the Adventurous Founding*, 84.

36. Hoefnagel, *Eleazar Wheelock and the Adventurous Founding*, 84.

37. Fenn, *Pox Americana*, chaps. 2–4.

38. Hoefnagel, *Eleazar Wheelock and the Adventurous Founding*, 84–87; Chase, *History of Dartmouth College*, 1:362–64, 530–33; Wheelock, Aug. 5, 1776, Ms. 776455.2 (laws re: smallpox; forbids Dr. Laban Gates to treat students).

39. Fenn, *Pox Americana*, 138–40.

40. Fenn, *Pox Americana*; Colin G. Calloway, *One Vast Winter Count: The Native American West before Lewis and Clark* (Lincoln: University of Nebraska Press, 2003), 415–26.

41. Excerpts from Wheelock's diary reprinted in Chase, *History of Dartmouth College*, 1:352–53.

42. James Dean to Walcutt, Apr. 6, 1775; pass by Gov. Carleton, June 15, 1775, Thomas Walcutt Papers, Massachusetts Historical Society, reel 2.

43. Students to John Smith, Dec. 30, 1775, Ms. 775680.2.

44. Benj. Walcutt to Thomas, May 8, 1777, Walcutt Papers, reel 2.

45. Elizabeth Walcutt to Thomas, Sept. 23, 1777, Walcutt Papers, reel 2.

46. Walcutt to Nathan Dane, Sept. 22, 1787, Walcutt Papers, reel 2; George Dexter, ed., "Journal of Thomas Walcutt in 1790," *Proceedings of the Massachusetts Historical Society*, Oct. 1879, reprinted in Archer Butler Hulbert, *Pioneer Roads and Experiences of Travelers* (Cleveland: Arthur H. Clark, 1902) 2:43–63. On Ohio land fever see R. Douglas Hurt, *The Ohio Frontier: Crucible of the Old Northwest, 1720–1830* (Bloomington: Indiana University Press, 1996), chap. 6.

47. Walcutt's donation is mentioned in Ms. 817362. The collection was later removed to Bowdoin College: John King Lord, *History of Dartmouth College, 1815–1909* (Concord, N.H.: Rumford Press, 1913), 510.

48. Wheelock to John Sergeant, Jan. 29, 1778, Ms. 778129; Daniel Simon to Wheelock, Oct. 7, 1778, Ms. 778557.1; Simon to Wheelock, Dec. 7, 1778, Ms. 778657; George T. Chapman, *Sketches of the Alumni of Dartmouth College* (Cambridge, Mass.: Riverside Press, 1867), 22–23.

49. Brooks, *Collected Writings of Samson Occom*, 119–23.

50. Brooks, *Collected Writings of Samson Occom*, 133.

51. Joseph Johnson to Wheelock, May 2, 1774; Oct. 17, 1774, Ms. 774302, 774567; Brooks, *Collected Writings of Samson Occom*, 308; Brothertown Records, 1774–1804, Hamilton College Library, Clinton, New York, 1–2.

52. W. DeLoss Love, *Samson Occom and the Christian Indians of New England* (1899; reprint, Syracuse, N.Y.: Syracuse University Press, 2000), 284–85.

53. James W. Oberly, *A Nation of Statesmen: The Political Culture of the Stockbridge-Munsee Mohicans, 1815–1972* (Norman: University of Oklahoma Press, 2005), 22–23.

54. Brooks, *Collected Writings of Samson Occom*, 143, 155.

55. Anthony Wonderley, "Brothertown, New York, 1785–1796," *New York History* 80 (2000), 457–92, reviews the new community's difficult first decade; Blodgett, *Samson Occom*, 205–7.

56. Chapman, *Sketches of the Alumni of Dartmouth College*, 29; Levi Konkapot, Jr., to Rev. Cutting Marsh, Sept. 22, 1858, reprinted in *Boston Recorder*, in Peter Pohquonnappeet, Alumni file.

57. Blodgett, *Samson Occom*, 210; Brooks, *Collected Writings of Samson Occom*, 136–39.

58. Brooks, *Collected Writings of Samson Occom*, 26–27; Walter Pilkington, ed., *Journals of Samuel Kirkland, Eighteenth-century Missionary to the Iroquois, Government Agent, Father of Hamilton College* (Clinton, N.Y.: Hamilton College, 1980), 222–23.

59. Louis Vincent to Wheelock, Feb. 20, 1784, Ms. 784170.

60. "Letter of introduction for John Wheelock," Dec. 13, 1781, Ms. 781681.

61. Chapman, *Sketches of the Alumni of Dartmouth College*, 29–30; Kenneth C. Cramer, "Indian Students in the Post-Wheelock Years," *Library Bulletin*, in Rauner Misc. Material File, Rauner Library; Richardson, *History of Dartmouth College*, 1:202.

62. Chase, *History of Dartmouth College*, 1:589–93; "An act granting twenty three thousand acres of land to the Trustees of Dartmouth College, and the President of Moor's Charity School, to and for the use of the said College and School forever," June 14, 1785, in "Records of the Trustees of Moor's Charity School," bound volume, Moor's Indian Charity School Records, box 2, 1–2; Richardson, *History of Dartmouth College*, 219.

63. "An Act more effectually to define and improve the charitable establishment," June 9, 1807, in "Records of the Trustees of Moor's Charity School," Moor's Indian Charity School Records, box 2, 104.

## Chapter 4

1. Frederick Chase, *A History of Dartmouth College and the Town of Hanover, New Hampshire*, 2 vols. (Vol. 1, Cambridge, Mass.: John Wilson and Son, 1891), 1:298.

2. James Zug, ed., *The Last Voyage of Captain Cook: The Collected Writings of John Ledyard* (Washington, D.C.: National Geographic, 2005), 47.

3. On Ledyard, see James Zug, *American Traveler: The Life and Adventures of John Ledyard, The Man Who Dreamed of Walking the World* (New York: Basic Books, 2005); Bill Gifford, *Ledyard: In Search of the First American Explorer* (New York: Harcourt, 2007), 29 ("fostered the impression" quotation), 197 ("cloak of civilization" quotation); and Edward G. Gray, *The Making of John Ledyard: Empire and Ambition in the Life of an Early American Traveler* (New Haven, Conn.: Yale University Press, 2007).

4. Zug, *American Traveler*, 129; Zug, *Last Voyage of Captain Cook*, 46.

5. Colin G. Calloway, *One Vast Winter Count: The Native American West before Lewis and Clark* (Lincoln: University of Nebraska Press, 2003), 395–415.

6. Reginald Horsman, *Expansion and American Indian Policy, 1783–1812* (1967; reprint, Norman: University of Oklahoma Press, 1992); Anthony F. C. Wallace, *Jefferson and the Indians: The Tragic Fate of the First Americans* (Cambridge, Mass.: Harvard University Press, 1999).

7. Colin G. Calloway, *The American Revolution in Indian Country: Crisis and Diversity in Native American Communities* (Cambridge: Cambridge University Pres, 1995), 292–301.

8. Alan Taylor, *The Divided Ground: Indians, Settlers, and the Northern Borderland of the American Revolution* (New York: Knopf, 2006), 81–82, 165 (quotation), 212–14, 304–5; Laurence M. Hauptman, *Conspiracy of Interests: Iroquois Dispossession and the Rise of New York State* (Syracuse, N.Y.: Syracuse University Press, 1999), chap. 4; Karim M. Tiro, "James Dean in Iroquoia," *New York History* 80 (1999), 397–422; Christine Sternberg Patrick, "The Life and Times of Samuel Kirkland, 1741–1808: Missionary to the Oneida Indians, American Patriot, and Founder of Hamilton College" (Ph.D. diss., State University of New York, Buffalo, 1993), chaps. 7–8; J. David Lehman, "The End of the Iroquois Mystique: The Oneida Land Cession Treaties of the 1780s," *William and Mary Quarterly*, 3rd ser., 47 (1990), 523–47. The treaties and proceedings at Fort Stanwix and Herkimer are in Colin G. Calloway, ed., *Revolution and Confederation*, vol. 18 of Alden T. Vaughan, gen. ed., *Early American Indian Documents: Treaties and Laws, 1607–1789* (Bethesda, Md.: University Publications of America, 1994), 336 ("faithful services" quotation).

9. Patrick, "Life and Times of Samuel Kirkland," chap. 9; Pilkington, *Journals of Samuel Kirkland*, 25–27, 280 (George's later life); George T. Chapman, *Sketches of the Alumni of Dartmouth College* (Cambridge, Mass.: Riverside Press, 1867), 65.

10. Charles J. Kappler, comp., *Indian Affairs: Laws and Treaties*, 2 vols. (Washington, D.C.: Government Printing Office, 1904), 2:37–39.

11. Hauptman, *Conspiracy of Interests*, 73; Tiro, "James Dean in Iroquoia," 392, 415–22.

12. Davenport Phelps, Alumni file, 1775 ("red men" quotation); Isabel Thompson Kelsay, *Joseph Brant, 1743–1807: Man of Two Worlds* (Syracuse, N.Y.: Syracuse University Press, 1984), 546–47; Taylor, *Divided Ground*, 353–54, 357.

13. I am grateful to Rick Behrens for this information.

14. Leon Burr Richardson, *History of Dartmouth College*, 2 vols. (Hanover, N.H.: Dartmouth Publications, 1932), 1:219–20.

15. M. E. Goddard and Henry V. Partridge, *A History of Norwich, Vermont* (Hanover, N.H.: Dartmouth Press, 1905), 236–38.

16. Sevier to the warriors and cheifs [*sic*] of the Cherokee Nation, June 24, 1799, Governor John Sevier Papers, 1796–1801, Tennessee State Library and Archives, Nashville, box 1, folder 8.

17. Potter's expenses are recorded in ledger 1789–1851, Moor's Indian Charity School Records, 13. *A Vindication of the Official Conduct of the Trustees of Dartmouth College* (Concord, N.H.: G. Hough, 1815), 62–63; Josiah Dunham, *An Answer to the "Vindication of the Official Conduct of the Trustees of Dartmouth College," in confirmation of the "Sketches"; with Remarks on the Removal of President Wheelock* (Hanover, N.H.: David Watson, printer, 1816), 41.

18. Goddard and Partridge, *History of Norwich, Vermont*, 134.

19. *Christian Herald*, 1816, 93–94.

20. Walter Lowrie and Matthew St. Clair Clarke, eds., *American State Papers, Class II: Indian Affairs*, 2 vols. (Washington, D.C.: Gales and Seaton, 1832), 1:532; Dinsmoor's account of his public service [n.d.], Dinsmoor Family Papers, 1802–1853, Rauner Library, Dartmouth College, Ms. 40, box 4, miscellaneous file; Ms. 797118.1 (spinning wheels).

21. "Genealogies: Col. Silas Dinsmoor," Silas Dinsmoor, Alumni file, 1791.

22. Lowrie and Clarke, *American State Papers: Indian Affairs*, 1:639, 640–41.

23. Dinsmoor's account of his public service, Dinsmoor Papers, box 4, miscellaneous file.

24. Dearborn to Dinsmoor, May 8, 1802, in Clarence Edwin Carter, ed., *The Territorial Papers of the United States* (Washington, D.C.: Government Printing Office, 1937), 5:146, copy in Dinsmoor Papers, box 4, miscellaneous file.

25. Jefferson to Harrison, Feb. 27, 1803, in Francis Paul Prucha, ed., *Documents of United States Indian Policy* (Lincoln: University of Nebraska Press, 1975), 22–23. On Jefferson's Indian policy and Harrison's role in implementing it, see Wallace, *Jefferson and the Indians*, and Robert M. Owens, *Mr. Jefferson's Hammer: William Henry Harrison and the Origins of American Indian Policy* (Norman: University of Oklahoma Press, 2007).

26. "Genealogies: Col. Silas Dinsmoor," 452.

27. Thomas D. Clark and John D. W. Guice, *The Old Southwest, 1795–1830: Frontiers in Conflict* (Norman: University of Oklahoma Press, 1996), 256.

28. Quotation from Clark and Guice, *Old Southwest, 1795–1830*, 36.

29. Kappler, *Indian Affairs*, 2:79; Lowrie and Clarke, *American State Papers*, 1:697.

30. Kappler, *Indian Affairs*, 2:87–88; Lowrie and Clarke, *American State Papers*, 1:749; William S. Coker and Thomas D. Watson, *Indian Traders of the Southeastern Spanish Borderlands: Panton, Leslie and Company and John Forbes and Company, 1783–1847* (Pensa-

cola: University of West Florida Press, 1986), 255–56, 267–68; Arthur H. DeRosier, Jr., *The Removal of the Choctaw Indians* (Knoxville: University of Tennessee Press, 1970), 32.

31. "Genealogies: Col. Silas Dinsmoor," 452 (quotation); Silas Dinsmoor, Alumni file; Dinsmoor's account of his public service, Dinsmoor Papers, box 4, miscellaneous file.

32. Lowrie and Clarke, *American State Papers*, 2:180–81, 243; Clark and Guice, *Old Southwest*, 241; "Choctaw petition," Dinsmoor Papers, box 4, miscellaneous file. See also Thomas H. Williams to Dinsmoor, Dec. 19, 1820, Ms. 820669: "The Choctaw Treaty is under the hammer and I hope will be ratified. Until that happens, Gov. Holmes will do nothing in relation to your claim."

33. *New York Observer*, Apr. 27, 1839; Solomon Spaulding, Alumni file, 1785; Howard A. Davis, Donald R. Scales, and Wayne L. Cowdrey, *Who Really Wrote the Book of Mormon?* (Santa Ana, Calif.: Vision House, 1977). On the earth mounds, see George R. Milner, *The Moundbuilders: Ancient Peoples of Eastern North America* (London: Thames and Hudson, 2004)

34. Gary E. Moulton, ed., *The Lewis and Clark Journals: An American Epic of Discovery* (Lincoln: University of Nebraska Press, 2003), 114.

35. Edwin James, *Account of An Expedition from Pittsburgh to the Rocky Mountains, performed in the Years 1819 and '20 . . . under the command of Major Stephen H. Long*, 2 vols. (Philadelphia: Carey and Lea, 1823), 1:iv.

36. James, *Account of An Expedition*, 45; Colin G. Calloway, *The Shawnees and the War for America* (New York: Viking/Penguin, 2007).

37. James, *Account of An Expedition*, 59–66. On Cahokia see Biloine Whiting Young and Melvin L. Fowler, *Cahokia: The Great Native American Metropolis* (Urbana: University of Illinois Press, 2000), and Timothy R. Pauketat, *Cahokia: Ancient America's Great City on the Mississippi* (New York: Viking/Penguin, 2009)

38. James, *Account of An Expedition*, 174, 179–80.

39. James, *Account of An Expedition*, 160, 356.

40. James P. Ronda, "Exploring the American West in the Age of Jefferson," in John Logan Allen, ed., *North American Exploration*, 3 vols. (Lincoln: University of Nebraska Press, 1997), 3:67; James, *Account of An Expedition*, 361.

41. Paul E. Cohen, *Mapping the West: America's Westward Movement 1524–1890* (New York: Rizzoli, 2002), 108–9. For an assessment of Long's contributions to American scientific and geographic knowledge of the West, see Roger L. Nichols and Patrick L. Halley, *Stephen Long and American Frontier Exploration* (Newark: University of Delaware Press, 1980).

42. Richardson, *History of Dartmouth College*, 1:221; Chase, *History of Dartmouth College* 1:619, 635.

43. Timothy Dwight, *Travels in New-England and New-York*, 4 vols. (1821; reprint, Cambridge, Mass.: Harvard University Press, 1969), 2:73, 76–77.

44. Edward Augustus Kendall, *Travels through the Northern Parts of the United States*, 3 vols. (New York: I. Riley, 1809), 3:195–98.

45. Leon B. Richardson, "The Dartmouth Indians, 1800–1893," *Dartmouth Alumni Magazine* 22 (June 1930), 524–27.

46. "Notable Dartmouth Indians," list, Rauner Library.

47. "Scotch Fund" ledger (Moor's Charity School accounts abridged from College ledgers), 1799–1817, Ms. DA 403, box 3, 1–4. Expenses for these Abenaki students are also listed in ledger 1789–1857, Moor's Indian Charity School Records, box 2, 18–36.

48. Joseph Perry to Rev. Jedediah Morse, June 25, 1816, Ms. 816375.2.

49. "The Character Book of Governor George Simpson, 1832," in Glyndwr Williams, ed., *Hudson's Bay Miscellany, 1670–1870* (Winnipeg: Hudson's Bay Record Society, 1975), 200; Morag Maclachlan, "The Case for Francis Annance," *Beaver* 73, no. 2 (1993), 35–39 ("highest office"); Morag Maclachlan, ed., *The Fort Langley Journals, 1827–30* (Vancouver: UBC Press, 1998), 14; Jean Murray Cole, ed., *This Blessed Wilderness: Archibald McDonald's Letters from the Columbia, 1822–44* (Vancouver: UBC Press, 2001), 271. Annance had (or had had) a country wife of his own, who bore him three sons, one of whom drowned. At one point Stuart's wife, Mary Taylor, accused Annance of rape (Sylvia Van Kirk, *Many Tender Ties: Women in Fur-trade Society, 1670–1870* [Norman: University of Oklahoma Press, 1980], 168), but they seem to have had an ongoing affair.

50. "Account of Dartmouth College in America," *Christian Observer* 13 (1814), 23.

## Chapter 5

1. *Green Mountain Democrat*, Apr. 4, 1835, 2, col. 4, quoted in *Addendum to the Petition for Federal Recognition as an American Indian Tribe submitted to the Bureau of Indian Affairs by the Abenaki Nation of Vermont* (1986), pt. B, 308–9 (ms. in author's possession). The prospective student's name translates as St. Joseph St. John Baptiste Alanum. Thanks to John Moody for this.

2. Colin G. Calloway, ed., *After King Philip's War: Presence and Persistence in Indian New England* (Hanover, N.H.: University Press of New England, 1997); Rev. Jedediah Morse, *A Report to the Secretary of War of the United States, on Indian Affairs* (New Haven, Conn.: S. Converse, 1822), 64–75; Jean O' Brien, *First and Lasting: Writing Indians out of Existence in New England* (Minneapolis: University of Minnesota Press, 2010).

3. President Nathan Lord to Secretary of the SSPCK, Apr. 26, 1832; similar letter, Apr. 20, 1832; Society in Scotland for Propagating Christian Knowledge, Records, 1794–1892 (hereafter SSPCK Records), folder 1-3; *Petition of the Society in Scotland for Propagating Christian Knowledge to Settle Scheme for Application of Trust-Fund* (Edinburgh: T. and A. Constable, 1922), 4.

4. Rauner Library, Dartmouth College, *Dartmouth Catalogue* for 1831–32.

5. Lord to Codman, May 1, 1838, SSPCK Records, folder 1-3.

6. William G. McLoughlin, *Cherokees and Missionaries, 1789–1839* (1984; reprint, Norman: University of Oklahoma Press, 1995), 105–22 (Ross quotation at 121); McLoughlin, *Cherokee Renascence in the New Republic* (Princeton, N.J.: Princeton University Press, 1986), 254–58 (Ross quotation at 258); George T. Chapman, *Sketches of the Alumni of Dartmouth College* (Cambridge, Mass.: Riverside Press, 1867), 81; "Memoir of the Rev. Samuel Worcester, D.D.," *New Hampshire Repository* 2, no. 1 (October 1846), 9–28.

7. Chapman, *Sketches of Dartmouth Alumni*, 176.

8. *First Ten Annual Reports of the American Board of Commissioners for Foreign Missions* (Boston: Crocker and Brewster, 1834), 249 (Report for 1819). Grant Foreman, "Dwight Mission," *Chronicles of Oklahoma* 12 (Mar. 1934), 42–51; quotation at 47, 51; Hugh Park, *Reminiscences of the Indians by Cephas Washburn* (Van Buren, Ark.: Press-Argus, 1955), 64–89, quotations at 67, 76.

9. *General Catalogue of Dartmouth College and Associated Schools, 1769–1925* (Hanover N.H.: Rumford Press, 1925), 639.

10. W. B. Morrison, "The Choctaw Mission of the American Board of Commissioners for Foreign Missions," *Chronicles of Oklahoma* 4 (1926), 176; J. Y. Bryce, ed., "Our First Schools in Choctaw Nation," *Chronicles of Oklahoma* 6 (1928), 356, 367–68.

11. Lindsay G. Robertson, *Conquest by Law: How the Discovery of America Dispossessed Indigenous Peoples of Their Lands* (New York: Oxford University Press, 2005), 62–76, quotations at 70, 76. See also Robert J. Miller, *Native America, Discovered and Conquered: Thomas Jefferson, Lewis and Clark, and Manifest Destiny* (Westport, Conn.: Praeger, 2006), especially 50–53.

12. Theda Perdue and Michael D. Green, eds., *The Cherokee Removal: A Brief History with Documents* (Boston: Bedford Books, 1995), 105–14.

13. *Register of Debates in Congress, 1824–1837*, 14 vols. (Washington, D.C.: Gales and Seaton), vol. 6, pt. 1 (Senate), 456; vol. 6, pt. 2 (House), 383, 1133; 21st Cong., 1st sess., *Senate Journal*, 266–68; 21st Cong., 1st sess., *Journal of the House of Representatives*, 729–30; Ronald N. Satz, *American Indian Policy in the Jacksonian Era* (Lincoln: University of Nebraska Press, 1975), 40–41, 53 (Webster's stance); Chapman, *Sketches of the Alumni of Dartmouth College*, 67, 107, 109, 111, 133, 138, 144, 162.

14. Malcolm J. Rohrbough, *The Land Office Business: The Settlement and Administration of American Public Lands, 1789–1837* (New York: Oxford University Press, 1968), chap. 13, quotations at 283–84, default figures at 294.

15. Satz, *American Indian Policy in the Jacksonian Era*, 41.

16. James W. Oberly, *A Nation of Statesmen: The Political Culture of the Stockbridge-Munsee Mohicans, 1815–1972* (Norman: University of Oklahoma Press, 2005), 38; *Journal of John Sergeant, Missionary to the Stockbridge Indians*, 49 (Williams to the Oneidas).

17. Geoffrey E. Brueger, "Eleazar Williams: Elitism and Multiple Identity on Two Frontiers," in James A. Clifton, ed., *Being and Becoming Indian: Biographical Sketches of North American Frontiers* (Chicago: Dorsey Press, 1989), 112–36, quotation at 118; list of expenses paid to Eleazar Williams, "Caughnawaga Indian," for travel to Springfield, Mass., 130 miles away, "fitting there for a mission," ledger 1789–1851, Moor's Indian Charity School Records, 26.

18. "Marsh's Report to the Scottish Society, 1831," *Collections of the Wisconsin State Historical Society* 15 (1900), 48–50. Estimates of the Stockbridge population at Statesburg at this time range from 225 to 350; Oberly, *Nation of Statesmen*, 44.

19. "Marsh's Report to the Scottish Society," quotations at 72, 82, 201.

20. "Extracts from Marsh's Journal during the Black Hawk War," *Collections of the Wisconsin State Historical Society* 15 (1900), 60–65.

21. Ellen M. Whitney, ed., *The Black Hawk War 1831–32*, 2 vols. (Springfield: Illinois State Historical Library, 1970–75), vol. 2, pt. 1, 484–85, 583; vol. 2, pt. 2, 1050. Kerry A. Trask, *Black Hawk: The Battle for the Heart of America* (New York: Holt, 2006), 224.

22. "Expedition to the Sacs and Foxes," *Collections of the Wisconsin State Historical Society* 15 (1900), 104–55, quotations at 117, 127.

23. "Scottish Report for 1834," *Collections of the Wisconsin State Historical Society* 15 (1900), 94, 176; Marsh to Draper, Mar. 25, 1857, in *Collections of the Wisconsin State Historical Society* 4 (1859), 300–301.

24. Oberly, *Nation of Statesmen*, 63, 69, 77, 125–27; John E. Chapin, "Sketch of Cutting Marsh," *Collections of the Wisconsin State Historical Society* 15 (1900), 31; Leon B. Richardson, "The Dartmouth Indians, 1800–1893," *Dartmouth Alumni Magazine* 22 (June 1930), 526; Annual Meeting, 1848, Secretary's Book, SSPCK Records, folder 1-10; Tawse to Greene, May 4, 1849, SSPCK Records, folder 1-4. On the dispute between Marsh and Slingerland and for confirmation of other details on Slingerland, I am grateful to Jeffrey Siemers for providing me with a copy of his unpublished manuscript "Death of the Tribal Church: The Stockbridge Mohicans and the ABCFM."

25. Peter Paul Osunkhirihine to S. B. Treat, June 5, 1851, ABCFM Archives, Houghton Library, Harvard, microfilm, reel 79, unit 6, vol. 4, 88–91 (original p/DOC 25). I am grateful to John Moody for sharing with me with a copy of this letter, in which Osunkhirhine provides details on his early life. Osunkhirhine returned to visit Newport in April 1861; Edmund Wheeler, *The History of Newport, New Hampshire* (Concord, N.H.: Republican Press Association, 1879), 251.

26. President Tyler to Rev. John Codman, June 17, 1823, Ms. 823367; Nathan Lord to Codman, Sept. 1, 1827, Ms. 8277501; see also Lord to Codman, Apr. 1, 1829, Ms. 829251; Leon Burr Richardson, *History of Dartmouth College* (Hanover, N.H.: Dartmouth College Publications, 1932), 1:417.

27. Lord to Codman, Sept. 9, 1829, Ms. 829509.

28. Richardson, *History of Dartmouth College*, 1:418.

29. Lord to Codman, Apr. 5, 1832, SSPCK Records, folder 1-3.

30. Mason Wade, ed., *The Journals of Francis Parkman* (New York: Harper, 1947), 1:21, 332n20.

31. Osunkhirihine to S. B. Treat, June 5, 1851, ABCFM Archives, microfilm, reel 79, unit 6, vol. 4, 88–91; John Wheelock to Jedediah Morse, Feb. 25, 1811, Ms. 811175.1; National Archives, Canada, Records Relating to Indian Affairs, RG 10, vol. 7:3733–45, reel C-10999; vol. 11:10003–4, 10006, reel C-11000; vol. 15:11918–20, 11924, 11928, reel C-11002.

32. Lord to Codman, Oct. 1, 1829, Ms. 829551; Osunkirhine to Lord, Sept. 2, 1829, Ms. 829502; Lord to Jeremiah Evarts, Nov. 17, 1829, Ms. 829613; David Greene to Codman, May 11, 1830, Ms. 830311; Tawse to Codman, Feb. 3, 1831, SSPCK Records, folder 1-3.

33. Osunkhirhine to Lord. Apr. 6, 1831, Ms. 831256.

34. *Missionary Herald* 30 (1834), 141; 32 (1836), 29; 33 (1837), 79.

35. Lord visited St. Francis in 1837 and 1841. Lord to Codman, Oct. 23, 1837, SSPCK Records, folder 1-3; Lord to Codman, May 3, 1841, Ms. 841303.

36. *Proceedings of the Vermont Historical Society*, Oct. 8, 1872 (Montpelier, Vt., 1872): xiii–xiv. Rauner Library holds the following works by Peter Paul Osunkhirhine, a.k.a. P. P. Wzokhilain: *Wawasi Lagidamwoganek Mdala Chowagidamwoganal Tabtagil, Onkawodokodozwal Wji Po batami Kkidwogan.* (Boston: Crocker and Brewster, 1830); *Wobanaki Kimzowi Awighigan* (Boston: Crocker and Brewster, 1830); *Kagakimzouiasis Ueji Uo'banakiak Adali kimo'gik Aliuitzo'ki Za Plasua* (Quebec: Fréchette & Cie., 1832); *St. Mark* (n.p., n.d.); *Metaphysical Sermon by the Rev. P. P. Osunkhirhine, Native Preacher, Missionary of the American Board and Commissioners for Foreign Missions, St. Francis, Canada East* (Three Rivers, Quebec: printed for the author).

37. Masta to Kelly, Mar. 1, 1924, Native Americans vertical file; Henry L. Masta, "When the Abenaki Came to Dartmouth," *Dartmouth Alumni Magazine* 21 (Mar. 1929), 302–3.

38. Lord to Codman, Apr. 11, 1836, SSPCK Records, folder 1-3.

39. Lord to Codman, Apr. 15, 1839, SSPCK Records, folder 1-3.

40. SSPCK Records, folder 1-4, passim.

41. Lord to Codman, Mar. 25, 1845, SSPCK Records, folder 1-4.

42. Lord to Codman, Oct. 21, 1844, Ms. 844571; Lord to Codman, Mar. 25, 1845, Apr. 23, 1847; SSPCK Records, folder 1-4. I am grateful to Marge Bruchac for the connection to Dark Cloud.

43. Lord to Tawse, May 9, 1844, in Secretary's Reports, 1843–1892, SSPCK Records, folder 1-10; Lord to Codman, Oct. 21, 1844, Ms. 844571; Lord to Codman, Apr. 23, 1847, SSPCK Records, folder 1-4.

44. Lord to Tawse, May 9, 1844, in Secretary's Reports, 1843–1892, SSPCK Records, folder 1-10; Lord to Codman, Oct. 21, 1844, Ms. 844571.

45. Lord to Codman, Mar. 25, 1845, SSPCK Records, folder 1-4; Lord to Greene, Apr. 23, 1849, Ms. 849273; Lord to Greene, May 1, 1850, SSPCK Records, folder 1-4; Richardson, *History of Dartmouth College*, 1:419. I am grateful to Lee Witters for the information on Masta's thesis, which is in volume 13 of the collated medical school theses.

46. Osunkhirihine to S. B. Treat, June 5, 1851, ABCFM Archives, microfilm reel 79, unit 6, vol. 4, 88–91.

47. Lord to [unknown], May 5, 1856, SSPCK Records, folder 1-5.

48. Lord to Codman, Apr. 1, 1829, Ms. 829251.

49. Laurence M. Hauptman, *Conspiracy of Interests: Iroquois Dispossession and the Rise of New York State* (Syracuse, N.Y.: Syracuse University Press, 1999).

50. H. A. Vernon, "Maris Bryant Pierce: The Making of a Seneca Leader," in L. G. Moses and Raymond Wilson, eds., *Indian Lives: Essays on Nineteenth- and Twentieth-century Native American Leaders* (Albuquerque: University of New Mexico Press, 1985), 26; Hauptman, *Conspiracy of Interests*, 154–56.

51. "Scotch Fund" ledger (Moor's Charity School accounts abridged from College ledgers), 1799–1817, Ms. DA 403, box 3, 3–5; Joseph Perry to Jedediah Morse, June 25, 1816, Ms. 816375.2.

52. Frederick Chase, *A History of Dartmouth College and the Town of Hanover, New Hampshire*, ed. by John K. Lord, 2 vols. (Vol. 1, Cambridge, Mass.: John Wilson and Son, 1891), 1:636; James B. Seaver, *A Narrative of the Life of Mrs. Mary Jemison*, ed. June

Namias (Norman: University of Oklahoma Press, 1992), 127; William N. Fenton, ed., "Answers to Governor Cass's Questions by Jacob Jameson, a Seneca [ca. 1821–1825]," *Ethnohistory* 16 (1969), 114–16; Report of the Board of Examiners, Sept. 9, 1816, Ms. 816509.

53. Timothy Alden, *An Account of Sundry Missions performed among the Senecas and Munsees; In a series of letters* (New York: J. Seymour, 1827), 33; "Journals of Rev. Thompson S. Harris: His Missionary Labors among the Senecas at Buffalo Creek and Cattaraugus Reservations, 1821–1828," *Buffalo Historical Society Publications* 6, no. 11 (1903), 281–82, 343–45; Fenton, "Answers to Governor Cass's Questions by Jacob Jameson," 116.

54. Granville Carter, ed., *The Collected Speeches of Sagoyewatha, or Red Jacket* (Syracuse, N.Y.: Syracuse University Press, 2006), 243, 245–46, 256–57, 260, 262, 265–66.

55. Hauptman, *Conspiracy of Interests*, 154–56, 160.

56. Fenton, "Answers to Governor Cass's Questions by Jacob Jameson," 118; "Algiers Romance a Naval Tragedy: U.S. Surgeon, Forbidden to Wed Sheik's Daughter, Was Buried at Sea," *New York Times*, July 5, 1955," copy in Rauner Library, Native Americans vertical file.

57. Hauptman, *Conspiracy of Interests*, 176.

58. William N. Fenton, "Toward the Gradual Civilization of the Indian Natives: The Missionary and Linguistic Work of Asher Wright (1803–1875) among the Senecas of Western New York," *Proceedings of the American Philosophical Society* 100 (Dec. 1956), 567–81; Thomas S. Abler, "Protestant Missionaries and Native Cultures: Parallel Careers of Asher Wright and Silas T. Rand," *American Indian Quarterly* 16 (1992), 25–38, esp. 28; Tawse to Lord[?], Sept. 4, 1851, SSPCK Records, folder 1-5.

59. Vernon, "Maris Bryant Pierce: The Making of a Seneca Leader," 23–25; Lord to Codman, Apr. 11, 1836, Apr. [?], 1837, Oct. 19, 1838, Apr. 15, 1839, Apr. 23, 1840, SSPCK Records, folder 1-3; see also H. A. Vernon, "Maris Bryant Pierce: A Seneca Chief at Dartmouth," *Dartmouth Alumni Magazine* (Dec. 1983), 38–41.

60. Vernon, "Maris Bryant Pierce: The Making of a Seneca Leader," 26–28.

61. The fall term ran September 1 to November 25, followed by a seven-week vacation. Winter term began late January and ran for seven weeks, but students who were teaching were not required to be in residence. Spring term went from late March to late July, with a two-week vacation break in May. Vernon, "Maris Bryant Pierce: The Making of a Seneca Leader," 24, citing Richardson, *History of Dartmouth College*, 2:452.

62. Lord to Codman, Oct. 19, 1838, SSPCK Records, folder 1-3.

63. *Address on the Present Condition and Prospects of the Aboriginal Inhabitants of North America, with particular reference to the Seneca Nation. Delivered at Buffalo, New York, by M. B. Pierce, a Chief of the Seneca Nation, and a Member of Dartmouth College* (Philadelphia: J. Richards, 1839).

64. Maris Bryant Pierce, "Book of Memorandum, 1840," Mar. 10, April 5, July 19. Pierce's widow donated his memorandum book to the Buffalo Historical Society; Rauner Library has a photostat copy.

65. John W. Tawse and George Lyon, *Report to the Society in Scotland for Propagating Christian Knowledge, of a Visit to America by their Appointment, in reference to the Fund Under Their Charge for the Education of Native Indians* (Edinburgh: Printed for the

Society, 1839), quotation at 10; *Petition of the Society in Scotland for Propagating Christian Knowledge to Settle Scheme for Application of Trust-Fund* (Edinburgh: T. and A. Constable, 1922), 4.

66. Tawse to Codman, Oct. 24, 1840, Ms. 840574; Tawse and Lyon, *Report to the Society in Scotland for Propagating Christian Knowledge, of a Visit to America*, 24–28, 128–30.

67. *Extra Census Bulletin: Indians: The Six Nations of New York* (Washington, D.C.: U.S. Census Printing Office, 1892; reprint, New York: New-York Historical Society, 1992), 75.

68. Vernon, "Maris Bryant Pierce: The Making of a Seneca Leader," 34.

69. Christopher Mulveg, "Among the Sag-a-noshes: Ojibwa and Iowa Indians with George Catlin in Europe, 1843–1848," in Christian F. Feest, ed., *Indians and Europe: An Interdisciplinary Collection of Essays* (1989; reprint, Lincoln: University of Nebraska Press, 1999), 265–73; Brian W. Dippie, *Catlin and His Contemporaries: The Politics of Patronage* (Lincoln: University of Nebraska Press, 1990), 107–9; Donald B. Smith, "Maungwudaus Goes Abroad," *Beaver*, Outfit 307 (Autumn 1976), 4–9.

70. *Hartford Daily Courant*, Apr.18, 1850: 2; I am grateful to Donald Smith for providing me with a copy of this source. Lord to Greene, May 1, 1850, May 7, 1851, SSPCK Records, folder 1-4, 1-5.

71. Lord to Tawse, May 9, 1853, SSPCK Records, folder 1-5.

## Chapter 6

1. For an overview see Kathleen Garrett, "Dartmouth Alumni in the Indian Territory," *Chronicles of Oklahoma* 32 (1954), 123–41.

2. Lord to Rev. John Codman, Oct. 19, 1838, Apr. 15, 1839, Society in Scotland for Propagating Christian Knowledge, Records, 1794–1892 (hereafter SSPCK Records), folder 1-3; Garrett, "Dartmouth Alumni in the Indian Territory," 137–38.

3. Arthur H. DeRosier, Jr., *The Removal of the Choctaw Indians* (Knoxville: University of Tennessee Press, 1970); Donna L. Akers, *Living in the Land of Death: The Choctaw Nation, 1830–1860* (East Lansing: Michigan State University Press, 2004), chap. 2.

4. J. P. Folsom, "Sketch of His Early Life," Ms. 000094, 1–8.

5. Lord to Codman, Oct. 21, 1844, Ms. 844571.

6. Lord to Codman, Mar. 25, 1845, SSPCK Records, folder 1-4.

7. Folsom, "Sketch of His Early life," quotation at 10–11.

8. Lord to Tawse, May 9, 1853, Lord to Rev. Neal, May 9, 1853, SSPCK Records, folder 1-5.

9. Lord to Rev. David Greene, May 7, 1851; Lord to Neal, May 10, 1852 (commencement speech), SSPCK Records, folder 1-5; Leon B. Richardson, "The Dartmouth Indians, 1800–1893," *Dartmouth Alumni Magazine* 22 (June 1930), 526; Folsom, "Sketch of His Early Life," quotation at 16; John King Lord, *A History of Dartmouth College 1815–1909* (Concord, N.H.: Rumford Press, 1913), 306 (commencement).

10. W. N. Jones quoted in class report, copy in Joseph Pitchlynn Folsom, Alumni file; Angie Debo, *The Rise and Fall of the Choctaw Republic*, 2nd ed. (Norman: University of Oklahoma Press, 1961), 123, 166–67, 215–16; *Constitution and Laws of the Choctaw Nation. Together with the Treaties of 1855, 1865 and 1866. Published by authority and direction of the General council by Joseph P. Folsom . . . Chahta Tamaha* (New York: W. P. Lyon & Son, 1869).

11. Lord to Greene, May 1, 1850, SSPCK Records, folder 1-4.

12. "Indians at Moor's Charity School," Apr. 1852, SSPCK Records, folder 1-5.

13. Lord to [unknown], May 5, 1856, SSPCK Records, folder 1-5.

14. "Indians at Moor's Charity School," Apr. 1852, SSPCK Records, folder 1-5.

15. The records are not consistent as to whether Ward left in 1852 or 1853 and whether he dropped out of Dartmouth or left before entering, having been preparing at Moor's Charity School. Lord to Neal, May 10, 1852, May 9, 1853, SSPCK Records, folder 1-5.

16. Lord to Neal, May 9, 1853; Lord to [unknown], May 5, 1856, SSPCK Records, folder 1-5.

17. Garrett, "Dartmouth Alumni in the Indian Territory," 127–28; Lord to Neal, May 15, 1857, May 10, 1858, SSPCK Records, folder 105.

18. Lord to Neal, May 13, 1859, SSPCK Records, folder 1-5; Apr. 27, 1861, May 10, 1862, SSPCK Records, folder 1-6.

19. Lord to Neal, May 10, 1858, May 13, 1859, SSPCK Records, folder 1-5; Lord to Neal, May 10, 1862, SSPCK Records, folder 1-6; Richardson, "Dartmouth Indians," 526–27; DeWitt Duncan Alumni file, 1861.

20. Rauner Library, Class of 1861 Report; DeWitt Duncan, Alumni file; Garrett, "Dartmouth Alumni in the Indian Territory," 130–32.

21. See, for example, Clarissa W. Confer, *The Cherokee Nation in the Civil War* (Norman: University of Oklahoma Press, 2007).

22. Garrett, "Dartmouth Alumni in the Indian Territory," 128.

23. Garrett, "Dartmouth Alumni in the Indian Territory," 129.

24. Samuel L. Gerould, *Biographical Sketches of the Class of 1858, Dartmouth College* (Nashua, N.H.: Telegraph Publishing Co., n.d.), 139; *General Catalogue of Dartmouth College and the Associated Schools, 1769–1940*, 181.

25. James Ward, Jr., Alumni file, 1855; Rev. Edward Schwarze, *History of the Moravian Missions among Southern Indian Tribes* (Bethlehem, Pa.: Times, 1923), 277, 285–87.

26. Lord to Neal, May 10, 1862, May [?], 1863, SSPCK Records, folder 1-6.

27. Lord to Neal, May [?], 1863; Smith to Treat, June 15, 1865, SSPCK Records, folder 1-6; Richardson, "Dartmouth Indians," 527.

28. Smith to Neal, July 12, 1864, SSPCK Records, folder 1-6; Richardson, "Dartmouth Indians," 527.

29. Smith to Rev. J. B. Treat, Dec. 31, 1872, SSPCK Records, folder 1-7.

30. *Petition of the Society in Scotland for Propagating Christian Knowledge to Settle Scheme for Application of Trust-Fund* (Edinburgh: T. and A. Constable, 1922), 5.

31. Tawse to Treat, July 8, 1869, SSPCK Records, folder 1-6.

32. Colin G. Calloway, ed., *Our Hearts Fell to the Ground: Plains Indian Views of How the West Was Lost* (Boston: Bedford/St. Martin's, 1996), 105–10.

33. Smith to Treat, Oct. 17, 1870 ("half-blood"), SSPCK Records, folder 1-6; Oct. 21, 1870, SSPCK Records, folder 1-7; Robert Hawthorn, Alumni file, 1874.

34. Smith to Treat, May 25, 1869, SSPCK Records, folder 1-6; Smith to Treat, Oct. 21, 1871, SSPCK records, folder 1-7; Garrett, "Dartmouth Alumni in the Indian Territory," 139–40; Albert Carney, Alumni file, 1875; includes a list of manuscripts relating to Carney, mainly dealing with finances.

35. Smith to Treat, June 20, 1875, and July 12, 1875, SSPCK Records, folder 1-7; John Comstock to the editor, *Dartmouth Alumni Magazine* 22 (Feb. 1930), 282; Garrett, "Dartmouth Alumni in the Indian Territory," 132–33.

36. David E. Wilkins, ed., *Documents of Native American Political Development, 1500s to 1933* (New York: Oxford University Press, 2009), 133–41.

37. Smith to Treat, Feb. 6, 1876, SSPCK Records, folder 1-7; Garrett, "Dartmouth Alumni in the Indian Territory," 130.

38. Bartlett to Tawse, June 20, 1877, George Cummings to Rev. E. K. Alden, July 23, 1879, Bartlett to Alden, Dec. 19, 1879, SSPCK Records, folder 1-7; Bartlett to Rev. E. E. Strong, Jan. 20, 1881, S. C. Pautels [?] to Strong, Sept. 26, 1881, Bartlett to Strong, Nov. 17, 1881, Rev. H. Fairbanks, statement respecting W. H. Luckadoe, Feb. 1882, and Tawse to Strong, May 6, 1882, SSPCK Records, folder 1-8. Cherokee Alonzo Mitchell, class of 1886, also attended the Agricultural College.

39. Jan. 12, 1882, SSPCK Records, folder 1-8.

40. Gaines to Strong, Dec. 22, 1882, Gaines to Bartlett, Mar. 6, 1883, Strong to Bartlett, June 1, 1883, SSPCK Records, folder 1-8.

41. Bartlett to Strong, Jan. 9, SSPCK Records, folder 1-8; Bartlett to Strong, Mar. 30, 1893, SSPCK Records, folder 1-9; Richardson, "Dartmouth Indians, 1800–1893," 527; Harvey Shelton, Alumni file; Garrett, "Dartmouth Alumni in the Indian Territory," 135 ("go to hell story").

42. Bartlett to Strong, Jan 9, 1884, June 18, 1885, Sept. 22, 1888, SSPCK Records, folder 1-8; Bartlett to Strong, Mar. 30, 1893, SSPCK Records, folder 1-9; Garrett, "Dartmouth Alumni in the Indian Territory," 136.

43. Richard K. Behrens, "From the Connecticut Valley to the West Coast: The Role of Dartmouth College in the Building of the Nation," *Historical New Hampshire* 63 (Spring, 2009), 45–68; John Ball, *Autobiography of John Ball* (Grand Rapids, Mich.: Dean-Hicks, 1925).

44. Behrens, "From the Connecticut Valley to the West Coast," 49, 59–60; George T. Chapman, *Sketches of the Alumni of Dartmouth College* (Cambridge, Mass.: Riverside Press, 1867), 244, 348.

45. Chapman, *Sketches*, 349; Franck C. Lockwood, *The Apache Indians* (1938; reprint, Lincoln: University of Nebraska Press, 1987), 156 (long Goodwin quotation); Karl Jacoby, "'The Broad Platform of Extermination': Nature and Violence in the Nineteenth-century North American Borderlands," *Journal of Genocide Research* 10 (2008), 249–67, espe-

cially 253; Ralph Hedrick Cole, *Federal Control of the Western Apaches, 1848–1886* (Albu-
querque: University of New Mexico Press, 1970), 60 ("bow their necks" quotation). On
Goodwin's administration see Jay J. Wagoner, *Arizona Territory 1863–1912: A Political
History* (Tucson: University of Arizona Press, 1970), chap. 2.

46. Edwin Hyde Alden, Alumni file, 1859.

## Chapter 7

1. For a biography, see Raymond Wilson, *Ohiyesa: Charles Eastman, Santee Sioux*
(Urbana: University of Illinois Press, 1983); for an autobiographical account, Charles
A. Eastman, *From the Deep Woods to Civilization: Chapters in the Autobiography of
an Indian* (1916; reprint, Lincoln: University of Nebraska Press, 1977). On Eastman the
writer, see Bernd C. Peyer, "Charles Alexander Eastman (Ohiyesa)," in Peyer, "*The Thinking Indian": Native American Writers, 1850s–1920s* (Frankfurt: Peter Lang, 2007), chap.
5; Penelope Myrtle Kelsey, "Charles Eastman's Role in Native American Resistance Literature," in Kelsey, *Tribal Theory in Native American Literature* (Lincoln: University of
Nebraska Press, 2008), 43–61, and David Martinez, *Dakota Philosopher: Charles Eastman
and American Indian Thought* (Minneapolis: Minnesota Historical Society Press, 2009).

2. Gerald Vizenor, *Manifest Manners: Postindian Warriors of Survivance* (Hanover,
N.H.: University Press of New England, 1994), 51.

3. Carolyn Gilman and Mary Jane Schneider, *The Way to Independence: Memories of
a Hidatsa Family, 1840–1920* (St. Paul: Minnesota Historical Society Press, 1987), 153–54,
226.

4. Frederick E. Hoxie, *Parading through History: The Making of the Crow Nation in
America, 1805–1935* (Cambridge: Cambridge University Press, 1995), 233–34.

5. Eastman, *From the Deep Woods to Civilization*, 25.

6. Eastman, *From the Deep Woods to Civilization*, 46–47.

7. Eastman, *From the Deep Woods to Civilization*, 48.

8. Eastman, *From the Deep Woods to Civilization*, 54–55.

9. E. E. Ruggles to [unknown], Jan. 24, 1882, Gaines to Strong, Jan. 24 and 28, 1882,
Bartlett to Strong, Jan. 30 and 31, 1882, Strong to Bartlett, Feb. 1, 1882, Society in Scotland
for Propagating Christian Knowledge, Records, 1794–1892 (hereafter SSPCK Records),
folder 1-8; minutes of annual meeting, Jan. 1882, Secretary's Book, SSPCK Records,
folder 1-10.

10. Prof. M. R. Gaines, Mar. 7, 1882, SSPCK Records, folder 1-8.

11. Gaines to Strong, Dec. 22, 1882, Gaines to Bartlett, Mar. 6, 1883, SSPCK Records,
folder 1-8.

12. Eastman, *From the Deep Woods to Civilization*, 65.

13. Eastman, *From the Deep Woods to Civilization*, 66–67.

14. Sally Jenkins, *The Real All Americans: The Team That Changed a Game, a People,
a Nation* (New York: Doubleday, 2007); David Wallace Adams, "More Than a Game: The
Carlisle Indians Take to the Gridiron," *Western Historical Quarterly* 32 (2001), 25–53.

15. Eastman, *From the Deep Woods to Civilization*, 68.

16. Bartlett to Strong, Jan. 9, 1884, SSPCK Records, folder 1-8.

17. Wilson, *Ohiyesa*, 32; Eastman, *From the Deep Woods to Civilization*, 69, 72; *Boston Traveler*, June 12, 1919, copy in Rauner Library, Dartmouth College.

18. Eastman, *From the Deep Woods to Civilization*, 68–69.

19. Fred E. Winn, "Ohiyesa, By a Classmate" [n.d.], Rauner Library. Thanks to Ibrahim Elshamy for locating this source and other details about Eastman's education at Dartmouth.

20. Eastman, *From the Deep Woods to Civilization*, 69.

21. Indian Charity Fund, June 30, 1884, and misc. accounts, SSPCK Records, folder 1-8.

22. Eastman to Strong, July 14, 1887, SSPCK Records, folder 1-8.

23. Dawes and Roosevelt quoted in Colin G. Calloway, *First Peoples: A Documentary Survey of American Indian History*, 3rd ed. (Boston: Bedford/St. Martin's, 2008), 378; Morgan quoted in Michael C. Coleman, *American Indians, the Irish, and Government Schooling* (Lincoln: University of Nebraska Press, 2007), 51.

24. Emily Greenwald, *Reconfiguring the Reservation: The Nez Perces, Jicarilla Apaches, and the Dawes Act* (Albuquerque: University of New Mexico Press, 2002); Bonnie Lynn-Sherow, *Red Earth: Race and Culture in Oklahoma Territory* (Lawrence: University Press of Kansas, 2004), chap. 7.

25. For further discussion see Colin G. Calloway, "The Vermont Secretary and the Apache POWs: Redfield Proctor and the Case of the Chiricahuas," *Vermont History* 59 (1991), 166–79.

26. Eastman, *From the Deep Woods to Civilization*, 70.

27. Theodore D. Sargent, *The Life of Elaine Goodale Eastman* (Lincoln: University of Nebraska Press, 2005).

28. Quoted in Wilson, *Ohiyesa*, 52.

29. Wilson, *Ohiyesa*, 59–61; Eastman, *From the Deep Woods to Civilization*, 11–14.

30. "Statements of a Delegation of Ogallalla Sioux before the Chairman of the Committee of Indian Affairs, United States Senate, April 29–30, 1897, Relative to Affairs at the Pine Ridge Agency," 55th Cong., 1st sess., Senate Doc. 61 (Washington, D.C.: U.S. Government Printing Office, 1897).

31. S. C. Bartlett, "Statement in regard to Moor's Charity School," c. 1890, Moor's Indian Charity School Records, box 1; Bartlett to Strong, Feb. 10, 1892, and Nov. 15, 1892, SSPCK Records, folder 1-9; Bartlett to the SSPCK, Mar. 9, 1892, Correspondence between the American Board of Commissioners for Foreign Missions and the S.S.P.C.K. regarding the education of Indians at Moore's Indian School and Dartmouth College, 1890–1898, National Archives of Scotland, Edinburgh, GD95/12/16, 362–65, and SSPCK Records, folder 1-9; Sec. of the SSPCK (Nesbit) to Sec. of the Society Board of Commissioners in Boston (Strong), Mar. 8, 1893, Correspondence between the American Board of Commissioners for Foreign Missions and the S.S.P.C.K, GD/95/12/16: 372–75, and SSPCK Records, folder 1-9; Bartlett to Strong, Mar. 27, 1893, Correspondence between the American Board of Commissioners for Foreign Missions and the S.S.P.C.K, GD95/12/16, 380–85.

32. Leon Burr Richardson, *History of Dartmouth College*, 2 vols. (Hanover, N.H.: Dartmouth College Publications, 1932), 2:737.

33. Strong to C. C. Nisbet, Apr. 29, 1893, Correspondence between the American Board of Commissioners for Foreign Missions and the S.S.P.C.K., GD95/12/16: 378.

34. Bartlett to Strong, Mar. 30, 1893, SSPCK Records, folder 1-9.

35. Archibald Isaac, Alumni file, 1900.

36. Charles A. Eastman, *Indian Boyhood* (New York: McClure, Phillips, 1902), v.

37. Charles Eastman, "What Can the Out-of-doors Do for Our Children?" *Education* 41 (1920–21), 599–605, quotation at 604.

38. Wilson, *Ohiyesa*, 185.

39. "A Visit from Lord Dartmouth," in Edward Connery Latham and David M. Shribman, eds., *Miraculously Builded in Our Hearts: A Dartmouth Reader* (Hanover, N.H.: University Press of New England, 1999), 37–44.

40. Joanna Brooks, ed., *The Collected Writings of Samson Occom, Mohegan* (New York: Oxford University Press, 2006), 30.

41. *Dartmouth*, June 21, 1927; *Hanover Gazette*, July 14, 1927; "Art Gift to College Oil Painting Famous Living Indian Graduate," *Gazette*, July 4, 1935; "Dartmouth Alumni Entertain Bryant in Unveiling Fete," *Washington (DC) Herald*, May 22, 1935; Rauner Library.

42. Philip J. Deloria, *Indians in Unexpected Places* (Lawrence: University Press of Kansas, 2004), 60; Deloria, *Playing Indian* (New Haven, Conn.: Yale University Press, 1998), 123–26.

43. L. G. Moses, *Wild West Shows and the Images of American Indians, 1883–1933* (Albuquerque: University of New Mexico Press, 1996).

44. Lucy Maddox, *Citizen Indians: Native American Intellectuals, Race, and Reform* (Ithaca, N.Y.: Cornell University Press, 2005); Kelsey, *Tribal Theory in Native American Literature*, 50.

45. Peyer, "Charles Alexander Eastman," 334–35.

46. Kelsey, *Tribal Theory in Native American Literature*, 51.

47. Eastman, *From the Deep Woods to Civilization*, 195.

## Chapter 8

1. *Petition of the Society in Scotland for Propagating Christian Knowledge to Settle Scheme for Application of Trust-Fund* (Edinburgh: T. and A. Constable, 1922); 5–6; Rauner Library, Society in Scotland for Propagating Christian Knowledge: The Foreign Fund, typescript, 1980, probably written by R. J. B. Simpson, SSPCK secretary, Society in Scotland for Propagating Christian Knowledge, Records, 1794–1892 (hereafter SSPCK Records).

2. Leon Burr Richardson, *History of Dartmouth College*, 2 vols. (Hanover, N.H.: Dartmouth College Publications, 1932), 2:761; preface, Moor's Indian Charity School Records, 1760–1915.

3. *Petition of the Society in Scotland for Propagating Christian Knowledge to Settle Scheme for Application of Trust-Fund*, 7–9; Society in Scotland for Propagating Christian Knowledge: The Foreign Fund.

4. On the assault on Indian culture in the late nineteenth and early twentieth centuries see, for example, David Wallace Adams, *Education for Extinction: American Indians and the Boarding School Experience, 1875–1928* (Lawrence: University Press of Kansas, 1995); Brenda Child, *Boarding School Seasons: American Indian Families, 1900–1940* (Lincoln: University of Nebraska Press, 1998); Frederick E. Hoxie, *The Final Promise: The Campaign to Assimilate the Indians, 1888–1920* (Lincoln: University of Nebraska Press, 1984); Francis Paul Prucha, ed., *Americanizing the American Indian: Writings by the "Friends of the Indian," 1880–1920* (Lincoln: University of Nebraska Press, 1978).

5. Rayna Green, "The Tribe Called Wannabee," *Folklore* 99 (1988), 30–35.

6. Jere Daniell, "Dartmouth College," in Frederick E. Hoxie, ed., *Encyclopedia of North American Indians* (Boston: Houghton Mifflin, 1996), 171; Sarah Part, "The Influence of White Conceptions of American Indians on Dartmouth Student Life, 1880–1920: A Study of Student Scrapbooks," independent study, Native American Studies, spring 2008, Native American Studies Program, Dartmouth College, quotation at 42.

7. Philip J. Deloria, *Playing Indian* (New Haven, Conn.: Yale University Press, 1998); Renée Bergland, *The National Uncanny: Indian Ghosts and American Subjects* (Hanover, N.H.: University Press of New England, 2000); Alan Trachtenberg, *Shades of Hiawatha: Staging Indians, Making Americans, 1880–1930* (New York: Hill and Wang, 2004); Mick Gidley, *Edward S. Curtis and the North American Indian, Incorporated* (Cambridge: Cambridge University Press, 1998); Sherry L. Smith, *Reimagining Indians: Native Americans through Anglo Eyes, 1880–1940* (New York: Oxford University Press, 2000).

8. Deloria, *Playing Indian*, 2–7, 25–26; Part, "Influence of White Conceptions."

9. "Robert Frost 1896 Returns to the Campus," in Edward Connery Latham and David M. Shribman, eds., *Miraculously Builded in Our Hearts: A Dartmouth Reader* (Hanover, N.H.: University Press of New England, 1999), 71–72.

10. P. Curtis Herbert, "The Indian Symbol at Dartmouth College," student history paper, 1972, copy in Indian Symbol Files, Native American Studies Program.

11. Part, "Influence of White Conceptions."

12. Russell O. Ayers, "The Indian Yell Revisited," *Dartmouth Alumni Magazine* 65 (May 1973), 14–15.

13. Part, "Influence of White Conceptions," 29–39.

14. James T. Kloppenberg, "The Dartmouth Indian," student paper, spring 1972, copy in Indian Symbol Files, Native American Studies Program.

15. Quoted in *Orozco at Dartmouth: The Epic of American Civilization* (Hanover, N.H.: Hood Museum of Art/Dartmouth College Library, 2007), 6.

16. Thanks to Peter Carini for the information on Humphrey and the Indian head.

17. See, for example, *Aegis* (1947), 140–41.

18. Horace A. Nelson, Alumni file, 1904; Bunny McBride, *Molly Spotted Elk: A Penobscot in Paris* (Norman: University of Oklahoma Press, 1995) 17–18.

19. McBride, *Molly Spotted Elk*.

20. The items are on display in the Native American Studies Program building.

21. Lawrence S. Ritter, *The Glory of Their Times: The Story of the Early Days of Baseball Told by the Men Who Played It* (1966; reprint, New York: Morrow, 1984); R. J. Lesch, "Chief Meyers," Baseball Biography Project, bioprojsabr.org; "Real Indian Chief Will Play on Dartmouth Eleven," newspaper clipping, scrapbook of Dartmouth graduate, class of 1901, Rauner Library; Ralph Glaze, as told to Rolfe Humphries, "How the Chief Made the Major Leagues," *Denver Sunday Post, Empire Magazine*, Aug. 20, 1967, in John T. Meyers, Alumni file, 1909, 32–34.

22. Ritter, *Glory of Their Times*, 170–84; Bender quotation at 201; Lesch, "Chief Meyers"; Henry C. Koerper, "John Tortes Meyers: A Cahuilla in the Big Leagues," *News from Native California* 10 (summer 1997), 4–6. On Bender see Tom Swift, *Chief Bender's Burden: The Silent Struggle of a Baseball Star* (Lincoln: University of Nebraska Press, 2008).

23. Ritter, *Glory of Their Times*, 170, 172.

24. Alvis Kusic, Alumni file, 1909; Victor Johnson, Alumni file, 1910.

25. David Hogan Markham, Alumni file, 1915; Markham to Leon B. Richardson, June 18, 1920, Ms. 930368; John Hurd, "The Wheelock Dream, Sparsely Realized, Still a Force in the Life of the College," *Dartmouth Alumni Magazine* 58 (Oct. 1965), 35–39.

26. Oct. 23, 1914, Carlos Montezuma Papers, Newberry Library, Chicago, 383–85. I am grateful to Bernd C. Peyer for providing me with a copy of this letter.

27. "College Owes Indian Yell to Cherokee Chief," *Dartmouth*, Sept. 25, 1925, 3; Walkingstick obituary, *Dartmouth Alumni Magazine* 63 (Feb. 1971), 78; Ayers, "Indian Yell Revisited," 14–15.

28. *Dartmouth College and Associated Schools General Catalogue, 1769–1940* (Hanover, N.H.: Dartmouth College Publications, 1940), 433; Angus Splicer, Alumni file, 1916.

29. Walkingstick to Mrs. Law [?], Oct. 27, 1914, Ms. 914577.

30. War record, Simon Ralph Walkingstick, Alumni file.

31. Walkingstick to Rugg, Apr. 5, 1918, and Apr. 8, 1919, Simon Ralph Walkingstick, Alumni file.

32. Walkingstick to Rugg, Nov. 5, 1919, Simon Ralph Walkingstick, Alumni file.

33. Simon Ralph Walkingstick, Alumni file; *Dartmouth Alumni Magazine* 63 (Feb. 1971), 78.

34. Carolyn Thomas Foreman, *Indians Abroad, 1493–1938* (Norman: University of Oklahoma Press, 1943), 214.

35. Francis Philip Frazier, Alumni file, 1920; Thomas Alfred Tripp, "Sitting Bull's Successor: The Story of an Indian Pastor Who Preaches in the Old School Language," *Congregationalist*, Feb. 1943, 12–24, copy in Francis Philip Frazier, Alumni file.

36. Frazier to Paul Richter, Dec. 7, 1959, Francis Philip Frazier, Alumni file.

37. Press release, Dartmouth College News Service, June 12, 1964, Francis Philip Frazier, Alumni file.

38. Frell MacDonald Owl, interview by Dr. Blumer, May 1979; Thomas John Blumer Collection on the Catawba Nation, Native American Studies Archive, University of South Carolina, Lancaster. Thanks to archivist Brent Burgin for providing me with this quotation.

39. Dawnena Walkingstick, "A Pre-citizenship Certificate of Educational Competency," *Journal of Cherokee Studies* 1 (Fall 1976), 87–91; Adams, *Education for Extinction*, 145–46.

40. *Dartmouth Alumni Magazine* 61 (July 1969), 28; Frell Macdonald Owl, Alumni file, 1927; George W. Friede, "Dartmouth Indian with a Mission," *Dartmouth Alumni Magazine* 49 (Mar. 1957), 21–24.

41. Friede, "Dartmouth Indian with a Mission," 24.

42. Frell M. Owl, "Who and What Is an American Indian?" *Ethnohistory* 9 (1962), 265–84; quotations at 265, 272–73, 274.

43. Benedict Hardman, Alumni file, 1931.

44. Roland Burnett Sundown, Alumni file, 1932.

45. "Indians Who Have Attended Dartmouth in the Last Twenty Years," Native Americans—Alumni, vertical file; *Dartmouth College and Associated Schools General Catalogue, 1769–1940.*

46. John Elwood Snyder, Alumni file, 1936.

47. Everett E. White, Alumni file, 1937.

48. Alexander Augustine Sapiel, Alumni file, 1938.

49. Eddie O'Brien, "Remembering December 7, 1941," in Latham and Shribman, *Miraculously Built in Our Hearts*, 181–87.

50. "Indians Who Have Attended Dartmouth in the Last Twenty Years."

51. "Indians Who Have Attended Dartmouth in the Last Twenty Years."

52. Henry G. Perley, Alumni file, 1943.

53. Albert Andrew Exendine, Alumni file, 1943.

54. Henry G. Perley, Alumni file.

55. William John Cook, Alumni file, 1949.

56. Joseph H. Jacobs, Alumni file, 1950; "Indians Who Have Attended Dartmouth in the Last Twenty Years."

57. Thanks to Bruce Duthu for bring Durance to my attention. The PBS documentary *In the Light of Reverence* explores the controversy surrounding the site.

58. White River Junction, Vermont, *Valley News*, Dec. 5, Dec. 8, 1952, and other clippings, Native Americans vertical file.

59. Ewers's publications include: *The Horse in Blackfoot Indian Culture: with Comparative Material from Other Western Tribes* (Washington, D.C.: U.S. Government Printing Office, 1955); *The Blackfeet: Raiders of the Northwestern Plains* (Norman: University of Oklahoma Press, 1958); *Artists of the Old West* (Garden City, N.Y.: Doubleday, 1965); *Plains Indian Sculpture: A Traditional Art from America's Heartland* (Washington, D.C.: Smithsonian Institution Press, 1986); *Indian Life on the Upper Missouri* (Norman: University of Oklahoma Press, 1968); *Plains Indian History and Culture: Essays on Continuity and Change* (Norman: University of Oklahoma Press, 1997).

60. Washburn's publications include *Red Man's Land/White Man's Law: A Study of the Past and Present Status of the American Indian* (New York: Scribner, 1971); *The Assault on Indian Tribalism: The General Allotment Law (Dawes Act) of 1887* (Philadelphia: Lippincott, 1975); Wilcomb Washburn, ed., *The American Indian and the United States: A*

*Documentary History*, 4 vols. (New York: Random House, 1973); *The Indian in America* (New York: HarperRow, 1975); Wilcomb Washburn and Bruce G. Trigger, eds., *The Cambridge History of the Native Peoples of the Americas: North America*, 2 vols. (Cambridge: Cambridge University Press, 1996).

61. William N. Fenton, *Iroquois Journey: An Anthropologist Remembers*, ed. Jack Campisi and William A. Starna (Lincoln: University of Nebraska Press, 2007).

62. Gísla Pálsson, *Travelling Passions: The Hidden Life of Vilhjalmur Stefansson*, translated from the Icelandic by Keneva Kunz (Hanover, N.H.: University Press of New England, 2005).

63. Gordon M. Day, "The Dartmouth Algonkian Collection," in Rauner Misc. Material File, Rauner Library, Dartmouth College. On Day and his work, see Michael K. Foster and William Cowan, eds., *In Search of New England's Native Past: Selected Essays by Gordon M. Day* (Amherst: University of Massachusetts Press, 1998); *Western Abenaki Dictionary*, 2 vols. (Ottawa: Canadian Museum of Civilization, Canadian Ethnology Service, 1994–95).

64. Andrew Garrod and Colleen Larimore, introduction to *First Person, First Peoples: Native American College Graduates Tell Their Life Stories* (Ithaca, N.Y.: Cornell University Press, 1997), 8; Part, "Influence of White Conceptions," 44.

65. Charles Jay Kershner, "Eleazar Is Outdone," *Dartmouth Alumni Magazine* 63 (Oct. 1970), 33.

66. Hurd, "Wheelock Dream, Sparsely Realized," 35–39, 116.

67. Andrew Garrod and Colleen Larimore, introduction to *First Person, First Peoples*, 8.


*Chapter 9*


1. Francis Paul Prucha, ed., *Documents of United States Indian Policy* (Lincoln: University of Nebraska Press, 1975), 256–58.

2. Kemeny quotations from Charles Jay Kershner, "Eleazar Is Outdone," *Dartmouth Alumni Magazine* 63 (Oct. 1970), 32.

3. Alfred T. Quirk, "The Dartmouth Dilemma: Minority Enrollment from the 1960s," (1993), 128; Rauner Library, DA-7, Office of the Provost, Series 1736, Provost Subject Files, box 4938

4. Quirk, "Dartmouth Dilemma," 129.

5. Kershner, "Eleazar Is Outdone," 32–33.

6. Rosemary Lunardini, "A Place on the Plain," *Dartmouth Medicine* (Fall 1995), 24, 26, 28.

7. "Indians and the Ivy League," *American Indian Report*, Feb. 2000, 12.

8. A concise and insightful discussion of the Indian symbol and the issues it raised in the 1970s, much of which still applies today, can be found in Calvin Trillin, "The Symbol Is a Symbol," *New Yorker*, May 7, 1979, 132–40.

9. "Policy Statement from Native Americans at Dartmouth on the Dartmouth 'indian'

Symbol and Recommendations," Dec. 2, 1971, copy Native American Studies Program, Dartmouth College.

10. Michael Dorris, *The Broken Cord* (New York: Harper and Row, 1989), 31, 42.

11. Quoted in "Outline History of Native American Programs at Dartmouth College," Native American Council Minutes, Native American Studies Program, Dartmouth College.

12. Robert Kilmarx to Michael McGean, Mar. 1, 1972, and "Report and Recommendations of the Indian Symbol Study Committee, Approved by Dartmouth Alumni Council, June 15, 1972," Native American Studies Program. The report also appears in *Dartmouth Alumni Magazine* 64 (July 1972), 31–32.

13. Russell Ayers, Alumni file, 1929, especially alumni record and Ayers to "Charley," July 5, 1972.

14. Ayers to "Charley," July 5, 1972, Russell Ayers, Alumni file, 1929.

15. Ayers to Dudley, Aug. 26, 1974; Ayers to "Ort," and Ayers to Fran and Charley, Oct. 1, 1974, Russell Ayers, Alumni file.

16. Ayers to Charley, Oct. 13, 1976, Russell Ayers, Alumni file.

17. Ayers to Charles Dudley, June 28, 1972, Russell Ayers, Alumni file.

18. *Dartmouth Alumni Magazine* 64 (June 1972), 5, and in Indian Symbol Files, Native American Studies Program.

19. Ellis O. Briggs, "Goodbye to the Dartmouth College Indian," *Manchester Union Leader*, July 31, 1972, Indian Symbol Files.

20. *Dartmouth Alumni Magazine* 64 (May 1972), 2–3, and in Indian Symbol Files.

21. Eleanor R. Williamson, Juana D. Perley, Madalene F. Burnham, *Aboriginally Yours: Chief Henry Red Eagle* (Greenville, Me.: Moosehead Communications, 1997), xx, xxvi. I am grateful to the late Fred Stockwell, class of 1943, for providing me with a copy of this source, and for his support of Native American Studies at Dartmouth. His interest, like that of his classmates, was due in no small part to his association with and memory of Henry Eagle.

22. *Dartmouth Alumni Magazine* 65 (Jan. 1973), and in Indian Symbol Files.

23. Benedict Hardman to George H. Colton, Dec. 8, 1974, and letter to the editor, *Dartmouth Alumni Magazine* 66 (Mar. 1974), 2, and 69 (Mar. 1977), Indian Symbol Files.

24. Jack Manning, personal communication, Mar. 23, 2009.

25. Trillin, "Symbol Is a Symbol," quotations at 133.

26. N. Bruce Duthu, "The Good Ol' Days," in Andrew Garrod and Colleen Larimore, eds., *First Person, First Peoples: Native American College Graduates Tell Their Life Stories* (Ithaca, N.Y.: Cornell University Press, 1997), 239.

27. John D. Pope, class of 1954, *Dartmouth Alumni Magazine* 65 (Oct. 1972), 4, and in Indian Symbol Files.

28. Dorris, *Broken Cord*, 105 (quotation), 140–41.

29. *Dartmouth*, Feb. 28, 1978.

30. Quoted in *Sports Illustrated* 50, no. 19 (May 7, 1979), 12.

31. Elizabeth Carey, "I Dance for Me," in Garrod and Larimore, *First Person, First Peoples*, 127.

32. Hicks to Dorris, Aug. 1, Aug. 13, 1979; "Hicks Ponders the Old and New Dartmouth," interview with Jon Walcoff, *Dartmouth Fortnightly*, Feb. 6, 1981, 6–7; both in Indian Symbol Files.

33. *Dartmouth*, May 27, 1980, 1.

34. See for example the article by two *Review* editors, Gregory A. Fossedal and Dinesh D'Souza, "Dartmouth's Restoration," *National Review*, Sept. 18, 1981, 1071–77, and the essays on "The Indian Wars: The Meaning of a Symbol," in James Panero and Stefan Beck, eds., *The Dartmouth Review Pleads Innocent: Twenty-five Years of Being Threatened, Impugned, Vandalized, Sued, Suspended, and Bitten at the Ivy League's Most Controversial Conservative Newspaper* (Wilmington, Del.: ISI Books, 2000), 71–87.

35. *Dartmouth*, Nov. 3, 1983.

36. Richard Weissman and Donald Pomeroy to Dartmouth students, Sept. 21, 1984, Indian Symbol Files; *Dartmouth*, Sept. 24, 1984.

37. *Dartmouth*, May 23, 1984.

38. *A Way of Learning: A Film by Alanis Obomsawin* (Trustees of Dartmouth College, 1988).

39. Kendra Quincy Kemp, "The Smashing of a Tradition: Clay Pipes at Dartmouth College, 1992–1993," senior seminar paper, History Department, Dartmouth College, 2002.

40. *Dartmouth Life*, November 1992.

41. Marianne Chamberlain, "The Web of Life," in Garrod and Larimore, *First Person, First Peoples*, 157.

42. Native American Council letter, *Dartmouth*, Nov. 20, 2006; President Wright, Announcement to Dartmouth Students, Nov. 20, 2006; "Hundreds Converge on Dartmouth Hall for Rally," *Dartmouth*, Nov. 30, 2006; Catherine Faurot, "Native Voices," *Dartmouth Alumni Magazine* 99 (May/June 2007), 40–45, 109.

43. *The Dartmouth Review*, Nov. 29, 2006.

44. Louise Erdrich, "Foreword," in Garrod and Larimore, *First Person, First Peoples*, xii.

45. Garrod and Larimore, Introduction to *First Person, First Peoples*, 8.

46. Trillin, "Symbol Is a Symbol," quotation at 136.

47. Haynes Lund, class of 1974, letter to the editor, *Dartmouth Alumni Magazine* 72 (Apr. 1980), 12.

48. The full text of the American Psychological Association resolution is at www.apa. org/releases/ResAmIndianMascots.pdf.

49. S. L. Price, "The Indian Wars," *Sports Illustrated*, Mar. 4, 2002, 66–72; Carol Spindel, *Dancing at Halftime: Sports and the Controversy over American Indian Mascots* (New York: New York University Press, 2000); C. Richard King and Charles Fruehling Springwood, eds., *Team Spirits: The Native American Mascot Controversy* (Lincoln: University of Nebraska Press, 2001).

50. Fay G. Cohen, *Treaties on Trial: The Continuing Controversy over Northwest Indian Fishing Rights* (Seattle: University of Washington Press, 1986), 6–7, 90, 109–10, 120, 175.

51. Kallen M. Martin, "Under His Authority: Slade Gorton and the New Terminators in Congress," *Native Americas*, Sept. 30, 1996, 22.

52. "Senator Gorton's Ignoble Crusade," *New York Times*, Aug. 31, 1997, 8.

53. Quoted in N. Bruce Duthu, *American Indians and the Law* (New York: Viking/Penguin, 2008), 125.

54. Jeffrey St. Clair, "The Last Indian Fighter: Slade Gorton Is American Indians' Public Enemy No. 1," *In These Times*, Oct. 2, 2000, 14.

55. The Harvard Project on American Indian Economic Development, *The State of the Native Nations: Conditions under U.S. Policies of Self-Determination* (New York: Oxford University Press, 2008), 61–62.

56. "Dartmouth's Native American Program Celebrates 20th Anniversary," *Dartmouth Currents* 3, no. 2 (Oct. 25, 1990).

57. "Yellowtail Tabbed as MSU Endowed Chair in Native American Studies," *MSU News*, Oct. 10, 2006.

58. Lori Arviso Alvord, "Full Circle," in Garrod and Larimore, *First Person, First Peoples*, 216–17; Lori Arviso Alford and Elizabeth Cohen Van Pelt, *The Scalpel and the Silver Bear* (New York: Bantam Books, 1999), 26–27; Peter Mandel, "Native Americans at Dartmouth: The People and the Program," *Dartmouth Alumni Magazine* 78 (May 1986), 36–40.

59. *Beet Queen* (1986), *Tracks* (1988), *The Bingo Palace* (1994), *Tales of Burning Love* (1997), *The Antelope Wife* (1998), *The Last Report on the Miracles at Little No Horse* (2001), *The Master Butchers' Singing Club* (2003), *The Painted Drum* (2005).

60. Alvin Warren, interview, *First Voices* 1, no. 1 (Spring 2008), 12–13; Alvin Warren, "Cultivating the Next Generation of Leaders: Reflections of a Young Tribal Leader," *Grantmakers in the Arts Reader* 18 (Fall 2007), 89–95.

61. Garrod and Larimore, Introduction to *First Person, First Peoples*, 4.

62. Quoted in Colleen Larimore to Dave Smathers, Sept. 30, 1991, Native American Council Minutes.

## Conclusion

1. *Dartmouth Alumni Magazine* 89 (Mar. 1997).

2. Francis Paul Prucha, ed., *Documents of United States Indian Policy* (Lincoln: University of Nebraska Press, 1975), 33; Michael C. Coleman, *American Indians, the Irish, and Government Schooling* (Lincoln: University of Nebraska Press, 2007), 1 (quotation), 40; David Wallace Adams, *Education for Extinction: American Indians and the Boarding School Experience, 1875–1982* (Lawrence: University Press of Kansas, 1995).

3. K. Tsianina Lomawaima, *They Called It Prairie Light: The Story of Chilocco Indian School* (Lincoln: University of Nebraska Press, 1994); Brenda J. Child, *Boarding School Seasons: American Indian Families, 1900–1940* (Lincoln: University of Nebraska Press, 1998); Basil H. Johnston, *Indian School Days* (Norman: University of Oklahoma Press, 1989).

4. Luther Standing Bear, *Land of the Spotted Eagle* (1933; reprint, Lincoln: University of Nebraska Press, 1978), 236.

5. Vine Deloria, Jr., *Indian Education in America* (Boulder, Colo.: AISES, 1991), 20–21.

# SELECT BIBLIOGRAPHY

## Archival Sources

Massachusetts Historical Society, Boston
    Thomas Walcutt Papers.
National Archives of Scotland, Edinburgh
    Correspondence between the American Board of Commissioners for Foreign Missions and the S.S.P.C.K. regarding the education of Indians at Moore's Indian School and Dartmouth College, 1890–1898, GD95/12/16.
Native American Studies Program, Dartmouth College
    Indian Symbol Files.
    Native American Council Minutes.
Rauner Library, Dartmouth College
    Alumni Files.
    Dinsmoor Family Papers, 1802–1853.
    J. P. Folsom, "Sketch of His Early Life."
    McClure Collection.
    Moor's Indian Charity School Records, 1760–1915.
    Papers of Eleazar Wheelock.
    Papers of Samuel Kirkland, 1764–1808.
    Records of the Dartmouth College Treasurer.
    Samson Occom, "A Short Narrative of My Life" (1768).
    Society in Scotland for Propagating Christian Knowledge, Records, 1794–1892.
    Vertical files: Moor's Charity School, Native Americans, Native American Alumni, Native Americans at Dartmouth.

## Printed Sources

Axtell, James. "Dr. Wheelock's Little Red School." In Axtell, *The European and the Indian: Essays in the Ethnohistory of Colonial North America.* New York: Oxford University Press, 1981, 87–109.

Behrens, Richard K. "From the Connecticut Valley to the West Coast: The Role of Dartmouth College in the Building of the Nation." *Historical New Hampshire* 63 (Spring 2009), 45–68.

Blodgett, Harold. *Samson Occom: The Biography of an Indian Preacher.* Hanover, N.H.: Dartmouth College Publications, 1935.

Brooks, Joanna, ed. *The Collected Writings of Samson Occom, Mohegan.* New York: Oxford University Press, 2006.

Brown, Rebecca, ed. *Where the Great River Rises: An Atlas of the Connecticut River Watershed in Vermont and New Hampshire.* Hanover, N.H.: University Press of New England, 2009.

Calloway, Colin G. "Eleazar Wheelock Meets Luther Standing Bear: Native American Studies at Dartmouth College." In *Native American Studies in Higher Education: Models for Collaboration between Universities and Indigenous Nations,* ed. Duane Champagne and Jay Stauss. Walnut Creek, Calif.: Altamira Press, 2002, 17–27.

Chase, Frederick. *A History of Dartmouth College and the Town of Hanover, New Hampshire.* Ed. John K. Lord. 2 vols. Vol. 1: Cambridge, Mass.: John Wilson and Sons, 1891. (Often cited as a 2-volume work, although volume 2 has title and imprint: *A History of Dartmouth College, 1815–1909,* by John King Lord, being the second volume of *A History of Dartmouth College and the Town of Hanover, New Hampshire,* begun by Frederick Chase. Concord, N.H.: Rumford Press, 1913.)

Daniell, Jere R. "Eleazar Wheelock and the Dartmouth College Charter." *Historical New Hampshire* 24 (winter 1969), 3–44.

*Dartmouth Alumni Magazine.*

*Dartmouth College and Associated Schools General Catalogue, 1769–1940.* Hanover, N.H.: Dartmouth College Publications, 1940.

Day, Gordon M. "Dartmouth and Saint Francis." *Dartmouth Alumni Magazine* 52 (Nov. 1959), 28–30; reprinted in Day, *In Search of New England's Native Past: Selected Essays by Gordon M. Day,* ed. Michael K. Foster and William Cowan. Amherst: University of Massachusetts Press, 1998, 49–53.

Dexter, Franklin B., ed. *Diary of David McClure, Doctor of Divinity, 1748–1820.* New York: Knickerbocker Press, 1899. Reprinted as *Ohio Country Missionary: The Diary of David McClure 1748–1820.* Waterville, Ohio: Penobscot Press, 1996.

"Documents Relating to the Stockbridge Mission, 1825–48." *Collections of the Wisconsin State Historical Society* 15 (1900), 25–205. (Contains sketch, reports, and journal of Cutting Marsh.)

Eastman, Charles A. *From the Deep Woods to Civilization: Chapters in the Autobiography of an Indian.* 1916. Reprint, Lincoln: University of Nebraska Press, 1977.

Garrett, Kathleen. "Dartmouth Alumni in the Indian Territory." *Chronicles of Oklahoma* 32 (1954), 123–41.

Garrod, Andrew, and Colleen Larimore, eds. *First Person, First Peoples: Native American College Graduates Tell Their Life Stories.* Ithaca, N.Y.: Cornell University Press, 1997.

Hoefnagel, Dick, with the collaboration of Virginia L. Close. *Eleazar Wheelock and the Adventurous Founding of Dartmouth College.* Hanover, N.H.: Hanover Historical Society/Durand Press, 2002.

Hurd, John. "The Wheelock Dream, Sparsely Realized, Still a Force in the Life of the College." *Dartmouth Alumni Magazine* 58 (Oct. 1965), 35–39, 116.

James, Edwin. *Account of An Expedition from Pittsburgh to the Rocky Mountains, per-*

*formed in the Years 1819 and '20 . . . under the Command of Major Stephen H. Long.* 2 vols. Philadelphia: Carey and Lea, 1823.

Latham, Edward Connery. *A Guide to the Microfilm Edition of the Papers of Eleazar Wheelock together with the Early Archives of Dartmouth College and Moor's Indian Charity School and Records of the Town of Hanover, New Hampshire through the year 1779.* Hanover, N.H.: Dartmouth College Library, 1971.

Lord, John King, *A History of Dartmouth College 1815–1909.* Concord, N.H.: Rumford Press, 1913.

Love, W. DeLoss. *Samson Occom and the Christian Indians of New England.* 1899; reprint, Syracuse, N.Y.: Syracuse University Press, 2000.

Masta, Henry. "When the Abenaki Came to Dartmouth." *Dartmouth Alumni Magazine* 21 (Mar. 1929), 302–3.

McCallum, James Dow. *Eleazar Wheelock, Founder of Dartmouth College.* Hanover, N.H.: Dartmouth College Publications, 1939.

McCallum, James Dow, ed. *The Letters of Eleazar Wheelock's Indians.* Hanover, N.H.: Dartmouth College Publications, 1932.

McClure, David, and Elijah Parish. *Memoirs of the Rev. Eleazar Wheelock, D.D., Founder and President of Dartmouth College and Moor's Charity School; with a summary history of the College and School, to which are added copious extracts from Dr. Wheelock's Correspondence.* Newburyport, Mass.: Edward Little and Co., 1811.

Murray, Laura J., ed. *To Do Good to My Indian Brethren: The Writings of Joseph Johnson, 1751–1776.* Amherst: University of Massachusetts Press, 1998.

Occom, Samson. *A Short Narrative of My Life* (1768). In Colin G. Calloway, ed., *The World Turned Upside Down: Indian Voices from Early America.* Boston: Bedford/St. Martin's, 1994, 55–61.

*Petition of the Society in Scotland for Propagating Christian Knowledge to Settle Scheme for Application of Trust-Fund.* Edinburgh: T. and A. Constable, 1922.

Peyer, Bernd C. "The Betrayal of Samson Occom." *Dartmouth Alumni Magazine* 91 (Nov. 1998), 32–37.

———. *The Tutor'd Mind: Indian Missionary-writers in Antebellum America.* Amherst: University of Massachusetts Press, 1997.

Pilkington, Walter, ed. *Journals of Samuel Kirkland, Eighteenth-century Missionary to the Iroquois, Government Agent, Father of Hamilton College.* Clinton, N.Y.: Hamilton College, 1980.

Richardson, Leon Burr, *History of Dartmouth College.* 2 vols. Hanover, N.H.: Dartmouth College Publications, 1932.

Richardson, Leon Burr, ed. *An Indian Preacher in England: Being Letters and Diaries Relating to the Mission of the Reverend Samson Occom and the Reverend Nathaniel Whitaker to Collect Funds in England for the benefit of Eleazar Wheelock's Indian Charity School, from which grew Dartmouth College.* Hanover, N.H.: Dartmouth College Publications, 1933.

Schneider, Tammy, "'This Once Savage Heart of Mine': Joseph Johnson, Wheelock's 'Indians,' and the Construction of a Christian Indian Identity, 1764–1776." In Colin

G. Calloway and Neal Salisbury, eds., *Reinterpreting New England Indians and the Colonial Experience*. Boston: Colonial Society of Massachusetts, 2003, 232–63.

Sullivan, James, et al., eds. *The Papers of Sir William Johnson*. 15 vols. Albany: State University of New York Press, 1921–65.

Szasz, Margaret Connell. *Indian Education in the American Colonies, 1607–1783*. Albuquerque: University of New Mexico Press, 1988.

———. "Samson Occom: Mohegan as Spiritual Intermediary." In Szasz, ed., *Between Indian and White Worlds: The Cultural Broker*. Norman: University of Oklahoma Press, 1994, 61–78.

Tawse, John W., and George Lyon. *Report to the Society in Scotland for Propagating Christian Knowledge, of a Visit to America by their Appointment, in reference to the Fund Under Their Charge for the Education of Native Indians*. Edinburgh: Printed for the Society, 1839.

Vernon, H. A. "Maris Bryant Pierce: The Making of a Seneca Leader." in L. G. Moses and Raymond Wilson, eds., *Indian Lives: Essays on Nineteenth- and Twentieth-century Native American Leaders*. (Albuquerque: University of New Mexico Press, 1985, 19–42.

Wheelock, Eleazar. *A Plain and Faithful Narrative of the Original Design, Rise, Progress and Present State of the Indian Charity School at Lebanon, Connecticut*. Boston: Richard and Samuel Draper, 1763.

———. *A Continuation of the Narrative of the Indian Charity School*. London, 1769.

———. London, 1771.

———. (May 1771 to Sept 1772.) Portsmouth, N.H., 1773.

———. (Sept. 1772 to Sept 1773.) Hartford, 1773.

———. Hartford, 1775.

Wilson, Raymond. *Ohiyesa: Charles Eastman, Santee Sioux*. Urbana: University of Illinois Press, 1983.

# INDEX